OFFICIAL FERRARI SERVICE & REPAIRER

Maranello

As an official Ferrari dealer for over 50 years, Maranello ensures that Ferrari ownership remains a truly unique and rewarding experience.

Our Service Department offers an enclosed truck collection and re-delivery service plus a very competitive menu pricing on a wide selection of models.

We also offer car storage from our new purpose built facility, which is fully maintained by our Factory trained technicians for either your short or long term requirements.

For further information please contact Mandy, Shaun or Kuldip on: 01784 558432

Maranello Service Centre
Ten Acre Lane
Egham, Surrey TW20 8RJ
Telephone: 01784 558432
www.dealer.ferrari.com/maranello/egham

CONTENTS

Ferrari Supercars 2011

FROM THE PUBLISHERS OF

evo & *Octane*

Ferrari is on a roll. The FF has redefined what's
expected of a supercar, with genuinely innovative technology behind it, while the
599GTO shows just how good, how *focused*, a Ferrari can be. Meanwhile, in the
world of historic Ferraris, the status and value of all the models just keeps rising.

So what better time to sit yourself down and immerse yourself in this collection
of the very best Ferrari articles from *Evo* and *Octane* magazines, brought right up
to date with the latest models and news from Maranello.

The sheer variety of the articles should be enough to keep you glued to the pages
for hours. We have 1950s grand prix cars, iconic GTs of the 1960s, the then-new
breed of 'junior' Ferraris of the 1970s, the outrageous creations of the 1980s –
such as the 288GTO, the Testarossa and the F40 – and the surprisingly practical
supercars of the last couple of decades. What a mix!

What's important to remember is that each and every feature in here has been
written by people who *really* know their stuff. The piece on Ferrari in Formula 1 is
by Doug Nye, the world's foremost motor racing authority. The FF was driven by
Henry Catchpole, *Evo*'s road-testing ace. And who better to tell you what it's like
to own and drive Ferraris old and new than Pink Floyd drummer and car collector
extraordinaire Nick Mason? Enjoy the read!

Peter Tomalin & David Lillywhite

'Each and every feature in here has been written by people who really know their stuff'

Editorial office
Dennis Publishing, 5 Tower Court, Irchester Road,
Wollaston, Northants NN29 7PJ, UK
Tel: +44 (0)207 907 6585. Fax: +44 (0)1933 663367
Email: eds@evo.co.uk or info@octane-magazine.com
Websites: www.evo.co.uk and www.octane-magazine.com

Advertising office
Octane Media Advertising Dept, 19 Highfield Lane,
Maidenhead, Berkshire SL6 3AN, UK
Tel: +44 (0)1628 510080. Fax: +44 (0)1628 510090
Email: ads@octane-magazine.com

Co-editors	David Lillywhite
	and Peter Tomalin
Art editor	Rob Gould
Designer	Robert Hefferon
Production editor	Glen Waddington
Sub-editor	Sarah Bradley
Publishing assistant	Alex Lowit
Advertising director	Sanjay Seetanah
Advertising sales	Rob Schulp
Advertising production	Anisha Mogra
Publishing director	Geoff Love
Bookazine manager	Dharmesh Mistry
Associate publisher	Nicola Bates
Newstrade director	David Barker
Managing director	Ian Westwood
Group finance director	Ian Leggett
COO	Brett Reynolds
CEO	James Tye
Chairman	Felix Dennis

Ferrari Supercars is published under licence from Dennis
Publishing Limited, United Kingdom. All rights in the
licensed material belong to Felix Dennis, Octane Media
or Dennis Publishing and may not be reproduced, whether
in whole or in part, without their prior written consent.
Octane is a registered trademark.

Repro by Octane Repro
Printed by BGP, Bicester, UK
Distribution Seymour, 2 East Poultry Avenue,
London EC1A 9PT. Tel: +44 (0)207 429 4000

FERRARI
THE COMPANY

Ferrari is probably the most revered car company in the world. This is its story. Words: Glen Waddington

It's fair to say that no

other car maker's name resonates with quite the frisson of Ferrari. It embodies passion, excitement, glamour and pure damn driving pleasure like no other. The name's been attached to cars made by the company since 1947, but its history goes back further to founder Enzo Ferrari's days as an independent race team manager (Scuderia Ferrari was founded in Modena in 1929) and as Alfa Romeo's in-house racing chief in 1938.

That lasted just one season before differences between Enzo Ferrari and Alfa Romeo management forced his departure. Ferrari's contract barred him from producing racing cars under his own name for four years, so Scuderia Ferrari briefly became Auto-Avio Costruzioni. It produced two cars, called the 815 (they had 1.5-litre eight-cylinder engines, in effect made by mating two Fiat fours), which were fastest-in-class in the 1940 Mille Miglia though neither finished the race. One survives today. And thousands of Ferraris have followed.

THE EARLY YEARS

Ferrari moved to Maranello in 1943 only for his factory to be bombed a year later. It was rebuilt in 1946 and, on 16 September that year, the first Ferrari engine (a V12, you won't be surprised to hear) was fired up for the first time. Significantly, the new factory included space for building road cars – significant because Enzo Ferrari had respect only for racing. He would build road cars, but merely to fund Ferrari in competition.

That V12 was designed by Gioachino Colombo (a protégé of Vittorio Jano at Alfa Romeo), who had designed the successful two-stage supercharged Alfetta 158/159 racing engine. His V12 – a 1.5-litre, hence with 125cc per cylinder – founded a dynasty of enormously successful racing engines that would also be used in road cars. The legend was beginning.

Called the 125, it featured a single overhead camshaft per cylinder bank and twin spark plugs per cylinder: nothing too outrageous, but enough for a power output of 118bhp at a screaming 6800rpm. In 1947, remember. And it was attached to a simple twin-tube chassis with leaf spring suspension.

It revs with a malevolence that would make you believe its engine was at least three times the capacity. I once drove a 1947-'48 Tipo 166 Spider Corsa (166? This was a 2.0-litre, though still the same engine layout, and 145bhp at an even screamier 7500rpm), a car reckoned to be the earliest surviving Ferrari and also believed to have been based on the chassis and running gear of the very first Ferrari ever to have been built – Enzo recycled his racers in those days to keep the bills down.

No matter. It still tingled with the fizzing rawness of all the best racing Ferraris.

This was a landmark car: that 166 was the first Ferrari ever to be sold into private hands. And this was a landmark era. Ferrari scored its first victory in only its second race, at Piacenza, Rome, in May 1947, with Franco Cortese behind the wheel. Its first grand prix (non-F1) victory arrived in Switzerland, 1949, thanks to Alberto Ascari in a supercharged 125. And that same year marked the first of the firm's nine outright Le Mans 24 Hours victories. Yes, Ferrari had arrived.

FERRARI MATURES

Almost all Ferraris since the late-1950s were styled by Pinin Farina (one word from 1961), and the favoured coachbuilder was Scaglietti. A Ferrari style was emerging, and so was a Ferrari soul. And one model number above all others sums up the greatness of the marque: 250.

It's a cylinder capacity again, this time of Colombo's 3.0-litre V12, still with its roots in the 125 – although the first 250 was actually a sleeved-down version of the Aurelio Lampredi-designed 4.1-litre V12 used in the Type 342 America. The 250 debuted in the Type 250 Export and appeared almost simultaneously in the 250 Europa: Ferrari's first serious road-going GT, and the only road car ever to feature the small-bore Lampredi engine.

This became the era of Ferrari's great berlinettas. So far, Ferrari had produced single-minded sportscars for racing and more luxurious coupés for road use. The 250 Berlinettas could do both, best characterised by the Tour de France of 1955 to 1959 and the great 250GT SWB (1959 to 1963). But this same engine also proved its flexibility in such touring cars as the Pininfarina coupés and cabriolets, and also the California Spiders. In its ultimate form it powered the 250GTO to a class win first time out at the Sebring 12 Hours in 1962 and three consecutive World GT Championships.

Only 39 GTOs were built; understandably it has become one of the world's most sought-after and valuable cars. Driving one is an ultimate, and a privilege with a physical experience to match. The car is alive to the touch like few others, the symphony of its 300bhp V12 tangible. It is as glorious to drive as it is to look at, even though its wet T-shirt styling merely wraps the mechanicals as necessary. And yet the GTO had suffered a troubled birth: in 1961, year of the 'Palace Revolt', Ferrari lost his key engineer Giotto Bizzarrini. The GTO had been his last project.

The 250 series was succeeded by the 275, and the GTO in many respects by the 275GTB: ostensibly a road car, yet a class-winner at Le Mans in 1965, and third overall behind two 250LM prototypes. It was to be the last great berlinetta of Ferrari's years as an independent.

FIAT TAKES CONTROL

It could so easily have been Ford. During the early 1960s Ferrari scored six Le Mans victories in a row. The American giant wanted a piece of that action and bid $18m for Ferrari in 1963 but, when Ford refused to allow Enzo Ferrari to maintain control of the Scuderia's racing programme, the deal fell through. As legend has it, Ford responded by developing the GT40, which took over from Ferrari's Le Mans dominance by scoring four in a row from 1966 to 1969.

Ultimately Fiat took control, in 1968 paying £4m for a 50% stake in the operation that increased to 90% in 1988 – the year Enzo Ferrari died. The deal had always meant that Fiat would look after the road cars while Enzo took care of racing, and he remained managing director until 1971. In the public view, this also meant that Ferrari became better known for its road cars than for competition; Ferrari remained a strong if not dominant force in Formula 1 and endurance racing, and its F1 success receded for a few years after Jody Scheckter's Championship of 1979.

The Fiat era's first major launch was the 365GTB/4 – better known to many as the Daytona, though that's only a nickname. Why name an Italian supercar after an American race circuit? Simple. Ferrari had rubbed Ford's nose in the dirt by humiliating it with a 1-2-3 victory at Daytona in 1967. That's Ford's home territory. Bitter, Enzo?

The Daytona maintained the Ferrari tradition for conservatism, having a front-mounted V12 in an era of mid-engined supercars kicked off by the Lamborghini Miura. Yet by the time deliveries began in 1969, the 174mph Daytona had earned the status of the world's fastest production car. *Autocar* magazine tested it at the MIRA proving ground, for the first time achieving 150mph within the confines of the mile straight. »

'Ferrari embodies passion, excitement, glamour and pure damn driving pleasure like no other car maker'

Above: 1947 V12-powered 125S was first in long line of sporting machines. **Left:** 1961 156 F1 'Sharknose' replica was built for Chris Rea film La Passione.

THE MODERN ERA

Luca Montezemolo joined Ferrari in 1973 as Enzo Ferrari's assistant, taking over the running of the F1 team; a year later the Daytona was replaced with the mid-engined Berlinetta Boxer and, in 1975, the mid-engined, V8-powered 308 family replaced the 1960s V6-engined Dinos. The modern hierarchy of Ferrari models had arrived, with junior V8s and more upmarket 12-cylinders.

The wedgy Bertone-designed 308GT4 was a brief departure from Pininfarina's absolute dominance of Ferrari styling, though the more classically elegant Pininfarina-penned 308GTB ensured Bertone didn't get another chance. While the 2+2 GT4 gave way to the Mondial in 1980, the GTB continued until 1988, when it was replaced by the 348, which begat the F355, then the 360 Modena and the F430... until arriving at the current, spectacular 458 Italia, a fully-fledged 562bhp supercar capable of 202mph and featuring groundbreaking aerodynamics, with front spoilers that deform according to air pressure at speed, changing shape to increase downforce. Ferrari's junior ain't so junior any more.

Shortly before he died, Enzo signed off the F40 – the twin-turbo V8-powered supercar that celebrated the company's 40th anniversary. That left Luca Montezemolo free to take control and, following the brash Testarossa that replaced the Boxer in 1984, fulfil his desire once more to see Ferrari producing a more traditional type of V12-powered GT, in the shape of the 550 Maranello and the 456GT. Today's equivalents are the 599GT and the FF – a complete new direction again, as Ferrari's grandest tourer is a four-wheel-drive shooting brake. Expect to see plenty around Closters and Meribel in the next ski season.

Ferrari made a massive comeback in Formula 1, too. In 1996 the Scuderia signed driver Michael Schumacher and technical director Ross Brawn. The result? Five World Championships from 2000 to 2004, a period in which Schumacher won more races and Championships than any other driver in the history of the sport.

THE LEGACY

Ferrari is the only team to have competed in the Formula 1 World Championship continuously since its inception in 1950. The team's records include 15 World Driver's Championship titles (Alberto Ascari first in 1952, Kimi Räikkönen last in 2007); 16 World Constructor's Championship titles between 1961 and 2008; 215 F1 grand prix victories (the first in 1951, when Jose Froilan Gonzalez won the British GP; the last in 2010, when Fernando Alonso won the Korean GP); 205 pole positions, 225 fastest laps, plus a host of non-Championship GP wins. No other team can match that.

And no other car maker can match the respect and romance such success engenders. Yet Ferrari's road models are not mere poseur machines. They aren't stylistic halos with a hollow core. They might have been a means to Enzo's end of going racing, but racing has always informed the technology of the road cars, from those early 125s that shared their engines, via the 250 Berlinettas that made great cars for road *and* track, to today's supercars, with their circuit-bred transmissions, engine and suspension management and ingenious active aerodynamics.

Enzo himself may be long gone, but his spirit lives on in every single car that bears the *Cavallino Rampante*.

Below: for Enzo, road cars were a means to an end: motorsport was his over-riding passion.

Above: today's hi-tech Maranello factory is pride of Italy. **Right:** the F40 is reaching ever-higher auction prices.

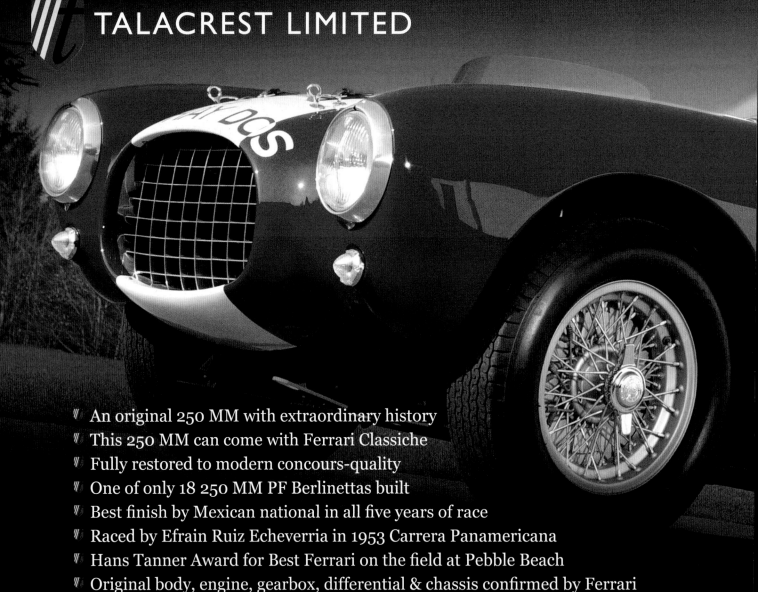

TALACREST LIMITED

- An original 250 MM with extraordinary history
- This 250 MM can come with Ferrari Classiche
- Fully restored to modern concours-quality
- One of only 18 250 MM PF Berlinettas built
- Best finish by Mexican national in all five years of race
- Raced by Efrain Ruiz Echeverria in 1953 Carrera Panamericana
- Hans Tanner Award for Best Ferrari on the field at Pebble Beach
- Original body, engine, gearbox, differential & chassis confirmed by Ferrari

Past thoroughbreds

We have over 30 years experience and have sold over $500 million worth of cars including five 250 GTO's. We are the biggest buyer of Ferrari in the world and have sold some of the most desirable, road and race Ferrari ever. The very best examples of classic cars and Ferrari similar to these shown here and on our website represent an enjoyable and rewarding haven for your money. If you have a Ferrari to sell or are looking for some thoroughbred horsepower trading then please contact Talacrest today for the best offer.

A famous winner of Italy's greatest motor race returns home to win Italy's greatest concours. Dale Drinnon tells the story of the Mille Miglia Ferrari 166 that wowed the judges at the prestigious Villa d'Este

Photography: Martyn Goddard

The stylish gentleman deep

in discussion in the hospitality suite on Sunday morning had the manner of someone who knew whereof he spoke. It was that confident, comfortable air of the insider, and when I realised his topic was what it takes to impress the jury at Villa d'Este, I leaned an ear a little closer. 'It is especially important to remember,' he was saying, 'that this is a concours d'elegance.'

He was, of course, absolutely correct; what he might have added to really drive the point home, however, was that elegance is a critical ingredient of the entire package, not just of the vehicle. And despite the latter-day popular tendency to confuse elegance with all sorts of other things, true elegance is like enlightenment: it can't be bought or even inherited, but if you live properly and don't chase after it, it will sometimes find you of its own accord.

Those circumstances agreed, it's only natural that Jack Croul and his Mille Miglia-winning blue Ferrari came away from the Sunday night awards dinner at the renowned BMW-sponsored Concorso d'Eleganza Villa d'Este with Best of Show. Jack is a tall, slim Californian from Newport Beach, who positively glows with the quiet dignity of the truly elegant. He is a former businessman and, although he never mentions this himself, a committed philanthropist who is especially active in educational giving. At age 19 he was navigating a B-17 out of Snetterton, and by the end of his rotation he had 33 combat ❯❯

Elegance
DEFINED

missions to his credit, and a Distinguished Flying Cross with three clusters – he doesn't mention those to me, either.

What Jack does mention is his cars; he has about 50 now, including a recently acquired MG TC ('The first sports car I ever owned was a TC...'), and he doesn't fly, but he has restored a P51 Mustang and a P38 Lightning, too. His real passion, though, is the Mille Miglia; he has participated in 14 consecutive runnings of the modern edition, 12 as the driver, and when Ferrari 166 chassis 0026M, the 1950 winner, came up for sale, his collection already included the 340 America that took Villoresi and Cassani to victory in 1951.

'I wasn't really looking for this particular car,' he said as we and his wife Kingsley sat in the sun beside it that afternoon, watching the endless throng of admirers who swarmed over 0026M during the weekend of the concours. 'I was attracted to it because I liked the idea of having two Mille Miglia winners. And now I can't believe how beautiful it is; the more I look at it, the more beautiful it becomes.'

Just then, the rare break in the crowd appeared that Jack had been waiting for; he raised his camera and snapped yet another photograph, this one from the rear quarter along the graceful arch of the accent line running down the car's tapered flanks. 'That's it, that's the angle, isn't it? Beautiful...'

It is indeed a stunning machine, as well as quite rare: only six Ferrari 166MM Berlinettas were built by Carrozzeria Touring. More importantly at a concours tracing its origins to the 1920s golden age of the genre, it has history. This is not an 'ordinary' Ferrari Mille Miglia winner: this is the famous Giannino Marzotto double-breasted-suit winner.

Yes, Giannino Marzotto did win the 1950 Mille Miglia in a tailored suit and a silk tie, and yes, he was one of four racing brothers from the fabulously wealthy Marzotto family, a major textile manufacturing and apparel concern then and an even bigger one now – Hugo Boss is among its many holdings. Legend has it the family connection is why Giannino chose a 166 painted in azzurro metallizzato, by the way: the father, Count Gaetano Marzotto, tells the four brothers with a fondness for fast Ferraris, 'I don't want you racing those awful red cars anymore', and young Giannino complies, in his own way.

But there's more to the Giannino Marzotto story than the hackneyed image of a playboy racing driver. He was 22 years old in 1950, and nonetheless had the chutzpah (and the brains) to stand up to all-knowing Enzo Ferrari and tell him 'two litres isn't enough, I'll need more power to win the Mille Miglia'. Giannino's 166, already displayed at the Geneva Show in March 1950 and DNF'd at April's Giro di Sicilia by Alberto Ascari with the standard engine, was uprated to the new 2.3-litre Type 195 »

'JACK SNAPPED A PHOTO FROM THE REAR QUARTER, ALONG THE ACCENT LINE: "THAT'S IT, THAT'S THE ANGLE! BEAUTIFUL..." '

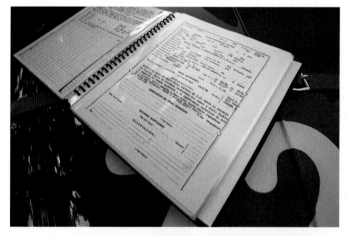

Above and right
Owner's 'bible' of researched material, hallmark of a Paul Russell restoration; hand-painted race numbers.

Above and left
Rear three-quarters angle shows delightful double curvatures; engine is correctly fitted with just one carburettor.

'PHOTOS TAKEN FOR CARROZZERIA
TOURING OF THE BRAND NEW
0026M PLAINLY SHOW THE
CONTROVERSIAL CHROME WHEELS'

unit immediately afterwards, and on April 23 Marzotto proved his argument. It snowed and hailed in the mountains on that Mille Miglia and rained almost everywhere else, and four-time champion Biondetti had far more speed on tap with his works Jaguar, but Giannino Marzotto came home first – and by over five minutes.

In 1953, he and navigator Mario Crosara did it again, joining Nuvolari, Pintacuda and Campari as two-time Mille Miglia winners, and only Biondetti managed better than that. Those others, you might notice, were all professionals who had lengthy careers; Marzotto raced only briefly and for the pure pleasure of it, and when the call came to quit motor sport and assume the family business, he moved smoothly on to become equally adept in that arena.

The fortunes of his blue Ferrari post-1950 Mille Miglia were a little more convoluted. Enzo did some interesting sales agreements in those days, and 0026M appeared on several more occasions for Ferrari's sole benefit over the following months: first at the Torino Show, still in race numbers and Mille Miglia mud; later at Le Mans with Raymond Sommer and Dorino Serafini as a Luigi Chinetti entry (a Did Not Finish after 12 hours).

Giannino also raced it one last time that year, winning at Rome, and its final outing under the Marzotto banner was a victory for brother Umberto at the Coppa Gallenga hillclimb in October. In January 1951, Giannino sold 0026M to a cousin, by then a second-tier race car and finally registered for road use as well.

**1950
FERRARI
166MM/195S
BERLINETTA
LE MANS**
SPECIFICATIONS

Engine
2341cc alloy V12, sohc,
single Weber 36DCF
carburettor

Power
130bhp @ 6000rpm
(published)

Torque
160lb ft @ 6000rpm
(as tested April 1950)

Transmission
Five-speed manual,
rear-wheel drive

Suspension
Front: independent
via double wishbones,
transverse leaf spring,
anti-roll bar, hydraulic
dampers.
Rear: live axle,
longitudinal leaf springs,
hydraulic dampers

Brakes
Drums all round

Performance
0-60mph c10 sec
Top speed 120mph (est)

Over the next few seasons, 0026M was raced sporadically around Europe by the cousin and by subsequent owners, usually in the smaller events; in 1957 it went to the USA, as obsolete Italian race cars of the period frequently did, to essentially the same routine. After two American keepers, the second of whom bought it from a used car lot and treated it to a Chevy driveline transplant – as old Italian race cars with tired engines frequently received – 0026M arrived in 1965 to the hands of John Andrews of Riverside, California.

It stayed there for roughly 36 years. Or more properly, in his mother's garage, piled up under layers of dust, old magazines and assorted household detritus, Mr Andrews eventually constructing a wooden box around it for a modicum of protection. He also mercifully retrieved the original engine and transmission from US owner number two, in exchange for a paltry $200, thereby proving their respective hearts were in the right places, regardless of their wherewithal to undertake Ferrari restorations.

Chassis 0026M might have forever stayed The Lost Marzotto Ferrari had marque expert Michael Sheehan not rediscovered it in 2000 and related the story in a magazine article. Once it surfaced, however, things started happening. Thomas Meade, an American famous for moving to Italy in the '60s and working in the very thick of the exotic car trade (the Thomassima specials were his creations), purchased it from Andrews early in 2001; it soon went to an unnamed Swiss buyer who got as far on a restoration as partial disassembly. That's where Jack Croul joins the plotline; in March 2003 he bought 0026M and

Spoilt for choice

IT'S TOUGH TO REJOIN the real world after three days of Concorso d'Eleganza Villa d'Este. The setting beside delightful Lake Como has enchanted visitors since the poet Virgil bought his first package tour, the hospitality of sponsor BMW and of the Hotel Villa d'Este was perfect in the best Old European tradition – unobtrusive yet unfailing – and the quality of the entrants must have kept the concours jury debating over a bottle of Valtellina Superiore until the wee hours of the morning. Poor things.

Alongside the Trofeo BMW Group award for Best of Show by the jury, won by Jack Croul's Ferrari, the other top four finishers all had a decidedly swoopy note.

The Coppa d'Oro Villa d'Este awarded by participants' vote went to the 1938 Mercedes 540K Autobahnkurier Coupé, another Paul Russell restoration, (main image, right), entered by Arturo Keller; the Trofeo BMW Group Italia, by popular vote of the public on Sunday's display at Villa Erba, was won by the 1937 Figoni et Falaschi Delahaye 135M of Peter Mullin (far right, middle). Continuing the aerodynamic theme on a modern note, the 2008 Bugatti Veyron Fbg Hermès took the Design Award, also by public vote at Villa Erba.

The most satisfying Class Winner was probably Chris Hrabalek's fluorescent, in-your-face, matt orange 1970 Lancia Stratos prototype, along with the Mention of Honour Ferrari 206S Dino Prototipo of James Glickenhaus (near right, bottom).

Meanwhile, the Attending Journalist's Personal Award goes to the engaging Dr Peter Heydon of Ann Arbor, Michigan, USA. His ex-Geneva Show Bentley MkVI Worblaufen Drophead won no trophies, but he brought his car 5000 miles for the joy of being there and charmed all he met. In the People I'd Like to Have Dinner With Class, he's right at the head of the field. Isn't that what this is all about?

MICHEL ZUMBRUNN

MICHEL ZUMBRUNN

commissioned Paul Russell and Company of Essex, Massachusetts, to complete the resto.

The car arrived that summer in boxes – 'not enough boxes' as Paul puts it; 'a lot of pieces were missing, although thankfully none of the major components or critical numbered pieces' – and a fair number of the incidentals would have to be chased or fabricated. That's obviously par for the course in the restoration game. In this instance, however, good Karma paid off all around: Paul's friend and regular Italian resource, the collector and historic racer Gabriele Artom, happens also to be good friends with Jack, and the Marzotto and Artom families go back for ages. There were times when Gabriele sent parts for Paul to reproduce by taking them off his own cars.

There was also the larger matter of researching and documenting the 'target' specifications for the restoration, especially difficult on competition machinery that sometimes changes during the course of an event, much less from one event to another. Which, one rather suspects, is the part of restoration that makes Paul the happiest; in another life he could have been a history professor or a forensic anthropologist.

Over the course of the three-year-plus project, he would unearth things like photos taken for Carrozzeria Touring of the brand new 0026M, plainly showing the controversial chrome wheels, and a test sheet for the single-carb version of the 195 engine marked 'for homologation Mille Miglia 1950 – G Marzotto'. Until then, questions existed as to whether the car ran with one Weber or three (and Paul being Paul, he had an example of each set-up ready just in case).

Likewise, a tiny smear of original colour found on the already-stripped bodyshell revealed that, while most Touring 166s were Le Mans blue, Giannino's 166 was actually metallic, and traces of the interior flocking »

'WHAT THE VILLA D'ESTE JUDGES WERE PRESENTED WITH IS AS CLOSE TO APRIL 23, 1950, AS HUMANS CAN GET'

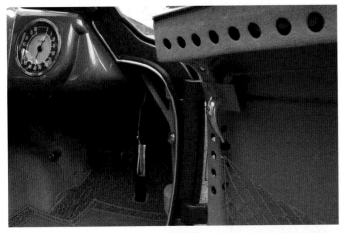

still trapped in crannies around the Superleggera tubing provided samples to match the fibre length and texture exactly. What the Villa d'Este judges, the participants and the public were presented with when they pressed around the Marzotto 166 that weekend, in short, is as close to April 23, 1950, as humans can get, right down to the brush strokes in the race numbers.

'You must be proud of the way the car turned out and the reception it's getting,' I said to Jack as he lowered his camera, 'and I'll bet you're looking forward to driving it in the Mille Miglia next month.' He checked the image on the tiny screen and smiled. 'Oh yeah, I'm very pleased, but I'm not driving this car in the Mille Miglia, I'm driving the 340; my brother Jim will be driving this car.'

Proof positive, I think you'll agree, that the Villa d'Este judges know true elegance when they see it.　　　　　　　　　　　　　　　△

Thanks to owner Jack Croul, to Gabriele Artom, and to Paul Russell and Company, Massachusetts, USA, www.paulrussell.com. Thanks also to BMW for hosting the magnificent event that is the Villa d'Este Concours. Best wishes to Giannino Marzotto, who was prevented by illness from attending this year's Villa d'Este.

Above and right
Few panels escaped some 'added lightness'; owner Jack Croul with his Villa d'Este winner.

There's a well-worn

adage that if it looks right, it probably is. Think back
through the history of man's mechanised movement and
picture the first Supermarine Spitfire, the Bugatti Type
35, the Jaguar D-type, the Hawker Hunter, the Lotus 25.
All of them effective, deadly even, and yet beautiful even
to the non-enthusiast's gaze. Whether it matters is a good
question, especially since all were tools required only to
perform better than their opposition.

The list above was necessarily short but there was
an obvious one missing, or an obvious type; the front-
engined Italian Grand Prix car of the 1950s. Long nose,
tall boat tail, big wheels and nary a straight line to be
found, all blended into a perfectly proportioned whole. To
a generation of wide-eyed youngsters, it was simply how a
real racing car looked.

1950 had been the start of Formula One as a category,
and if the decade of post-war austerity that followed
will be better remembered for the cold war, civil rights
and the bomb, it was nevertheless a glorious time for
Grands Prix. The Germans who had dominated pre-war
would not do it quite so easily this time; the English were
gearing up for action later on, and Maserati and Ferrari
were already better organised and spurred on by a battle
for Latin supremacy on the international stage. The men »

GRAND PRIX
GIANTS

The last of the great front-engined Grand Prix racers were proof positive
that engineering excellence goes hand in hand with physical beauty
Words: Mark Hales Photography: Matt Howell

who drove them simply wanted to win. A list that includes Fangio, Moss, Farina, Gonzalez, Ascari, Musso, Hawthorn and Collins is by no means complete, but is certainly exclusive.

In 1954 the rules were changed, and engines had to be 2.5 litres unsupercharged (or 750cc with a blower). This was the cue for Maserati to make the seminal 250F, which retained some of the powerful purpose of the big pre-war cars but shrank it into a more compact and elegant whole. The way the body's cigar shape sweeps and tapers along its length and the way the cockpit's opening peels its way from such compound curvature without spoiling it, is mesmerising. For me, the 250F is still the perfectly proportioned single seater.

Ferrari's Dino 246, which appeared four years later in 1958, was out of a similar mould but it was smaller and lighter, benefitting from progress in most areas. Yet the slightly more squashed look to the body and the prominent scoop on the bonnet to feed

the downdraught carburettors does not allow it quite the same uninterrupted purity of line.

The two types would compete against each other – just. The 250F was probably nearing the end of its competitive life before the factory officially withdrew from Grand Prix racing in 1957 to concentrate on business. Engine development was continued to assist the privateers, but the front-engined era was drawing to a close, too. Ferrari retired the Dinos in 1960 and a golden period gave way to the introduction of lighter and more nimble mid-engined cars. The two in the pictures are thus the perfect pair. The blood red best that Italy could produce at the time.

This Maserati, which belongs to Pink Floyd musician Nick Mason, is a relatively late model – probably one of those converted by the factory for V12 engines in 1957 in an unsuccessful attempt to take on Ferrari, but later refitted with a six. The layout is conventional for the time; a long-stroke in-line engine

sits tall beneath the bonnet, topped with twin overhead camshafts which also drive twin magnetos to feed twin plugs per cylinder. This last is another period convention, necessitated by the hemispherical combustion chamber which was then thought optimum. The large hump on the piston to gain the required compression with this design compromises the flame travel in the chamber, and the best defence was another plug on the other side to speed up the burning. Almost everybody used a similar arrangement, and would do so for another ten years.

The length of the engine and the need to accommodate the driver immediately behind it led Maserati to put the gearbox in-unit with the axle at the back of the car and spin the propeller shaft – which runs between the driver's legs – at engine speed. Suspension is independent at the front with double wishbones and coil springs (although the telescopic dampers are mounted separately), de Dion at the back via a transverse leaf »

'The men who drove them simply wanted to win.
A list which includes Fangio, Moss, Farina,
Gonzalez, Ascari, Musso, Hawthorn and Collins is
by no means complete, but it is certainly exclusive'

spring pinned in the middle. Big 16in wire wheels complete the picture and are filled with simply huge aluminium finned drum brakes.

The Ferrari has been owned by the same family for over 20 years and was assembled out of spares in the 1980s which makes it real, if not exactly official. At first sight it looks to have a similar layout to the Maserati's, but delve a little deeper and you see some more modern thinking. The engine is a V6 – unusually with an angle of 65 degrees rather than the more normal 60 and a concept pioneered by Enzo Ferrari's son Dino and designer Vittorio Jano, hence the soubriquet. The vee gets the weight lower and, because the engine is half the length, further back towards the centre – remove the bonnet and that long nose is filled with not much at all. The engine's layout is also why the carburettors and bonnet air scoop are where they are.

A single two-stage magneto driven from the back of one camshaft supplies the 12 sparks. It is exclusive to the engine and is now so rare that one changed hands recently for £20,000 – Dino ownership is clearly not for the faint of wallet. Transmission is also in the fashion of the time and lays at the back, in-unit with the axle like the Maserati's, but mounted across the car rather than in-line, which again helps shift weight forward. In addition, because drive goes to one end, the propeller shaft runs at an angle across the floor. That is why the engine is skewed under the bonnet.

The Maserati hangs its oil and fuel tanks right out the back inside that rivet-encrusted abdomen, which has to be the worst possible place to put them. Not only are they doing a fine impression of a pendulum, but it's an influence that will change as the fuel burns. Races in those days were long and cars might start with anything up to 40 gallons, which is a bit like riding a bike with a 270lb saddlebag.

The Ferrari moves that mass closer to the car's centre of gravity where it can't swing like a bobweight, putting the fluid inside panniers, one each side of the driver. On this car one is for oil, the other petrol, but depending on the length of the race Ferrari might have filled both with fuel and put a smaller tank for oil behind the driver. The science of weight distribution seems so obvious now and yet, at the time, requiring a driver clad in a polo shirt to sit in a bath of high-octane petrol may not have seemed like obvious progress. It would be interesting to know whether Fangio or Musso or Moss really thought about such things.

Yet more modern touches are the

Dino's big disc brakes inside smaller 15in wheels and the fully adjustable double-wishbone suspension at both ends, all sprung by modern-style coilover spring/damper units. This was the beginning of an exciting time in motor sport when the technology of design was about to gain ascendancy over complexity of engineering as a means to an end. Except maybe in the tyre department, where the very public nature of failure probably ensured a conservative approach. Ferrari would also try 16in wheels but the tyre section would remain, at 5.50 front and 6.50 rear, similar to those on the Maserati.

The Dino's driving position is another modern touch. The seat is much lower down than it is in the 250F, and instead of splaying the knees to clear a big wheel, you stretch the arms to find it straight in front, level with your chest. Gearshift is then down and to the left and needs a

moment's pause for thought; first gear is to the far left and back behind a spring-loaded detent, then it's right, all the way across the gate and forward for second, straight back for third, then back across the gate to the left and forward for fourth. Fifth is then straight back. All of which is fine when you are thinking about it but easy to forget when you are busy.

GTO Engineering's John James says to stay where I am and he'll just roll the car forward. I turn the switch to both sets of plugs, let the clutch up at walking pace and the engine bursts immediately into life. Let it warm, then out of the paddock towards Cadwell Park's delightful collection of serpentine gradients. There's a slight judder from a clutch which is heavy underfoot and which sends a gentle jangling through the propeller shaft over which you sit, but it's easy enough and the engine is completely devoid of temperament. At

least it is until you invite it to move a little faster...

The track is wet for the moment, and any more than half throttle in any gear sends the rear wheels spinning crazily, the needle on the big rev counter flicking towards the 8500rpm limit and the tail waltzing one way or the other. I try and get a drift going by taking some more speed into the longer corners and holding it there with a gentle dose of that wonderful V6 urge, but the front doesn't point either and then the rear wheels spin anyway if you try and help it.

Probably it's too wet for the time being to feel the benefits of better weight distribution and, as ever, I can't help wondering whether it was like this for Fangio and Moss, or whether the cars were set up differently. (I do remember reading how Fangio had made a pit stop for tyres in which the mechanics had been hurriedly hand-cutting deeper

Below
At Cadwell, Ferrari leads Maserati... the 250F's engine was equal to the Ferrari's by 1958, on paper at least. It doesn't feel it today. »

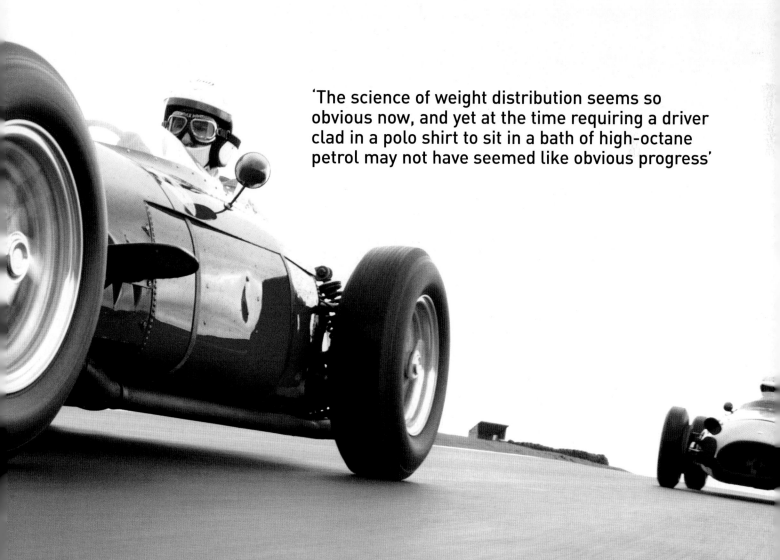

'The science of weight distribution seems so obvious now, and yet at the time requiring a driver clad in a polo shirt to sit in a bath of high-octane petrol may not have seemed like obvious progress'

'You sense the lower overall weight and the lesser inertia which makes the Dino feel quicker in its responses, but means the window of opportunity to get the car braked, pointed and the power on is narrower'

Above:
Minimal gauges are harder to see on low-set Ferrari dash. Note angled propshaft running across floor.

Far right:
Network of pipes pump oil and fuel from the remote tanks. Leaks were a common source of retirement.

grooves while he was on track.) A lap or two more just to savour the noise of the engine and the slickness of the right to left shift which, like all good dog boxes, gets slicker the faster you flick the lever. We resolve to let the track dry a little while we do some static photography.

That done and rain abated, it's time to try the 250F. There's a taller cockpit and a bigger vault to place a foot on the seat and step in – then a squat behind a much bigger wooden-rimmed wheel which is closer to you and tilted forward at the top. The cockpit's sides are then further away and you sit higher which somehow feels less intimate, more vintage. Gears are down on the floor to the right and the shift pattern is conventional H-pattern with a gate which also starts with a spring-loaded detent to the left-and-back for first. The straight-six doesn't fire quite as easily and both Ten Tenths' Charlie Knill-Jones and GTO's James puff a little together before it catches, and then it isn't quite as smooth as the V6 when it does. There's a similar jangling from the prop, although the clutch is lighter and so is the steering, but the 250F is just as simple to motivate.

Out on the circuit, which is now damp only in places, and the Maserati

immediately feels lighter to the touch. The steering takes less muscle although the elbows move further with that big wheel, and you can feel the car rolling and pitching more in response to your inputs. I head for the driest patches, which are round the long corner at the top of Cadwell. The straight engine rasps and thrums through the seat, sending a hum through the propshaft.

Keep a good eye on the rev counter now; the good guys used eight and more in the day, but we'll stick to seven-two like we're asked, by which time the engine is feeling a touch breathless anyway. Reach down towards the floor and cup a hand round the aluminium knob, kick the clutch pedal and flick the wrist. The shift is instant like a modern Hewland's, but the lever moves further and it doesn't snick. There might be no gears at all in the box, so light is the action. It feels even slicker than the Ferrari's, which is saying something.

Meanwhile the car is surging forward, engine crackling and wailing and popping out of that long black pipe which trails behind my shoulder. Look up the road and remember the technique: don't brake even though I want to, but keep the pedal planted hard to the floor. Ease the big rim and aim the front end at a

point somewhere way up ahead.

Oh yes. The nose doesn't point and dive like it does on some of the older cars, but instead the whole body seems to swivel gently round a point somewhere in its middle, somewhere between your knees. Elbows and instinct catch the motion with that big wheel, but I mustn't slap it back into line as swiftly as possible, mustn't do what I've been doing for years, just rein it in to stop the yaw angle getting any bigger but let it all keep coming. Monitor the amount with little massages of that big rim and, whatever you do, don't lift off. We've found the zone and we want to stay there.

It's a joy in a completely different style to an aggressive, wheelspinning powerslide because it works the fronts almost as hard as the rears, and as the road's sweep unravels the car almost straightens itself. But then the tighter corners which follow are a little less homogenous. The big drums tend to grab and twitch the car one way and another until you have all the shoes squashed against all the drums, then you have to be careful not to let that energy dive on the laden front wheel and pivot the car round the front end. That will only give you a dose of snappy oversteer on the exit. Better to brake a ❯❯

1960 FERRARI DINO 246 FORMULA ONE

SPECIFICATIONS

Engine
2417cc V6. Double overhead cams, two valves per cylinder. Dry sump lubrication. Three twin-choke downdraught Weber carburettors

Power
Approx 280bhp @ 8000rpm

Torque
n/a

Transmission
Five-speed dog-engaged gearbox, rear-mounted in-unit with differential

Suspension
Front/rear; independent via double wishbones with coilover spring/damper units

Brakes
Steel discs front/rear. Two-pot calipers No servo

Weight
6780kg (wet, see text)

Performance
0-62mph 3.9 secs (estimated)
Top speed (depending on gearing) 160mph

1957 MASERATI 250F FORMULA ONE

SPECIFICATIONS

Engine
2493cc in-line six. Twin overhead camshafts, two valves per cylinder. Dry-sump lubrication. Three twin-choke sidedraught Weber carburettors

Power
Approx 230bhp @ 7200rpm (1954), 270bhp @ 8000rpm (1956), 290bhp @ 8000rpm (1958)

Torque
n/a

Transmission
Five-speed dog-engaged -manual gearbox, rear mounted in-unit with differential

Suspension
Front: independent via double wishbones, coil springs and telescopic dampers. Rear: de Dion with transverse leaf spring and telescopic dampers

Brakes
Drum brakes with finned aluminium cladding. No servo

Weight
780kg (wet, see text)

Performance
0-60mph 4.3 secs
Top speed (depending on gearing) 155mph

'Look up the road and remember the technique: don't brake even though I want to, but keep the pedal planted hard to the floor. Ease the big rim and aim the front end at a point somewhere way up ahead'

little earlier and let the car settle, then power it through. Savour the crackle and the slick shift which soon follow.

Time for another go in the Dino, this time on a drier track. Here, hopping from one to the other highlights differences which are more subtle than you might expect. The steering is still heavier, but the driving position is more comfortable and you can brace the body better with legs outstretched and foot hard against a substantial footrest. The brakes you now find are firm underfoot, yet they are tireless and accurate and allow you to place the car better.

You sense the lower overall weight and the lesser inertia which makes the Dino feel quicker in its responses, but that does mean the window of opportunity to get the car braked, pointed and the power on is narrower. The tail-out oversteer which you can still have on the exit of the corner is more insistent and does need slapping firmly back into line. It's a more modern ambiance and you drive it accordingly, using those discs late and hard then leaning on a front end which at first understeers quite strongly, but invites you to bring in the power of that sublime engine.

And sublime it certainly is. Harsh yet musical under load, crackling a fusillade every time you back off, you twist your head in an attempt to lessen the aural assault drilling its way from the underslung exhaust nearest you and through the defence of helmet and earplugs. Utterly and completely

smooth and ever more muscular as it sears through the midrange, the V6 pulls and pulls seamlessly towards eighty-five with such eagerness you need to anticipate the shift, and think about which way to move the lever.

It's much revvier and bigger in the mid and upper ranges than the Maserati's in-line engine, but the exact numbers as ever depend on where you look. Maserati variously claimed 220-240bhp at 7200rpm in 1954, 280bhp at 8000rpm in 1957 and 290bhp in 1958. The stillborn V12 was reputed to push out 320bhp at 10,000rpm which, if events hadn't overtaken, should have made it a winner. Ferrari claimed 280 or 290bhp at 8500 or 8300rpm for the carburettored Dino 246 throughout its two-year life.

Weight has a bearing on acceleration as well as handling, and here we encounter another potential revision of history. When we rolled Mason's car onto Cadwell's scales (certified for MSA-approved championships), the readout said 780kg. The Dino read 680kg with exactly the same amount of fluids on board which meant that on the day there was 100kg between them – a massive difference. I couldn't discover any official figures for Ferrari, but Maserati claimed 630kg dry for the 250F of 1954-56 and 550kg for the 1958 'lightweight' T2 model. Assume 30kg for the 40 litres of fuel and 7kg for the two gallons of oil, and you have about 740kg dry for Mason's car – which is about 100kg more

than Maserati claimed. Like people, cars usually put on weight in later years, but it's still difficult to see where the 250F might have gained that much.

Engine and brakes apart though, the differences between them were not as clear cut as I had expected when I saw the respective layouts, and as I so often have, I began to wonder whether the intervening four decades had simply added some stiffness to the Ferrari's suspension. Or maybe this really was how they were at the time. Perhaps progress had already wrought its course and deliberate drifting as a means of gaining a handling balance on the hoof was about to become a thing of the past. Perhaps the two cars straddled the moment at which braking and pointing was about to take over, ready for the mid-engined revolution about to dawn.

There's no doubt, though, that on the day the Dino felt the lighter, more powerful car, more modern and faster round the lap. It wasn't, however, as much fun to drive as the older, heavier, less comfortable, slower Maserati, or at least, it was a different kind of fun. So let's just say that each had its own magic, and that cannot necessarily be measured by the scales, the dynamometer or the stopwatch. Then, as now, there is just something about the red cars.

Our thanks to GTO Engineering, John James, Ten Tenths, Charles Knill-Jones, Adrian Hamilton and Cadwell Park circuit. △

Above
Gearchange in Maserati has conventional H-pattern and is a total delight.

Far left
Twin magnetos each feed one set of plugs per cylinder to promote better combustion.

Ferrari 250

The '250' simply represents cylinder size, but Ferrari's range of
V12s have star quality, from the first Mille Miglia to the last Lusso
Words: David Lillywhite   Photography: Michel Zumbrunn

If ever there was a line-up of models that managed to be both highly evocative and deeply confusing, it's those from the prancing horse with '250' in their designation. So here we bring ten landmark cars, from the first to wear the '250' moniker, through GTO to the last-of-the-line Lusso. We've kept away from the out-and-out racers, like the 250 Testa Rossa and the 250LM, but brought together examples of all the major road cars.

This is a range that encompasses a staggering variety of body styles, created by masters of coachbuilding such as Vignale, Pinin Farina and Zagato. There are clear links between the models, but chassis changed, wheelbases altered and levels of trim varied enormously. Surprisingly, given that the cars are named '250' by the cubic capacity of a single cylinder of their 3-litre V12s, there are even two different engines used in the range.

Ferrari 250s are associated with greatness. Some represented firsts in Ferrari history, others have achieved legendary status through race victories or simple beauty. Curiously, few actually show great innovation, but that doesn't stop a 250 of some sort featuring in most people's lists of their most desirable cars. »

250 Mille Miglia

In the early 1950s, the fledgling Ferrari company was a constructor of competition machinery, with a small sideline in road cars, and already establishing a reputation for race track domination – Formula One and Le Mans victories had been chalked up in 1948 and '49 respectively.

To deal with the variety of race disciplines being attacked, the company had developed two engines: the original Gioacchino Colombo-designed 'short-block' V12 and the later, larger-capacity Aurelio Lampredi 'long-block' V12. Gradually the smaller unit was enlarged from its original 1.5-litre capacity, through 159, 166, 212 and 225 (2.7) designations. Meanwhile, the large, torquey Lampredi engines, as used in the 4.1-litre Ferrari 340 for example, were gaining a reputation for troublesome behaviour; not so much due to design shortcomings, but because their high torque was breaking transmissions.

The answer was to enlarge the Colombo unit once more, to 3 litres, and to change the head design from siamesed to individual ports. This gave the engine a new lease of life and set it up for use in the following 250s. Using this more compact motor in the lighter chassis of the smaller-engined cars resulted in the very first 250, a Vignale-bodied coupé initially named the 250S. This was the car that Ferrari entered in the 1952 Mille Miglia, driven by Giovanni Bracco who, legend has it, chained-smoked and brandy-swigged his way to a heroic win. The result was so important, Ferrari named all subsequent versions of the 250S as 250 Mille Miglias.

A total of some 32 of these cars were subsequently produced, some as Berlinettas (pictured) built by Pinin Farina (plus-two from Vignale), others as open-tops. The chassis were typical of Ferraris of the time, with oval tubing, a transverse leaf spring at the front, leaf springs at the back and Houdaille lever-arm dampers all round. A new four-speed gearbox was developed too, in place of the existing five-speed transmission.

The 250 Mille Miglia went on to score a number of important victories, particularly in America in the hands of Phil Hill.

'Ferrari entered the 250S in the 1952 Mille Miglia, driven by Giovanni Bracco who, legend has it, chain-smoked and brandy-swigged his way to victory'

250 Europa

It might not be one of the better known 250s, but really the 1953 Europa is the true start of the model line, because it was the first of the Gran Turismos, aimed at fast cross-country touring. Surprisingly, though, it used the Lampredi V12; a good engine but not necessarily as suitable for road use as the 'short block' Colombo.

The way this came about is simple, if a little illogical in hindsight. Ferrari's first real road car, the 147 166, was based around a 2400mm-wheelbase tubular chassis and the 2-litre Colombo V12. It was an expensive, sometimes troublesome machine that nonetheless rewarded those who could match its abilities.

As explained in the 250 Mille Miglia section, the engine was enlarged over the years to give the 195 (2.3-litre), and the 212 (2.5), while the bodies were supplied by an array of coachbuilders. The chassis remained virtually unaltered, although wheelbases changed, with two versions of the 212 built, the Inter and the Export – the latter with a shorter wheelbase.

When the time came to develop the next stage of road car, the 3-litre version of the Colombo V12 was still being experimented with for the 250 Mille Miglia. It seemed a safer option to use the Lampredi V12, which was already doing sterling service in the 4.1-litre 340 and 342. The result was the short-lived 250 Export and more popular 250 Europa.

Although Michelotti and Vignale styled the first Europa, Pinin Farina dominated production. The basic, long-serving chassis continued, now stretched to 2800mm (Export 2400mm) and, with the addition of a better appointed interior with extra soundproofing, weight was up by a fifth on previous road cars. The pay-off was that the Europa was by a wide margin the easiest Ferrari to live with so far and capable of 135mph and 0-60mph in less than eight seconds.

However, it was clear that Ferrari customers needed a little less in the way of thoroughbred behaviour from their Grand Tourers, and the Europa was phased out by the similarly named but otherwise quite different GT Europa.

'The pay-off was that the Europa was by a wide margin the easiest Ferrari so far to live with, and capable of 135mph and 0-60mph in less than eight seconds'

>>

250GT

The 250 Europa established Ferrari as a maker of serious, upmarket Grand Tourers – but the quality of the ride, the standard of the trim and the reliability of the all-alloy Lampredi engine left a little to be desired.

The Colombo engine – more responsive, lighter and shorter than the Lampredi unit – was better suited to a relatively compact Grand Tourer. So, for 1955 the car was revised, using the 3-litre Colombo motor from the 250 Mille Miglia and independent coil spring front suspension instead of Ferrari's traditional transverse leaf set-up. The shorter engine also allowed a reduction in the wheelbase, down to 2600mm.

Confusingly named GT Europa, the new car was a massive improvement and, at 140mph, even faster than the outgoing Europa. After 28 had been made, the Europa tag was dropped, and the model became known simply as 250GT. But there's little which was simple about the range of styles that the 250GT was available in...

Ferrari had settled on Pinin Farina as its coachbuilder of choice by this time so, predictably, of the 28 GT Europas built, 27 were from that coachbuilder. The other car was a one-off special by Vignale for Princess Liliane de Rethy of

Belgium. There were also seven lightweight 'Berlinettas' built in alloy by Pinin Farina – and three of these had an unusual rear wing treatment with a very prominent kick-up line from sill to sail panel (like the Tour de France over the page).

For the 250GT, Pinin Farina once again got the ball rolling, continuing the distinctive rear wing styling of the previous three GT Europa Berlinettas. But the company was struggling to keep up, its workshops packed and order books overflowing, so work was farmed out to local Carrozzeria Boano, where 250GTs (with flush rear wing styling) were produced until mid-1957.

Then Mario-Felice Boano left to become chief stylist at Fiat, and his business partner Luciano Polla was joined by Boano's son-in-law, Ezio Ellena. The firm became Carrozzeria Ellena yet production of 250GTs continued for another 12 months, unchanged except for an almost undetectably higher roofline for better headroom. This period of 250GTs are known as Boano and Ellena models, with the former company's cars called 'low roof' and the latter 'high roof'.

Pinin Farina, meanwhile, had been building a new factory to enable production of the 250GT to return 'home'. To mark the change, a new

design was launched with clean, notchback styling, 2600mm wheelbase, the best appointed interior so far and performance of 150mph and 6.7 seconds for 0-60. You can see this car above.

The 250GT Pinin Farina, or PF, as it became known, was launched in 1958, gaining twin distributors and then the 'outside-plug' engine (referring to the position of the spark plugs) in 1959, disc brakes, telescopic dampers and revised steering in 1960. It went on to sell more than 350 examples, all in left-hand-drive form.

'It was massively revised, using the 3-litre Colombo V12 of the 250 Mille Miglia and coil springs instead of Ferrari's traditional transverse leaf'

250GT Cabriolet

Usually when we think of road-going 250s, we think of muscular, coupé styling. But there were several versions of lithe, sexy, open-top 250s built too, which started with a one-off convertible from the Boano era.

Once Pinin Farina was back on the 250 scene, an open-top version was quickly produced. Initially four prototypes were created, each featuring unique body and interior treatments.

The first was chassis number 0655 GT, which was built for Ferrari racing ace Peter Collins. It featured a cut-down driver's door, a crackle-black dashboard and unusual styling creases in the wings. The windscreen did without a chrome top rail and Collins later equipped it with Dunlop disc brakes and alloy wheels (Borrani wire wheels had always been a 250 staple).

Another of the prototypes was built with a cut-down windscreen and a faired driver's headrest (like a D-type's). The third was made for the 1957 Paris Salon and the fourth was sold to the Aga Khan.

However, these four cars were simply interesting experiments ahead of a run of 36 open-top 250GT Cabriolets, which are now known as Series 1 (pictured).

The kicked-up rear wings of the earlier coupés remained, perfectly suiting the svelte styling, yet all but the very last of the Series 1 models featured headlights equipped with gorgeous Perspex cowls.

In the meantime, the California Spider had been introduced (see over page), based heavily on the competition variant of the 250, the Tour de France. Ferrari needed to differentiate between these two models which, although produced by different coachbuilders, looked remarkably similar. The solution was unfortunate in many ways, for the Cabriolet was revised with more sober styling – and no headlight cowls. This was the Series 2.

By way of compensation, the Series 2 was made more practical, with a more accommodating interior and improved boot space for grand touring. It was first shown at the 1959 Paris Salon but production didn't start until 1960, lasting until 1962.

Despite the improved comfort, many find the Series 2 a little too soft, and few disagree that the Series 1 is easily the best looking.

'Another of the prototypes was built with a cut-down windscreen and a faired driver's headrest, like a D-type'

»

250 Tour de France

Trading on the success of the 250GT, Ferrari produced a handful of tuned, lightweight Competizione versions. They used Pinin Farina-designed bodies built by Scaglietti in alloy, and entered them into International GT racing. Quite a turn-around from previous policies of producing road cars merely to finance the racing...

In 1956, the prestigious Tour de France was dominated by 250GT Competiziones, with one winning in the hands of de Portago and third place being taken by the very car that had been seen at the 1955 Paris Salon.

This success prompted Ferrari to name subsequent Competiziones with the Tour de France moniker. Initially they followed the style of the 250 Mille Miglia (some with Plexiglas cowled headlights), based around the 2600mm wheelbase chassis with drum brakes, coil spring front suspension and a leaf sprung axle at the rear. Power outputs initially varied between 230 and 240bhp.

Some of these early cars used plastic sliding side windows, others had wind-up glass, and all eight Scaglietti-built cars of the

Series I Tour de France received varying numbers of vents in the sail panel behind the side windows. Cabin appointments were basic.

For 1957, a Series II was introduced, which featured 14 sail panel vents, an extended nose, bonnet scoop (supplying air into a carburettor surround pan) and heavily re-profiled rear wings. Customers could specify a Testa Rossa spec engine, with lightweight pistons and con-rods and six oversize downdraught Weber carburettors.

Over the following years, until 1959, Ferrari continued to evolve the Tour de France. The Series III brought headlights set further back in the wings and covered by Plexiglas covers, rear wings with prominent fins and a three-vent sail panel. The Series IV moved to a single vent and power output crept up to between 240 and 260bhp, while the Series V (pictured) lost the light cowls.

All this for fewer than 100 cars, even including the handful of Zagato-built models. And yet, the Tour de France is now known as the finest long-wheelbase Ferrari GT that was ever produced.

'Ferrari produced a number of Competizione 250GTs. Quite a turn-around from previous policies of building road cars merely to finance the racing...'

250 **California**

It's the late 1950s, and Ferrari's 250GT Tour de France is beginning its now-legendary domination of GT class competition. There's a drop-top version of the 250 on the way but, in California, dealer Jon von Neumann (of Ferrari Representatives of Hollywood) has an idea that just won't go away. He wants Ferrari to build a convertible version of the Tour de France. Crucially, North American Ferrari importer Luigi Chinetti backs his idea.

Of course, the result is the 250GT California Spider, a more focussed, more hard-core drop-top than the GT Spider Pininfarina. Compare this California with the Cabriolet on the previous spread, and you'll see they look similar. However, the California was not just built by Scaglietti of Modena (which produced many of the Pininfarina designs), but designed by Scaglietti too.

The California was initially based around a 2600mm wheelbase chassis and equipped with a 240bhp engine, and in this form was given its formal debut in late 1958. Customers could specify all the options that buyers of a Tour de France were offered – from race-spec

camshafts to full Competizione set-ups – plus an additional elegant glassfibre hardtop. Some Californias were fitted with cowled headlights, some were left uncovered, but what's now known as the long-wheelbase California (pictured) continued until 1960.

In tandem with California production, though, Ferrari was developing a new short-wheelbase chassis. This would lead to the replacement for the Tour de France, referred to as the 250GT SWB (see the next page) and, unsurprisingly, the new 2400mm chassis founds its way to the California Spyder.

This ushered in a new era of Californias, which tended to appear to sit lower, with a more aggressive stance. As with the long-wheelbase Californias, the SWBs were built with both open and closed headlights, so the best way to differentiate is to count the vents behind the front wheelarch – a LWB should have three, while an SWB has only two.

Fittingly, the highest-specification 250GT California ever built was ordered by Luigi Chinetti for the 1960 Le Mans. With 280bhp, it was as quick as a tin-top SWB.

'In California, Jon von Neumann has an idea that just won't go away. He wants Ferrari to build a convertible version of the 250 Tour de France'

250 **SWB**

Ferrari's lightweight GTs were always known as Berlinettas which, between 1956 and '59 were well represented by the all-conquering Tour de France models. But in the last days of those 250s, seven 'Interim' Berlinettas were produced to a new, more modern style.

These cars performed well in racing in 1959 yet they were replaced by a new model that looked near-identical but would go on to even greater success and admiration. That model was the 250GT SWB – the last three letters standing for short wheelbase.

The SWB was based on a new chassis with a wheelbase of 2400mm, 200mm shorter than before. Pininfarina (renamed from Pinin Farina around this time) simply chopped out the extra length from the middle of the Interim's body, losing the quarter windows and in the process producing what is arguably the finest combination of good looks and muscular aggression ever seen.

Between late 1959 and early 1963 the SWB was produced in two forms, the Competizione and the Lusso (or 'street' spec). As the former, it was built by Scaglietti in aluminium, usually

with a 275bhp engine, a strengthened version of the familiar four-speed gearbox, bucket seats and sliding side windows.

The Lusso, not to be confused with the later 1962-64 Lusso seen elsewhere in this feature, was produced in steel except for an aluminium bonnet, doors and bootlid, and was more opulently equipped. With a lower compression ratio and smaller carbs, a Lusso engine typically produced 240bhp. Specifications were often mixed around though, so steel-bodied cars came with competition engines and vice versa.

But to give itself the best chance of winning the coveted International GT Championship, Ferrari produced a batch of 21 special SWBs for 1961. These were the SEFAC Hot Rods, with smaller-diameter chassis tubing for reduced weight, ultra-thin aluminium panelling and an engine equipped with Testa Rossa cylinder heads and bucket-sized carburettors that gave 285-295bhp.

These cars were good for 160mph, and won at Spa, Mille Miglia, Monza, Le Mans (GT class), Riverside and Tour de France. And yes, Ferrari won the GT Championship.

'Pininfarina simply chopped 200mm from the middle, losing the quarter windows and producing a car with the finest combination of looks and aggression'

250GTE

If any model demonstrates Ferrari's changing attitude towards commerciality, as well as the public's acceptance of the brand as a serious manufacturer of road cars, it's the 250GTE. Other than a few special-order 195s, 212s, 340s and 342s, the GTE was the first of the marque to be equipped with anything in the way of rear seats.

The car was a commercial success too, with more than 950 GTEs sold between 1960 and '63. The profits were usefully put towards the increasingly high-budget Ferrari race team.

The GTE kept to the 2600mm wheelbase of the 250GT and the Tour de France, but the cabin was made more roomy by moving the engine forward in the chassis by 200mm and widening the track of the front and rear wheels. Engine output was an impressive 240bhp at 7000rpm, which took the GTE from 0-60mph in just over seven seconds, with a top speed of almost 140mph – not bad for a four-seater.

Rear seats aside, the GTE represents the archetypal spec for a 1960s Ferrari: Pininfarina steel body with aluminium bonnet, doors and

boot, disc brakes, Nardi steering wheel, leather-covered seats and transmission tunnel, chrome-rimmed Veglia instruments and Borrani wire wheels. It pushes all the right buttons...

It was revealed as a new model at the 1960 Le Mans 24 Hours where a prototype GTE was used as a course car, before being officially launched five months later at the Paris Salon, Ferrari's favourite show. Little changed during the car's first two and a half years, even when the Series II was launched, the main update being the dashboard.

For the 1963 Series III a number of changes were phased in, some of them seen during Series II production. The rear leaf springs were changed for more responsive coils, the back wings reprofiled, the tail-lights changed and the driving lamps moved from the grille to directly under the headlights.

During production, an overdrive operating on fourth gear was introduced and this, with the disc brakes and boosted suspension, made the GTE the most useable 250 thus far. Now it's one of the most affordable in the range.

'The car was a commercial success, with the profits usefully put towards the increasingly high-budget Ferrari race team'

250GTO

In a line-up of iconic, highly collectible and astonishingly capable machines, the GTO is the version of the 250 that stands above the rest. It's the 250 that most enthusiasts think of first, the 250 that deservedly tops every wish list.

As successor to the great 250 SWB Competizione (and the SEFAC Hot Rods in particular), the GTO was aimed fair and square at the important GT championship. The 'O' of GTO stands for 'Omologato' (homologation) which, in hindsight, is an ironic nod to the FIA's qualifying rules – these stated that 100 cars had to be built for homologation to be granted. Ferrari got around these rules by convincing the FIA that the GTO was really a slightly modified 250 SWB. In many ways, that was true, although within the terms of FIA rules it was stretching the truth.

At least the evolution was there to see. The chassis of the GTO was little different from the SWB's, despite some extra bracing around damper and engine mounts and various other minor mods to stiffen the chassis. The engine, too, was the same Colombo V12 built to Testa Rossa specifications as used in the SWB Competizione. But larger valves and higher-lift cams brought power up to around 300bhp (later, one of two

4-litre GTOs would produce a stunning 390bhp). With a new five-speed gearbox, the GTO was capable of more than 170mph, and the acceleration was as rapid as five seconds from 0-60mph.

But the biggest difference of all between the GTO and its SWB predecessor was its bodywork. Despite the dominance of Pininfarina designs throughout the 250 range (and indeed all Ferraris of the era), the GTO was styled by Giotto Bizzarrini. He worked closely with experts at the university in Milan, using their wind tunnel to reduce drag produced by the new body.

The cowled lights and low front helped the low-drag cause, while weight was pared to a minimum with aluminium panels, Plexiglas side windows and rear screen, and a stripped-bare interior. Bizzarrini had done a superb job, but fell foul of Enzo Ferrari's famous cull of top employees and was sacked in November 1961. This left 25-year-old Mauro Forghieri in charge of the project.

Forghieri didn't quite get the GTO ready for the first race of the next season, at Daytona in February 1962, but the SWB/GTO development mule, driven by Stirling Moss, finished first in the GT class and fourth overall. When the genuine GTO was ready, Phil Hill and Oliver Gendebien

finished first in class and second overall at Sebring, and the wins kept on coming; Ferrari won the GT manufacturers' championship with GTOs in 1962 and '63.

For 1964, the GTO's body shape was revised to reduce drag still further. The '64 car was shorter, wider and lower, with more vents around the body, a flatter rear deck and a less curvy front end. Some prefer it, others feel the original was best. The changes worked, though, for Ferrari won the championship once again.

In all, 37 250GTOs were made between late 1961 and early '64, three of which were to 1964 spec. For many years the GTO held the record for the highest-ever selling price at auction (£6 million in 1990), but it's best to think of it as one of the greatest GTs ever built.

'Bizzarrini fell foul of Enzo Ferrari's famous cull of top employees and was sacked in November 1961, leaving 25-year-old Mauro Forghieri in charge of the GTO project'

'The GTO was styled by Giotto Bizzarrini, who worked closely with the experts at the university in Milan, using their wind tunnel to reduce the drag of the new body'

250GT Lusso

Take the bare bones of a 250GTO and re-clothe it in an elegant body of more civilised intention, and the result is the 250 Lusso – often said to be the best-looking 250 ever produced.

The Lusso is an incredible machine, with similar levels of comfort and performance to the 250 SWB. Chassis were to the same design as the GTO's, but the engine was placed slightly further forward to aid cabin space. Pininfarina penned the style, introducing a smart Kamm tail with neat circular rear lights and a wonderfully simple front end with a tiny bumper and separate overriders.

Lusso engines were generally ordered with outputs of 240bhp, which was enough to give performance figures of 150mph and a sub-seven-second 0-60mph. Coil springs and disc brakes all round were by then the 250 norm, but the interior of the Lusso set a new standard for the range. The bucket seats were trimmed in high-quality leather, as was the transmission tunnel and the doors, while the luggage area behind the seats was covered in vinyl with leather straps. The dashboard was also hide-trimmed, but the real point of interest here is

its unique Pininfarina styling, with a large speedometer and matching revcounter mounted in the centre, cocooned in sweeping cowls, and five minor instruments ahead of the driver, visible through the aluminium spokes of the gorgeous Nardi steering wheel.

There were 362 Lussos produced, 23 of which were right-hand-drive models.

As the last 250 road car to be introduced, the Lusso represents the results of ten years of development, which took the Ferrari GT from being a sometimes temperamental, haphazardly produced road-racer to a sophisticated, predictable (in the best sense of the word), high-performance Grand Tourer.

Funny, though, that in all those years, the outright performance didn't change significantly and the sense of style and character never diminished. That's why all 250s are, and always will be, so special.

Thanks to Ferrari specialist Paul Baber (www.250swb.com), Justin Platt of THRE, all the car owners, Lukas Hüni and photographer Michel Zumbrunn.

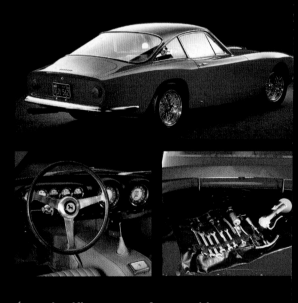

'...a significant step forward in comfort from the 250 SWB 'Lusso' and yet only a small step down from the performance of a GTO'

We're 6000 miles from the race tracks of Europe. And it's been 49 years since Ferrari chassis number 2689 GT hit 160mph time and time again down Le Mans' Mulsanne Straight to take a podium place and a first in the hard-fought GT class. But the magic is still there. Good grief, is it there!

These are the canyon roads of north-west Los Angeles: car and bike heaven where the tarmac is smooth and grippy, the locals tolerant and the views spectacular. The riptide of aural violence that blasts out of the Ferrari's quadruple tailpipes bounces off the rockfaces to clash with the cacophony of V12 mechanical madness, a whirr of thrashing valvetrain and dinky-sized pistons flying up and down at 5000, 6000, even 7000rpm.

We're grown adults, but still we drop the Plexiglas door windows to take in the noise, grinning like kids at every blip of the throttle. Foot down and the triple Webers suck so hard it's a wonder that the »

Ferrari's HOT ROD

This is the holy grail of 250 SWBs, one of the near-mythical Comp/61
'SEFAC Hot Rods' built to dominate European endurance racing. And could
it (whisper this) actually be better than the all-conquering 250GTO?

Words: David Lillywhite Photography: Mark Dixon

super-light aluminium bonnet doesn't turn concave, the intake bellow briefly drowning out both engine and exhaust, before they fight back screaming and roaring. And so we continue on our noisily rapid way, sometimes pushed hard into the bucket seats by the acceleration and occasionally backing off to take in the view.

What a machine! When a 250-series Ferrari is good, it's very, very good; even the crude early MMs and Europas with their transverse leaf spring front suspension and drum brakes are impressive when on fine form. But when you get to the 250GT Berlinettas, from the first 250GT and its competition 'Tour de France' (TdF) derivative to the GTO and the wonderfully complete 250GT Lusso road car... well, it's just heaven!

So how does the 250GT SWB (standing, of course, for short wheelbase) fit in? It's basically the link between the TdF and the GTO, a halfway house in evolutionary terms with a raft of minor changes over its predecessor that add up to much, much more than you'd ever expect.

Before the SWB was launched in late 1959, a small number of 'Interim' Berlinettas were built on the old 2600mm-wheelbase chassis, their Scaglietti-made bodies showing off the new Pininfarina styling that would grace the SWB to come.

Even on this longer wheelbase these Interim cars look considerably more together than the TdF, despite the addition of a small rear quarter window that neither the TdF nor the SWB ever featured. Taking 200mm out of the wheelbase to produce the SWB only added to the effect, the trailing edges of the doors now just a few inches from the taut rear arches, and the driver's backside even closer to the back axle.

Compared with the TdF the SWB just looks considerably more stylish and aggressive, unmistakably a car of the early 1960s. Gone are the TdF's '50s-style kicked-up rear wings, the sleekly recessed headlights and the bulbous roof and shallow screen. Instead, the front of the SWB (in hindsight) appears more conventional but blends in more comfortably with the trademark eggcrate grille, the sensuously curved front wings and the more muscularly bulbous back wings. Close your eyes and think about the shape of the rear sections of the roof and boot – it's easy to conjure up thoughts of gorgeously curved panelwork, but in fact the line from the trailing edge of the roof, down the rear window and along the boot lid is surprisingly straight and simple. Works, though!

In the California sunlight, the gleaming silver paint of 2689 GT shows off the lines to their very best. We have just left one of LA's trademark Sunday morning automobile gatherings, where the SWB was, of course, star of the show in a shopping mall car park absolutely packed with exotica. Out on the open road, with room to view the model properly, it just gets better.

But the fine looks aren't really the point of an SWB. It was designed to keep Ferrari at the very top of sports car racing, and the changes under the body are what matters. The reduction in wheelbase made the model lighter and easier to hustle through the bends than the TdF – just that little bit more alive and responsive.

> 'Foot down, and the triple Webers suck so hard it's a wonder that the super-light aluminium bonnet doesn't turn concave, the intake bellow briefly drowning out both engine and exhaust'

Below, clockwise
2689 GT (foreground)
gets fast exit at 1961
Le Mans; in the pits
with Jean Guichet; as
delivered to LA, 1965.

The SWB's chassis is still the same basic tubular ladder design of all the 250GT Berlinettas, but new Koni telescopic dampers in place of the old Houdaille lever arms keep the live rear axle in check and stopping is more powerful and predictable thanks to Ferrari's first use of disc brakes. It's interesting to find that, a full six years after Jaguar introduced discs on the C-type, the 1959 Paris 250GT SWB show car was still equipped with drums, even though all following SWBs had discs.

Power was up, too, by using yet another evolution of the Colombo 3-litre, single-overhead-cam, 60° V12. At between 260 and 280bhp it was a good 20bhp up on equivalent TdFs thanks to higher compression and larger carburettors. Two versions were available, both in widely varying specifications according to the customer's requirements. The Tipo 168B was the race engine, fitted to the Competizione version of the SWB, while the Tipo 168 was for street use in the (only slightly) more luxurious Lusso.

Competiziones had all-aluminium bodywork, built by Scaglietti, while Lussos were part steel, usually made down the road at Pininfarina but with their aluminium doors, boots and bonnets supplied by Scaglietti.

In keeping with this, the Tipo 168B engine was lighter than the 168, with some components cast in magnesium. It used still larger carbs, usually a line-up of three twin-choke Weber 40DCZs or DCL6s, where the Lusso's Tipo 168 made do with the same number of 36DCLs.

The very first SWB made was a Competizione, and it was these lighter, faster models that continued to dominate production for the first year of manufacture. This was largely because the new chassis meant that the

SWB didn't immediately qualify for homologation, and it wasn't until June 1960 – just in time for Le Mans – that it received its homologation papers and was able to switch from 'open class' international races to GT class. In that year SWBs won the Tourist Trophy, the Tour de France and the 1000km of Paris at Montlhéry. Not bad...

More Lusso versions followed, with extra attention paid to panel gaps and interior fittings, but GT class competition was fierce and success vital to the credibility of Ferrari. And so, along came something a little special... Less weight, more power: it's a classic, obvious recipe for success, and in this case it was beautifully executed.

So here we are, because today's terror of the canyon roads is one of these very cars, one of just 22 SWBs built to Comp/61 or 'SEFAC Hot Rod' specification, the ultimate derivative of the SWB and just a short step away from the 250GTO. In case you're wondering, SEFAC stood at this time for Società Esercizio Fabbriche Automobili e Corse, the name of the Ferrari company when it was restructured as a public corporation in 1960.

No single 250GT SWB SEFAC is the same, but crucially we know that the majority of them were built on a chassis of smaller-than-standard-diameter tubing, with extra bracing to compensate, and revised rear suspension pick-up points. Bodywork is generally an ultra-thin 1.1mm aluminium alloy, door windows are simple drop-down Plexiglas, operated by leather straps, and interiors are basic, some with bare aluminium floors, dashboards and firewalls. What is clear is that as production continued the specifications became less rather than

Right
Drop-down windows operated by leather strap; originals were probably fixed in place for Le Mans.

'Today's terror of the canyon roads is one of just 22 SWBs built to Comp/61 or "SEFAC" specification'

more radical, to the point that some of the last cars were built on standard Competizione chassis and bodies.

For many years there was much debate over the exact power output of the Tipo 168B/61 engines used exclusively in the SEFACs, but it is now usually agreed that it was around 290bhp. The increase came from Testa Rossa cylinder heads, high-lift Tipo 130 camshafts, larger intake tracts, two-piece large-diameter exhaust headers and triple twin-choke Weber 46DCF3s. The sump, valve covers and timing case were cast in magnesium, while the gearbox was the same four-speeder used in the SWB Competiziones, differing from the Lussos only in the lighter, ribbed cases.

At least 2689 GT's history and spec are well known and understood. It seems to have been the sixth SEFAC to be built, and we know that it was completed on 30 May 1961, just 11 days before that year's Le Mans 24 Hours, its planned first outing. Several SEFACs were built for that year's Le Mans; 2689 GT was sold jointly to experienced racers Jean Guichet and Pierre Noblet. They had previously individually owned and raced TdFs and pre-SEFAC SWB Competiziones, but had paired up only once before, in an unsuccessful attempt at the 1960 Montlhéry 1000km.

They were more triumphant in 2689 GT. The SEFAC cars proved perfectly suited to Le Mans, their extra 20bhp or so and lower weight making them noticeably quicker than the previous year's SWB entries. Guichet and Noblet's experience shone through as they carefully preserved their car, initially changing drivers at two-and-a-half hour intervals, but later reducing the gaps to one-and-a-half ▶▶

hours as tiredness set in. Noblet later claimed the surface at Le Mans was so smooth in 1961 that they had to change the tyres only once. The pair carefully worked up from tenth place at the end of three hours to first in GT class and third overall, at an average speed of 110.245mph.

Over the following year or so, the two went on to race 2689 in Monza's Coppa Intereuropa (finishing first), the Montlhéry Coupes du Salon, the Coupes de Bruxelles (first again), the Spa 500km, the Nürburgring 1000km and the six-hour Trophies d'Auvergne Clermont Ferrand. Noblet found the Nürburgring and Spa races tougher than Le Mans, yet no other SEFAC achieved such a distinguished racing history – although the famous dark blue Rob Walker team car, chassis 2735 GT, that Stirling Moss campaigned comes close.

But of course the highlight in 2689 GT's history is still that first outing at Le Mans, and it's the '61 Le Mans specification that previous owner John Upton settled upon for what turned out to be a nine-year restoration: silver livery with Gordini French Blue stripe and racing number 14 on the doors.

It wasn't an easy rebuild. 2689 GT had really suffered over the years between Guichet and Noblet's ownership and the beginning of the restoration in 1975, and at that time little was known of the SEFAC spec. Upton embarked on a near-fanatical programme of research, investigating every last unique detail of 2689 GT, and taking the time to quiz Pierre Noblet, fellow SWB gentleman driver George Arents and SWB collector Lou Slyker, among many others, to confirm his findings.

In 1984 Upton's labours were rewarded with a third in class at the Pebble Beach Concours and a reuniting with Pierre Noblet, who flew in from France to drive 2689 GT in a special Ferrari celebration at the Monterey Historics.

John Upton no longer owns 2689 GT; in 2003, renowned California car collector Bruce Meyer was holidaying in France and happened to pick up an early issue of *Octane*. There, advertised by Duncan Hamilton Ltd, was 2689 GT – and Bruce

had to have it. He flew from France to the UK to buy it. 'In college we lived in fraternity houses, and our alumni adviser in 1961 had just bought a new SWB,' recalls Bruce. 'I fell in love! 'In 1970 I bought my four-cam [Ferrari 275GTB]; in hindsight, I probably should have bought one of these [an SWB] or a 250GTO, because after that I followed their prices from the reasonable to the unreachable. When I spotted this car in *Octane* I knew I had to have it, even though its price was really beyond my budget. I could have afforded a steel SWB, but to me this is the most important of the SWBs.'

He's done little to change the car, other than a 'freshen-up', though he notes that before he bought 2689 GT it had a lower rear axle ratio to reduce the fearsomely high Le Mans gearing and make the car more useable. And use it Bruce does: 'I take it to a lot of events – I think I have a responsibility to do that,' he says, proving the point a little bit more by taking us to the infamous Rock Store once our photography sessions are over, gatecrashing the biker hang-out to remarkably popular reaction.

Could you make such varied use of a 250GTO? Well, maybe, but even the SEFAC SWB is quieter and more comfortable than the Omologato special that followed, and actually a little lighter in weight, though about 10bhp down in power. When the GTO was launched its looks were deemed disappointing after the dramatic SWB, but its more focused racing design brought in the results – and the rest is history...

2689 GT's celebrity continues apace: it was even part of a special 250GT SWB 50th anniversary celebration at the Pebble Beach Concours in August 2010. This featured eight SWBs in all, including two other SEFACs, an early Competizione, the Paris Motor Show SWB and examples of early and late Lussos. With fewer than 160 SWBs built, that was quite an occasion! △

Thanks to Bruce Meyer and family, the Ferrari Club of America, Kim Button and Kandace Hawkinson at Pebble Beach Concours, and Bruce Canepa.

1961 FERRARI 250GT SWB COMP/61 'SEFAC'

SPECIFICATIONS

Engine 2953cc 60° V12, SOHC, 24 valves, three twin-choke Weber 46DCF3s
Power 295bhp @ 7000rpm **Torque** 200lb ft @ 6000rpm **Transmission** Four-speed manual, rear-wheel drive
Suspension Front: independent by double wishbones, coil springs, Koni telescopic dampers. Rear: live axle, semi-elliptic
leaf springs, Koni telescopic dampers **Brakes** Discs front and rear, alloy calipers **Weight** 1020kg
Performance Top speed 160mph, 0-60mph 5sec (depending on gearing)

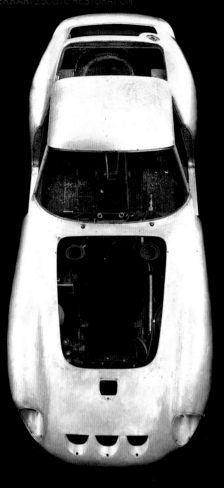
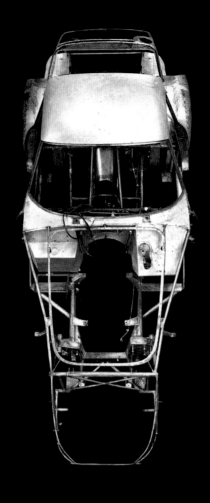
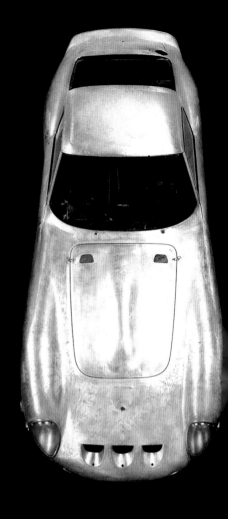
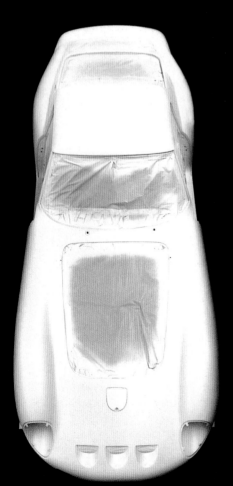
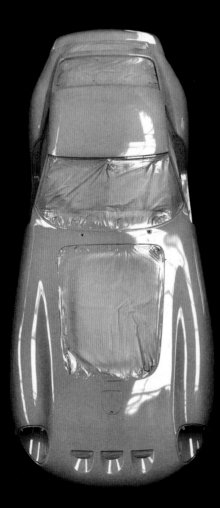
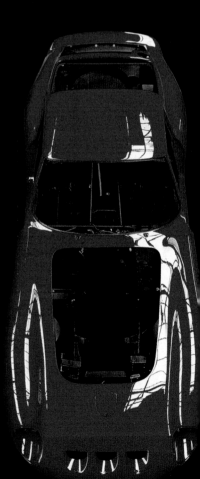

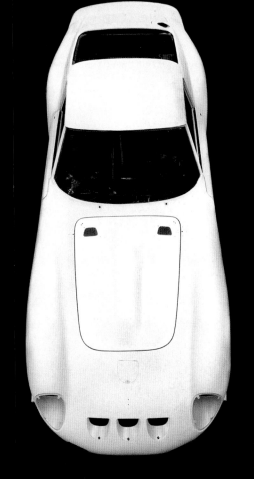

Reborn...

How do you set about restoring one of the most valuable cars in the world?
Robert Coucher charts the progress of 2450 hours in the life of a Ferrari GTO
Photography courtesy of Kevin O'Rourke

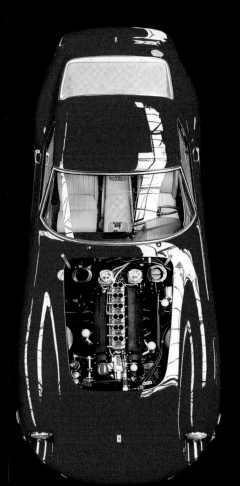

There is a fair old debate

going on in the world of historic cars at the moment. Should models be restored or preserved? In Britain and Europe we grumble when some of our American cousins completely rebuild their historic machinery, chroming the cam covers and wire wheels in the process. We profess to liking our historics careworn and patinated. The best proponents of this 'fit for purpose and nothing more' ethos are the lovely old contraptions found at any VSCC meeting in Britain. Or the scruffy vintage Bugattis enjoyed by the elegant drivers in the French Bugatti Club. Every grease nipple is oozing, but the paint is wretched and chrome has been wantonly rubbed through to the brass!

The Americans have responded with a special Preservation Class at Pebble Beach, and with the Pebble Tour which – rather shockingly – encourages entrants to actually drive their cars. The good news is that most do, with gusto. Other top-flight concours events have followed suit but, to be fair, the genteel motor cars in the Preservation arena are usually vintage automobiles that have led a ridiculously sheltered life doing little or no mileage, let alone having had to face the ravages of Driving Miss Daisy... Stored in sympathetic conditions, a mere wipe of Duck Oil and some of this century's air in the tyres sees them ready for the judges on the lawn.

Of course, this sort of debate intensifies when a tremendously rare and important historic machine like the Ferrari 250GTO here is »

'With a motor car of this magnitude, the best in the business were called upon to work their magic'

Ferrari 250GTO

SPECIFICATIONS

Engine
2953cc V12, sohc per
bank, two valves per
cylinder, six twin-choke
Weber carburettors

Max power
290bhp@7500-8000rpm

Transmission
Five-speed manual,
rear-wheel drive, LSD

Brakes
Servo-assisted discs

Weight
1050kg (2314lb)

Performance
0-60mph 6.5sec
Top speed 170mph

Value
£7,000,000-plus

Above: 3527GT
in good company
at Mototechnique's
workshop: experience
counts for everything.

concerned. As with all 39 Ferrari GTOs constructed, chassis number 3527GT's history has been detailed in various books. The previous owner, Stephen Pilkington – obviously a proper car chap who enjoyed his GTO properly and fast – had owned the special Ferrari since 1984. It has long been regarded as a 'lovely original car', which Pilkington drove on many Ferrari and GTO events in Europe. Quickly.

Purchasing the model in 2005, the new owner was faced with a quandary. Leave it as is or restore it. A tough decision, made more so when you consider a GTO is worth north of £7 million – if you can ever persuade one of the owners to sell. If this were a Ferrari that had been cossetted and gently exercised from new, then the decision would have been simple. Leave it alone. But the reality check is that Ferrari GTOs were built as racing cars, to last one season, over 40 years ago.

So, while 3527GT was a lovely original car, it had survived a tough racing life. It was sold new to Gottfried Koechert in May 1962 and was promptly entered in the Nürburgring 1000Km but retired. In September it was entered in the Tour de France, piloted by Lucien Bianchi and Claude Dubois, who led the fierce road-race until the last day, when they collided with a milk lorry. The lightweight aluminium nose of the Ferrari was stoved in but, with victory within their grasp, the pair leapt out and cut most of the front of the car clean

off. Unfortunately they could not manage better than seventh overall.

The car continued to race, winning the Angolan GP in Luanda in 1962 with Bianchi at the wheel. Then in 1965 it retired from racing and Graber, the Swiss coachbuilder, exacted some modifications, turning the old racer into a more comfortable tourer. 'One big advantage of the GTO is the noise level inside. It doesn't allow the passenger to speak and this leaves the driver in peace to savour the permanent and unique pleasure of driving the GTO on the road,' says GTO expert Jess Pourret. Quite.

In order to quieten the interior din, Graber soundproofed and carpeted the cabin, fitted panels to most exposed inner surfaces, replaced the Perspex side windows with wind-up glass and reupholstered the racing seats in leather. Rather optimistic little nerf bars were fitted to the front, and the rear lights were replaced with assemblies from a Volkswagen camper van. Ouch. Pilkington returned the exterior to original but kept the sensible Graber-modified interior, enjoying the GTO as such for 20 years.

The current owner, a successful individual and amateur historic racing driver, wanted a GTO as a touring car to add to his collection. With its history, 3527GT was just the model, a straight and original example in need of a little refreshing. And with a motor car of this magnitude the best in the British restoration business were called upon to work

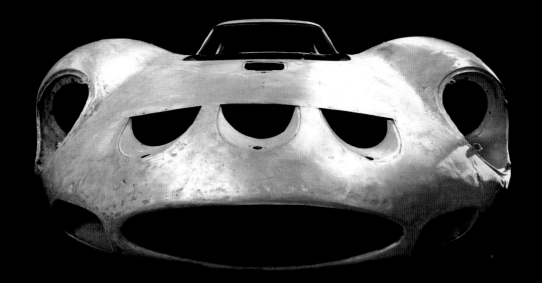

'As with most old racing cars, the nose and tail sections needed some love and attention, but overall the GTO was in remarkably good condition'

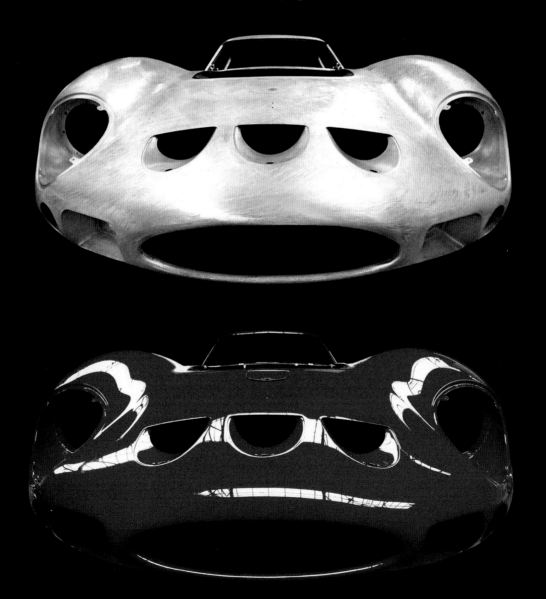

The restoration

'The non-original paint was micro-blistered and cracking, so it had to come off. We applied stripper and discovered the extent of all the repairs that had been necessary over the years'

This page: specialist work such as trimming was contracted out to known and trusted friends and colleagues.

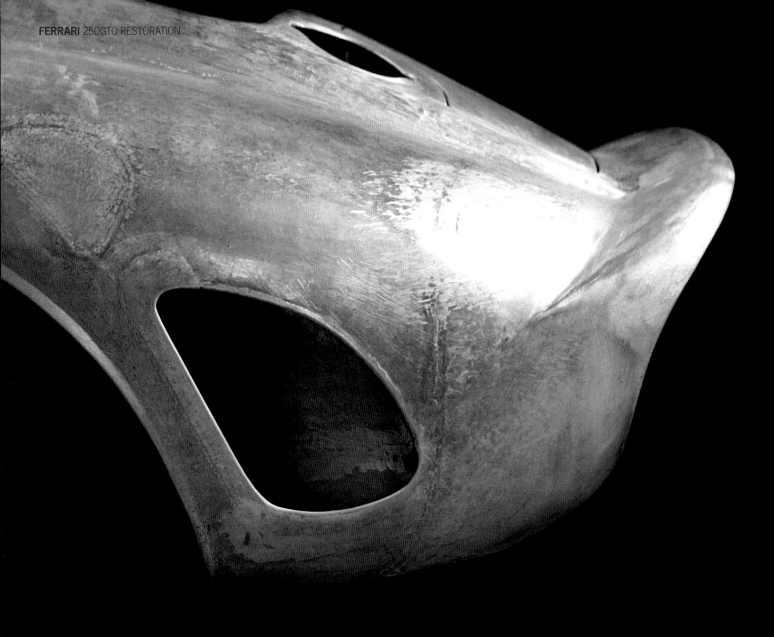

their magic: Kevin O'Rourke of Mototechnique in West Molesey near Richmond, son Rob (Rorky) O'Rourke of O'Rourke Coach Trimmers in Cranleigh near Guildford, and Martin Greaves of Classic Performance Engineering in Northamptonshire. The engine had previously been rebuilt by Ferrari specialist Greypaul and was in fine fettle, so the GTO went into O'Rourke's for a fresh coat of paint. But, as we all know, the real problems materialise once you scratch the surface...

'The non-original paintwork was micro-blistered and cracking, so it had to come off,' says Kevin O'Rourke. 'But first the body and chassis were digitally measured and recorded: both proved to be remarkably close to tolerance but not perfect. So we applied paint stripper and, once the car was in bare aluminium, discovered the extent of all the repairs that had been necessary over the years.

'Unfortunately, there was evidence of electrolytic corrosion where the aluminium skin wraps around the steel spaceframe. We would need to cut out this corrosion and let in new ally in numerous places. At this point it was decided to remove all the body panels so we could make an informed judgement as to what needed repairing and what could be conserved.'

He continues: 'With the panels removed we were able to gain full access to all inner panels, spaceframe and chassis tubes, in order to strip, straighten, repair, paint and protect the inner areas properly. It is imperative you have clean welds throughout the process to ensure none of the flux gets trapped in the ally, to burst through later. And as with most old racing cars, the nose and tail sections needed some love and attention. But overall the GTO was in surprisingly good condition.'

Once everything was lined up, a protective roll cage was designed and fabricated. At the request of the owner, this carries adjustable mountings for inertia-reel seat belts, while concealed mountings for three-inch racing harnesses are incorporated elsewhere in the car.

With the chassis refurbished, the original, carefully repaired body panels were refitted utilising all the factory rivet holes. These panels were all prepared and pre-painted internally to prevent any future electrolytic reaction. Next, a polyurethane primer was applied and baked at 90°C for an hour, then abraded and made ready for the polyester primer filler. This was hand sanded and shaped before a further grey sealer primer was applied. Grey is the best base for a red finish.

'The GTO was originally finished in Rosso Cina, which is unusual because it is a Fiat colour. We gave the client a number of swatches to choose from, and he went for this

Above: stripping back to bare metal was the only way to assess the true condition of vulnerable nose and tail sections.

> The GTO was originally finished in Rosso Cina, a Fiat colour. We gave the owner a number of swatches and he went for this lovely deep burgundy. It's known as Rosso Kev...'

lovely deep burgundy. It's known as Rosso Kev,' Kevin laughs. Four coats of base colour were applied and then coated in clear two-pack lacquer for protection. The Ferrari was then sanded and polished, and underbody stone protection applied.

With the GTO's bodywork renovated, re-assembled and painted, the car went up to Martin Greaves at Classic Performance Engineering for the rebuilt mechanical components to be refitted. 'Our intention was to make the GTO safe, reliable and great to drive,' says Greaves. 'We knew the engine was in fine condition with good oil pressure but, just to be sure, we removed the cam covers and sump for a quick look-see, and rebuilt all the ancillary components. The gearbox was stripped and crack-tested, and we found third gear was cracked. Gears are not generally available, but I eventually sourced one through our contacts.

'With the engine out we discovered the linkages operating the six twin-choke Weber carburettors were worn and had to be rebuilt and rebushed. These GTOs are renowned as being balanced and lovely to drive, so we did not alter the camber or suspension settings. We simply stripped, crack-tested, rebuilt and refreshed everything, then reassembled it all carefully.'

The exhaust system had to be replaced because it had been patched up rather too often, and special heat shields were inserted between the pipes and the passenger floor. All tanks were stripped, acid dipped and repainted. The rear ally fuel tank – now foam filled – is a work of art, as are the beautiful Borrani wire wheels, which were reshod with correct Michelin XWX tyres. The original Koni dampers were overhauled and the entire braking system was refreshed.

'The owner intends using the Ferrari for fast road events, so we carefully engineered in some heating and cooling fans. They are completely hidden in the existing cooling ducts and do a good job of increasing the flow of cool air, or hot, at the flick of a switch. On the Tour Auto, for example, a properly demisted windscreen is more important than an extra 50 horsepower,' adds a knowing Greaves.

With fresh mechanicals and wiring loom, the Ferrari was sent down to O'Rourke the younger in Cranleigh. 'As it had been converted to road use years ago, my brief was to do the same but add a few improvements and subtle upgrades to the interior: the sort of thing Ferrari would have done itself,' says Rorky. 'We unpicked most of the Graber interior and wrapped up all the sections for storage. Then we soundproofed the cockpit and made up new ally panels for the door cards and interior. The ones for the roof were fine.

»

so we reused those.'

Graber had panelled up most surfaces, leaving precious little storage space. O'Rourke opened up all these little binnacles, covering any exposed chassis tubing with hand-stitched and Connollised tan leather, using diamond-pattern stitching where appropriate. GTOs have fixed racing bucket seats, which are not a realistic option for long runs down to the South of France. Modern adjustable seats were sourced, which Rorky retrimmed in sumptuous leather and mounted on runners. They look simpatico and are very effective.

With the interior beautifully appointed and the original rear Perspex windscreen polished and refitted, the GTO went back to Mototechnique for final assembly of doors and side windows, bonnet and boot lid. Detailing complete, it made a last trip to Martin Greaves for final setting up.

At this point, real patience is required from both the owner and engineer. Little progress is visible for the hours of workshop time required to get the myriad detailed components to work in harmony. Things like the windscreen wiper action, the heating and demisting, properly bled and adjusted brakes, damper settings and all the other small details that turn a good car into a special one.

The final thing to do was to run up the V12 powerplant, debug it and get the carburettor tuning spot on. Initially there was a slight misfire at high rpm; however, optimising ignition and carburation settings have ensured clean running all the way to 7500rpm.

'The Ferrari is fabulous on the road,' says Greaves. 'Running on original-spec Michelins, you drive the GTO through the seat of your pants and it responds beautifully. The engine is remarkably tractable and, being a V12, it's lovely and smooth. But, saying that, it does like about 3000rpm showing on the clock, and above five-thou' it really comes alive. It's one of the best GTOs I have yet driven.'

So how much does a project like this cost? Well, it would be rude to discuss money, but think along the lines of 1500 hours in the bodyshop, 200 with the trimmer and 750 hours for mechanical work and set-up. Considering the magnitude of the task, this seems entirely acceptable.

On completion, 3527GT was presented at Goodwood House, making its first appearance at a special function hosted by Lord March. Martin Greaves then delivered the Ferrari to Ashford for collection by its new owner. 'He had a quick look around the car as I pointed out various controls, then popped his bag and laptop into the boot and disappeared off to the Channel Tunnel. No tentative drive around the car park, he was straight off to France! We didn't hear from him for a while and were all sick with worry,' says Greaves.

Two days and over 1000 miles later, the O'Rourkes and Greaves each received an e-mail from the owner: 'I have just completed a rather-too-warm trip to the South of France, arriving Friday lunchtime in the GTO. The car drove faultlessly throughout the trip (including very heavy traffic in Paris) and arrived in perfect order... Everything about the car is splendid. And I am certain much, much better than when it left Modena. Your teams have done a cracking job and I am very grateful. The Ferrari is perfect...'

'On completion, 3527GT was presented at Goodwood House, making its first appearance at a special function hosted by Lord March'

Hamann
CLASSIC CARS

965 Ferrari 275 GTS,
a wonderful restored example, one of only 200 cars built.

1967 Ferrari 275GTB/4,
One of the most desirable Ferrari road cars.

OTHER CARS AVAILABLE:

- Bizzarini 5300GT Strada
- Ferrari 250SWB Berlinetta
- Ferrari 250MM Spyder
- Jaguar D-Type
- Lamborghini Miura S
- Maserati 300S
- Mercedes 300SL Gullwing,
- Mercedes 300SL Roadster
- Porsche 356 Carrera Coupe

955 Porsche 550RS Spyder, Ex factory team
car. 1st in class at '55 Le Mans and
56 Mille Miglia factory entry.

1967 Ferrari 275 GTB/4 Alloy ex N.A.R.T., One of 11
alloy cars built, 1st in class at Daytona 24 hours.

1964 AC Shelby Cobra 289
Rare dual quad options, low miles
and clean history.

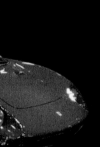

65 Ferrari 250 LM,
rare opportunity to own the 1st mid engine
rrari built in the company's history.

1956 Ferrari 250GT Boano Alloy Competizione, One
of three factory built cars with alloy body and
competition specs. Entry in '56 Mille Miglia.

With more than 30 years of experience in the industry Thomas Hamann has established himself as one of the leading international dealers and brokers of European classic race- and sports cars. With his extensive knowledge, contacts and excellent reputation many collectors from all over the world seek his advise and help when it comes to buying or selling a classic automobile or entire collection. Some of the most amazing and sought after, as well as valuable cars, found their way into the hands of satisfied customers with the help of Mr. Hamann. Let us also help you with your needs. Whether is comes to selling, buying or trading your classic automobile or entire collection, we are your reliable partner to do so.

mail: thomas@ferrari4you.com
st Coast, USA   Tel: +1-203-918-8300

www.ferrari4you.com

Baby Talk

More than thirty years ago, **John Simister** was tempted to blow his student grant on a half-share in a Ferrari Dino. He didn't, of course, but will a decent drive in a fine example convince him that he should have done?

Photography: Michael Bailie

I nearly bought a Dino once.

Half a Dino, anyway. You could purchase a sad one for laughably little in the post-energy crisis mid-1970s, and a friend and I worked out that if we didn't eat or drink all term we could buy a Dino with our student grants.

Fortunately sense prevailed, so I stuck with my souped-up Imp and he with his BSA C15. Next time I looked, Dinos were out of *Exchange & Mart* and reaching stratospheric heights in classic car emporia. And with that realisation vanished any hope of ownership. Stratospheric – yes, the Lancia Stratos had a Dino engine, too.

Years later, in 2001, I drove a lovely metallic blue example belonging to prestigious British Ferrari specialist Maranello Concessionaires before its collection got sold. What a delight that Dino was, fluid and sonorous and ground-huggingly low, but frankly not as quick as I expected, despite the promise of a 2.4-litre, 195bhp, Lampredi-designed V6 in a not very big car. Box ticked, memory filed away.

Maybe that Dino 246GT would have been faster had it been red. You know how cars can feel livelier, smoother, better on some days than on others, even though nothing has changed? The only variable in this is the human and his/her mood at the time. Given the importance of perception, then, it is entirely natural that a red Dino should be

'It's as crisp-edged a V6 as you could want, all intake snort and quad-exhaust howl and valvegear fizz; it sounds like half a V12 with a touch of dirty disharmony for extra intrigue'

Left
The first mid-engined Ferrari road car: you have to drive it quickly for it to work properly.

'First thought; isn't it small? I love small, fast cars, and I'm glad the Dino can now be counted as one'

faster. One way to find out: drive one.

Which is how I come to be at Philip Moir's classic-car 'timeshare' company Parc Ferme, coincidentally located in Egham, Surrey, very close to Maranello Sales' service department. Not that Philip uses his near-neighbour to maintain the Dino he hires out to hopelessly car-struck souls, because most service knowledge for this model resides elsewhere today. That blue-Dino drive lasted barely half an hour. This time, I'll get to know the beautiful beast properly.

THE 'BABY' FERRARI is a staggeringly good-looking car. Its shape set the template for the 308 and 328 that followed, and there's even some of its influence in the F40's lines. But the Dino is more delicate, more subtle than any of them, with its slender front grille, similarly slender (and useless) bumpers, thin screen pillars and seemingly almost no sills. You open a door by pulling a tiny, curved, chrome handle set into the side window's waistline trim; then you lower yourself into a huggy seat so low you feel you're almost

sitting on the road. But there was nothing to climb past on the way. Like I said, where are the sills?

This is an amazingly airy cabin for a car so low-slung. Partly it's the lack of a centre console, partly it's the surprising glass area. No other mid-engined coupé is so easy to see out of and manoeuvre. There's an embankment of brown suede forming the dashboard – which has faded from the original black, but Philip likes the patina. Switches are scattered semi-randomly; horizontal stripes – that Italian motif of automotive sportification – mark the seats, the door trims and much else.

The steering wheel is offset to the left, like the pedals, and its rim obscures the speedometer and tachometer, but the driving position is bearable once you've got used to the required knees-up, shins-straight-out pose. And the view forward, dominated by the mountainous front wings that rise out of the low plain of the bonnet, is like nothing else. Why on earth did later Ferrari fronts become so flat?

I've always thought the Dino's to be a timeless shape, the » way you do when something wonderful embeds itself in your brain at an early age. So it's strange to be close and alone with a Dino now: it's really here, I'm really about to drive it and certain parts of my brain are about to be re-ordered. First thought: isn't it *small*? I love small, fast cars, and I'm glad that the Dino can now be counted as one. Second thought: those wheels are both wonderfully retro and utterly ridiculous for an aspirant supercar, given the way rims have since evolved. The wheels are a mere 14in diameter, the Michelin XWX balloon tyres they wear are 205/70 in section. Seventy! And we used to think that was a low profile.

I'M ON MY WAY home from Egham, it's raining and frankly I'm not enjoying the drive. The heating and demisting are hopeless, the clap-hands wipers equally so, given their tiny blades, their inability to self-park and the lack of a flick-wipe. And the steering is very strange: I turn the wheel on a wet bend, turn some more, and still there seems to be no bite. Eventually there's a response and we're not, after all, in terminal understeer, but trust is taking a while to build. If this is one of those cars that leaps from massive understeer to massive oversteer with nothing inbetween, and sabotages

Below
Simister at speed: several days with the Dino confirmed that it's a challenging but rewarding car to drive really well.

my efforts at salvage with the steering's low gearing, then we're not going to get on.

Enzo Ferrari apparently resisted making a mid-engined road car to begin with, because he thought it would be too dangerous for his customers. It was only when the idea came along of using the Dino engine Ferrari had developed for Fiat and Formula Two, of relatively low power at first (2.0 litres and an optimistically claimed 180bhp for the Dino 206), that he relented. And even then he clearly wanted to make sure there was no twitchiness in the steering response. Well, he succeeded.

I go to sleep bemused. Maybe the wet road overly exaggerated that part of the Dino's dynamics. And the engine did sound fantastic, revving to 6000rpm in a blink, on to 7000 with verve, short-legged gearing making the most of the revviness. It's as crisp-edged a V6 as you could want, all intake snort and quad-exhaust howl and valvegear fizz; it sounds like half a V12 with a touch of dirty disharmony for extra intrigue. Nor is the gearchange quite the cantankerous control of popular legend. It's said to be impossible to get into second when the 'box is cold, but in reality that's not true at all. You just need to be gentle but firm, and maybe help with a double-declutch on the way down. Easy.

'Next morning, the Dino looks utterly seductive as its red paint glows in the mist. I'm going for a proper open-road blast and I'm going to find out what the Dino is really like'

Ferrari Dino 246GT

SPECIFICATIONS

Engine
2418cc, 65deg V6, iron
block, aluminium heads,
four overhead cams
driven by gears and
chains, two valves per
cylinder, three Weber
40 DCF carburettors

Power
195bhp @ 7600rpm

Torque
166lb ft @ 5500rpm

Transmission
Five-speed manual,
rear-wheel drive

Suspension
Double wishbones, coil
springs, anti-roll bar,
telescopic dampers

Brakes
Ventilated discs
all round, vacuum
servo assisted

Performance
0-60mph 7.1sec
Top speed 148mph

Value
Cost new £5486
at launch in 1969
Value now c£65,000

NEXT MORNING, the Dino looks utterly seductive as its red paint glows in the mist. I'm going for a proper open-road blast, and I'm going to find out what the Ferrari is really like once free of suburbia. The roads are drying, which helps, and I remember now that the later 328 and Mondial also had this sluggish-steering thing. So did the Honda NSX, come to that.

The idea is that the faster you go, the better the steering becomes. That's as it should be, because a Ferrari is meant to be driven quickly. At speed on the M4 motorway, the Dino sits with surprising stability but snicks easily from lane to lane as needed. It's all coming together.

And the engine is proving a very fine thing, torquey despite its massively oversquare bore/stroke ratio and seemingly desperate for action. It's as if the car has been kept cooped-up for too long and is finally filling its lungs. Certainly it seems to go better the more I drive it, its overrun exhaust haze one clue to the looseness that is behind its burgeoning pace. Maybe this is why LYX 117K feels quicker than I remember the blue Maranello car to be. The brakes are improving, too, with more bite and a shorter pedal travel. It just proves that cars need to be used to keep them fit.

Up on the beautiful Lambourn Downs there are long straights linked by some delicious bends. Along one of the bumpier straights the Dino is feeling a touch underdamped (I think new dampers might sharpen it considerably), but the steering is redeeming itself quickly. It still seems slow and lazy

Above
Airy cabin a pleasant surprise; neat, delicate detailing and raised front wings set Dino apart from later Ferraris.

at first, yet there's lots of road feel now the tyres are working properly. Dive into a corner and the front tyres' slip angle is initially large, but then they bite, the front end loads up and the threatened understeer turns tail and runs away.

That's not to say the tail takes over, though. The balance is actually quite benign, the Dino going where pointed with a surprising lack of tail-snap if you try to provoke it by lifting off the power. There's too much traction for a proper powerslide, as well. It would be hard to get into trouble in this car on a dry road, although a fast, wet bend could well be another matter.

Nevertheless, driving the Dino is a more physical activity than you might expect. The unassisted steering is garrulous once woken up, and not light. The brakes, likewise. And the gearchange, which requires constant analysis of engine speeds and timings, is always stiff. That open-plan gate is not just for show: were it not there, I suspect the ratios would be a lot harder to find given the apparent flexibility of the gear linkage. Lovely smooth clutch, though.

I ENDED UP loving the Dino. Its Pininfarina-penned shape leads you to expect something light and effortless to use, but no pre-Dino Ferrari had been like that so why should the company's first mid-engined road car be different? The Dino 246 is full of such contrasts: delicate but physical, modern yet vintage, frustrating but absorbing. I wanted one back in 1976, and more than 30 years later nothing has changed.

Ferrari 365GTB/4
Daytona

For at least half its 40-year history, the 365GTB/4 has been an indicator of the state of the classic car market. Where does it stand now, and why does it have such a hold over enthusiasts?

Words: Robert Coucher Photography: George Bamford

D 69

It is probably true to say that the Ferrari 365GTB/4 has been a bellwether of classic car prices for the last couple of decades. When the collector market rose to dizzying heights in the late '80s, the 365GTB/4 was at the front of the grid. It is often remembered as the million-buck Ferrari that fell ignominiously to 50,000 bucks virtually overnight. In Britain, prices peaked at £400,000 in 1990 – a lot of money back then.

Paul Osborn of Cars International Kensington says: 'When I was working at Chequered Flag in West Hollywood in 1989, I sold a bronze 5000-miler to the owner of Popeye Fried Chicken for $1 million. It was a perfect car, even if the colour was a bit of a challenge, and that was a fortune in those days. In America the Spider always commanded more money, whereas in Europe they

»

'*The Daytona was largely handmade: the upshot is that seasoned Daytona drivers say each car feels very different*'

were seen as hairdressers' cars, although that perception has now largely changed. But only 121 Spiders were manufactured, so they are rare and collectable and now command over $1 million. For some years the Americans did not fancy the early Plexiglas model (which gets the frontal light treatment), as they were never officially imported into the US. But that's exactly what the Japanese buyers want.'

When the crash came, the 365GTB/4 certainly dropped in value and remained at around £50,000 to £80,000 for years thereafter. 'But in the last 12 months or so [at time of writing, in 2008], the Ferrari has pretty much doubled in value and has performed better than any other '70s Ferrari by far,' adds Osborn.

Within a very short space of time the values of decent 365GTB/4s have risen from about £80K to £160K. Graeme Hunt of Bramley of Kensington explains: 'In November last year we sold a mint, silver 365GTB/4 for £197,500, which was the top price at that point. But when these cars were selling for £400,000 in 1990, think what a decent flat in London or apartment in New York cost. Those properties have more than doubled in value, whereas cars like these Ferraris still have only half the value they had 18 years ago.' Does make you think.

Not that we should be banging on about value and cost above all

else, but these big V12 Ferraris were very much at the forefront of the boom and bust of the past. Dealer Martin Chisholm says: 'I did some research for a customer which showed that Ferrari 365GTB/4 prices peaked at £400,000 in 1990, Aston Martin DB5s hit £100,000 and Mercedes-Benz 300SL Gullwings topped out at £150,000. Today the Aston is around £200,000, the Gullwing is north of £300,000 but a good Ferrari can be had for £150,000 to £170,000.

'I personally own a Ferrari Daytona because it epitomises the early '70s,' says Chisholm. 'While the Ferraris of the '50s and '60s are curvy and beautiful, the Daytona is mean and it looks the business. It is the car I have always wanted and I enjoy driving it immensely. With its fat back end planted under power, that long bonnet and great revvy engine, the Daytona is a proper man's car.'

Those of you who have been paying attention will have noticed the word 'Daytona' popping up in the last paragraph. Launched at the Paris Salon in 1968, this Ferrari was officially a 365GTB/4. In 1967 Ferrari's 330 P4 racing cars finished first and second, with a privateer 412P third, on American soil, finally breaking the Ford GT40's dominance. The word Daytona became Ferrari's internal designation for the 356GTB/4 during development, but apparently was leaked by

the press, incensing Enzo Ferrari, so it was never an official moniker. Today, however, this Ferrari is universally known as the Daytona.

When launched in Paris the Daytona was not met with rapture because it was rather conservative in terms of both looks and engineering. Lamborghini had stolen Ferrari's thunder with its rock star-esque Miura, featuring a mid-mounted V12, which did make the 365 Grand Touring Berlinetta four-cam look a bit straight-laced. Of course, we now know that a proper Ferrari has to have a lusty great V12 mounted up front, and the current awesome 599 has exactly that.

Look at George Bamford's exquisite photographs here and you will have to agree that Pininfarina's design is superb. The design drawings were completed on December 10, 1966, and the first prototype was finished in 1967, the bodywork being done by Scaglietti, effectively Ferrari's in-house bodyshop.

Amazingly, even in the late '60s the Daytona was largely handmade and there were never any press tools. Rather, sections of metal were shaped over a wooden buck and then welded together on a jig. The upshot is that no two machines are the same and that's why, when you speak to seasoned Daytona drivers, they all say that each car feels very different. Most are good, while others are less so.

As well as its striking bodywork, the Daytona features that superb 4.4-litre V12, which pumps out 352bhp at a heady 7500rpm. As with the preceding 275GTB/4, the transmission is situated at the rear. This

transaxle is linked to the clutch and engine via a torque tube, all in an effort to spread the car's considerable weight of 1550kg throughout the chassis. Interestingly, the Daytona was the first Ferrari to feature glassfibre inner body sections, which include the front and rear bulkheads plus the floors and transmission tunnel.

In total 1400 Daytonas were manufactured, 121 of which were Spiders as we said. Only 158 were right-hand drive, including seven Spiders. When new, many Daytonas were painted dark brown and other strange colours. 'You know when a car is on the up,' says Paul Osborn, 'when they all suddenly start to appear in "retail red" with biscuit hide interiors! Many Daytonas are on their second restorations, and the good ones are probably better than when they came out of the factory.'

Generally Daytonas are tough old things, with no real mechanical vices. Ferrari expert David Cottingham of DK Engineering warns of rust and accident damage. The gearboxes can wear and weak synchros are common. A full engine rebuild will set you back £25,000 and a transaxle is £5000. A Luppi interior will be about the same.

Terry Hoyle of TDH Classics is a Daytona fan. 'They are iconic cars with superb, powerful engines. Ferrari claimed 352bhp for the road engines, and every time we rebuild one the power sheets show exactly 352bhp. We generally don't modify them because Ferrari did such a good job to begin with. Ferrari is not where it is today because it did its design engineering on the back of a cigarette packet. These cars are

'Many Daytonas are on their second restorations, and the good ones are better than when they came out of the factory'

*'Driving a Daytona is
always an experience. Detractors
say that it is big and heavy.
Well, it is'*

beautifully executed in every detail.

'Sometimes the limited-slip diff can be felt thunking when you turn the car in tightly. People get worried and think there's something wrong, but it is just the LSD doing its job. It's a good idea to allow the box to warm up – just miss out second gear for the first five miles. And give the car ten miles or so to let the dampers and bushes start working properly. Rust? Not as bad as Dinos, but the intricate exhausts can rot through lack of use. Some owners have complained that the cars are heavy at parking speed, especially when the wider seven- and nine-inch rims are fitted. But we have a power steering kit which makes a big difference – and no, I'm not going to tell you how we do it!'

Beautiful as the Ferrari Daytona is, its whole raison d'être is driving. Fast. The car might have looked a little conservative when launched, although the early ones did have that clever Plexiglas front-end treatment (replaced for 1970 with pop-up lights), but it would do 174mph flat-out and 0-60mph in about 5.5 seconds. Fast today, sensational in 1968. And driving a Daytona is always an experience.

Detractors say that it is big and heavy. Well, it is. If you want a nimble little sports car, a Dino might suit better. The Daytona is a grand tourer designed to cover huge mileage at great speed. The steering is heavy when parking and a bit woolly around the straight-ahead position. Yes, the clutch is he-man and the gearshift needs a firm hand, but get the engine on the cam at four thou' and hold on: the Daytona gets serious and simply takes off. Handling is pretty neutral and the brakes take punishment when trying to haul it all back down again. But when the free-revving V12 goes for 7000rpm, you know you are in a special car.

Because of their great strength and speed, the Daytonas proved to be excellent long-distance racers at Le Mans. In 1971 'Coco' Chinetti, son of American Ferrari importer Luigi, drove a NART Daytona to a class win in the Index of Thermal Efficiency. In 1972 Daytonas took the top five places in the GT category, with the winning car timed at 183mph down the Mulsanne Straight, and in 1973 the British-entered, JCB-sponsored Daytona, driven by Neil Corner and Willie Green, retired at the 18th hour. But that car, chassis number 15681, is still very much with us, and is still raced and rallied to great effect.

Below
Quad tailpipes, Borrani wires with triple-eared knock-offs... this superbly restored example ticks all the 'proper car' boxes.

**Ferrari
365GTB/4**
SPECIFICATIONS

Engine
4390cc dohc all-alloy
V12, dual ignition, six
Weber 40 carburettors
Power
352bhp @ 7200rpm
Torque
318lb ft @ 5500rpm
Transmission
Five-speed manual, rear
mounted in transaxle
Suspension
Front: independent
via wishbones, coil
springs, telescopic
dampers, anti-roll bar.
Rear: independent via
wishbones, coil springs,
telescopic dampers
Brakes
Discs all round
Weight
1600kg (3527lb)
Performance
0-60mph 5.4sec
Top speed 174mph

Dark Horses

In among the iconic Maranello machines that we know and love, there are one-offs and special-bodied cars that only true enthusiasts recognise. These are a few of our favourites...

Words: Jack Carfrae

» P4/5 by Pininfarina

Ferrari Enzo not quite distinctive enough for you? Then why not have it rebodied with the flavour of the glorious late-60s 330 P3/4 sports-racer? That's what one super-rich American enthusiast did. Car collector James Glickenhaus located the last remaining box-fresh Enzo, still shrouded in white plastic and undriven, and had it shipped to Pininfarina, where it was fitted with a Jason Castriota-designed body.

Little separates the car from the Enzo mechanically. The 660bhp V12 and F1-style six-speed gearbox remain. However, the P4/5's kerbweight undercuts than that of the Enzo, and the revised body is both lower and more aerodynamic, as well as being arguably more attractive.

Glickenhaus has a deep love of the P3/4 and P4 Ferraris – he owns chassis no 0846, worth £6 million. Which explains why he was willing to part with more than £500,000 for an Enzo and an additional £2.4 million for its conversion... »

'Volpi commissioned Bizzarrini to cannibalise his 1961 Ferrari 250SWB and build something that would be faster than a GTO'

250 Breadvan

The Breadvan came about largely as a result of Enzo Ferrari's famous bloody-mindedness. Count Giovanni Volpi di Misurata was its instigator after Enzo refused to deliver a pair of 250GTOs. Enzo's argument was that the Count financed the company ATS, which employed ex-Ferrari types such as Bizzarrini, Chiti and Gardini. So Volpi commissioned Bizzarrini to cannibalise his 1961 Ferrari 250SWB and build something that would be faster than a GTO.

Bizzarrini's flair for aerodynamics resulted in the deep curves, knife-edged nose and high, truncated tail. The engine was moved back much further than in a standard 250SWB to sit behind the front axle, improving the handling. The number of carbs doubled to six dual-throat Webers, which required an unusual teardrop-like clear cover to house them. Suspension was tweaked, GTO wheels and tyres were added and the whole car sat much lower than in standard form. In competition it proved as fast as the GTOs, but unreliable.

»

575GTZ

Zagato's long-standing association with Ferrari was reignited in 2005 after a 12-year hiatus. The Milanese coachbuilder is renowned for producing striking and distinctive bodywork, and the GTZ is no exception.

It was Japanese collector Yoshiyuki Hayashi who contacted Zagato with the commission. Hayashi already owned a standard 2004 Ferrari 575M, which became the platform for the Zagato body. Noriko Harada, head of design at Zagato, took the responsibility of penning a new body for the 575.

The brief was simple: to make a completely individual car, and this allowed Zagato free rein with the design. The 575 was inspired by the hallowed Ferrari 250GTZ, arguably one of Zagato's best-looking cars, which just happened to be approaching its 50th anniversary. The 575GTZ has Zagato's trademark 'double-bubble' roof and two-tone paintwork. »

» 375 America Agnelli Speciale

Whilst it is difficult to identify the most valuable or exotic of Gianni Agnelli's cars, almost certainly the most *individual* is the Ferrari 375 America. The 375 was far from his only Ferrari, or even his only coachbuilt one. He bought a 166MM Barchetta, bodied by Touring of Milan in 1950, and a 212 Inter coupé by Vignale two years later.

However, the Speciale was Agnelli's first truly bespoke Ferrari. Easily the fastest of his collection, the Speciale was revealed on Pinin Farina's stand at the Turin Motor Show in 1955. Agnelli ordered 'a Ferrari that doesn't look like a Ferrari'. The deep green and dark red colour combination, sloping pillars and clear roof panel are all unique.

The Speciale was easily the most elaborately styled of Pininfarina's Ferraris, and had the blistering performance to back up its appearance with a 6.5-second 0-60mph time. »

'The Speciale was easily the most elaborately styled of Pininfarina's Ferraris, and had the blistering performance to back up its appearance'

'Robert Jankel claimed to have used only the windscreen, A-pillars and doors from the donor vehicle. Of all the bespoke Ferraris, this was the most outlandish'

» Daytona Shooting Brake

Over a decade after the original 250SWB Breadvan, Luigi Chinetti Junior, son of the renowned New York Ferrari dealer, decided to turn his hand to automotive design. He found a willing backer in Florida property developer Bob Gittelman, who liked Luigi's design for a 330GT estate but wanted it adapted for a Daytona chassis.

To build the creation, they turned to the Surrey-based Jankel Group, a subcontracting coachbuilder for Rolls-Royce and also home to Panther Westwinds. The finished machine was an unusual but impressive piece. Robert Jankel, the craftsman behind the car, claimed to have used only the windscreen, A-pillars and doors from the donor vehicle, while the interior was completely reworked with unorthodox but tasteful use of wood and leather. Of all the bespoke Ferraris, this was probably the most outlandish.

FERRARI'S JUNIOR SUPERCAR

308

Enzo's baby was the first Ferrari road car to receive a V8 engine, and was a huge step forward from the Dino 206/246 – but today the 308 lives in its predecessor's shadow. Perhaps now is the time for a rethink

Words: Keith Adams Photography: Paul Harmer

If you're a dedicated follower of fashion, it can't have escaped your attention that, after years of languishing in the doldrums imagewise, Ferrari 308s are becoming hot property again. Perhaps the whiff of 1980s consumerist excess has dispersed enough to allow the very obvious beauty of these cars to shine through.

But that's the world of classic cars – everything is cyclical. And that's what makes the Ferrari 308 so appealing right now. They can be bought for very reasonable money; they are useable in a way that few others from the Scuderia were before; and as long as you're sensible and keep the miles down, running costs are not out of the ordinary.

Here is the story of the 308 and its 328 kissing cousin, the car that Enzo did not initially want to call a Ferrari. But from those faltering steps, a true great has emerged. And without wanting to sound clichéd, now really is your chance to own *and enjoy* a genuine Ferrari legend without breaking the bank.

»

Pity the poor design and engineering teams at Ferrari. They were given one of the toughest briefs imaginable in the early 1970s, when they were tasked with replacing the Dino 206/246. The V6-powered junior supercar combined concept looks with a neat and tidy mid-engined chassis to create one of the greatest models ever to emerge from Fiorano. It didn't wear a prancing horse badge, but then it didn't need to – the 206 and 246 were 'proper' Ferraris that just happened to be priced to fight the Porsche 911.

But Ferrari was on a roll at the time, and the company oozed confidence. If it was going to replace the Dino, then it would start with a clean sheet – and everything about the new car would need to be upscaled or boldly re-invented. Where there were two seats before, four would confidently reside. A V6 might have been good enough for the original, but nothing less than a V8 would do for the '70s. As for the styling – Bertone was on form at the time, and Ferrari decided that it should be entrusted to drag the Scuderia kicking and screaming into the wedgy modern era. That would prove a controversial decision.

Styling aside – and we will get back to that – the GT4's biggest leap forward was its engine. It had a vee-angle of 90 degrees, and with a bore and stroke of 81x71mm it came in at 2927cc, just under the three litres that Formula 1 cars were running at the time. It cannot have gone uncommented within the factory that this would be far easier to package in a racer than Enzo's beloved flat-12.

The light-alloy power unit was powerful and free-revving. With an ample 255bhp on tap at a suitably racy 7700rpm, the belt-driven four-cam was a driver's dream. Ferrari eschewed fuel injection, relying on four double-choke Weber 40DCNF carburettors for fuelling, and the result was a magical soundtrack.

The GT4 was compact – as a Dino should be – measuring 4320mm long and 1800mm wide. But, most importantly, its kerbweight was a sylph-like 1150kg. The upshot was an excellent power-to-weight ratio and performance truly befitting of a (Dino-badged) Ferrari. Unlike the 246, which might make it to the high 130s given a long enough run, the 308GT4 could crack 150mph and get from nought to 60mph in comfortably under seven seconds.

Ferrari believed it had the right product for the time, and during the final stages of the 308's development seemed to be vindicated in going for a more grown-up approach, as ever more powerful versions of the 911 hit the market. More intriguingly, in 1972 Maserati wheeled out the 190bhp Citroën SM-engined Merak – clearly a junior league supercar – and Sant'Agata had already shown its hand by revealing the Urraco in prototype form in 1970.

It took another three years before the baby bull went on sale, making its debut in Turin in 1973. But Ferruccio's company – like Maserati – underestimated how much power even a junior supercar needed, and the 2.5-litre V8 trailed the Ferrari considerably, putting out 220bhp. Fiorano would start the battle with a clear advantage.

And so it came to pass. The 308GT4's first public appearance was at the Paris Salon in October 1973, and it was clearly worth the wait. Besides the new F1-derived engine, the GT4 broke new ground for being a four-seat transverse-mid-engined car – a first for Ferrari. However, much as the punters admired what was under the skin, they struggled to come to terms with the Bertone-designed, Scaglietti-built body, which looked suspiciously similar to the Carrozzeria's new Urraco – another proponent of the '70s wedge.

And it was that design which sowed the seeds of the GT4's relative lack of success in the coming years. The '70s might have been financially tough, but they were a golden

'Bertone was on form, and Ferrari decided that
it should be entrusted to drag the Scuderia kicking
and screaming into the wedgy modern era'

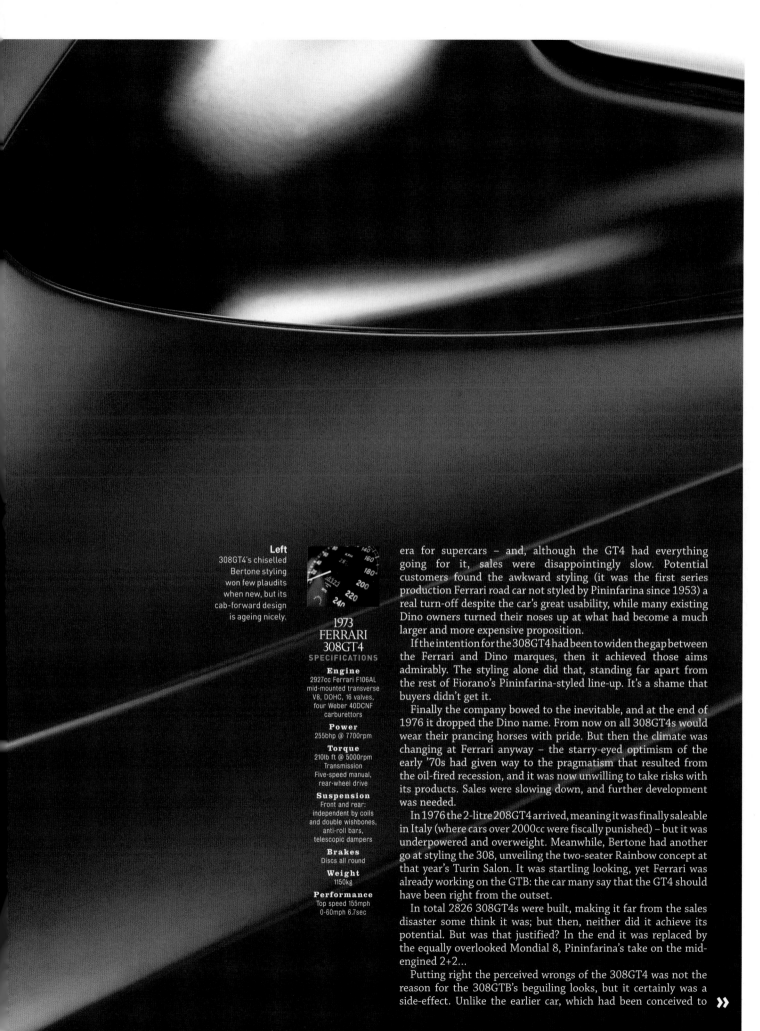

Left
308GT4's chiselled Bertone styling won few plaudits when new, but its cab-forward design is ageing nicely.

1973 FERRARI 308GT4

SPECIFICATIONS

Engine
2927cc Ferrari F106AL mid-mounted transverse V8, DOHC, 16 valves, four Weber 40DCNF carburettors

Power
255bhp @ 7700rpm

Torque
210lb ft @ 5000rpm
Transmission
Five-speed manual, rear-wheel drive

Suspension
Front and rear: independent by coils and double wishbones, anti-roll bars, telescopic dampers

Brakes
Discs all round

Weight
1150kg

Performance
Top speed 155mph
0-60mph 6.7sec

era for supercars – and, although the GT4 had everything going for it, sales were disappointingly slow. Potential customers found the awkward styling (it was the first series production Ferrari road car not styled by Pininfarina since 1953) a real turn-off despite the car's great usability, while many existing Dino owners turned their noses up at what had become a much larger and more expensive proposition.

If the intention for the 308GT4 had been to widen the gap between the Ferrari and Dino marques, then it achieved those aims admirably. The styling alone did that, standing far apart from the rest of Fiorano's Pininfarina-styled line-up. It's a shame that buyers didn't get it.

Finally the company bowed to the inevitable, and at the end of 1976 it dropped the Dino name. From now on all 308GT4s would wear their prancing horses with pride. But then the climate was changing at Ferrari anyway – the starry-eyed optimism of the early '70s had given way to the pragmatism that resulted from the oil-fired recession, and it was now unwilling to take risks with its products. Sales were slowing down, and further development was needed.

In 1976 the 2-litre 208GT4 arrived, meaning it was finally saleable in Italy (where cars over 2000cc were fiscally punished) – but it was underpowered and overweight. Meanwhile, Bertone had another go at styling the 308, unveiling the two-seater Rainbow concept at that year's Turin Salon. It was startling looking, yet Ferrari was already working on the GTB: the car many say that the GT4 should have been right from the outset.

In total 2826 308GT4s were built, making it far from the sales disaster some think it was; but then, neither did it achieve its potential. But was that justified? In the end it was replaced by the equally overlooked Mondial 8, Pininfarina's take on the mid-engined 2+2...

Putting right the perceived wrongs of the 308GT4 was not the reason for the 308GTB's beguiling looks, but it certainly was a side-effect. Unlike the earlier car, which had been conceived to **»** carry forward the Dino name, the GTB was meant to be a Ferrari. Almost as soon as the GT4 appeared, scoop shots of its two-seater cousin made the press. The Boxer-like design was a welcome departure from the origami styling that dominated the '70s, and clearly exactly what Ferrari customers wanted.

When the 308GTB surfaced at the 1975 Paris Motor Show, it was greeted with a collective sigh of relief, its elegant styling dominating the proceedings for all the right reasons. Once again the 308 was a landmark car, this time for its glassfibre body, a Ferrari first. Scaglietti excelled itself by creating resin-work so good that only its sound and feel differentiated it from steel.

Leonardo Fioravanti was responsible for the shape and, as expected from the man whose portfolio includes the Daytona and BB, it looked absolutely right – especially with those shapely air intakes that graced the flanks. There were no concessions for practicality, and that allowed the gifted designer to indulge himself; not a luxury Gandini had when he conceived the GT4. And that's why the two-seater was longer but had a shorter wheelbase than the car which sired it – overhangs were needed for the most impactful styling.

The GTB had little interior room and was very much a two-seater for those who travelled light. There was minimal stowage space, and that broad central tunnel denied any kind of intimacy between driver and passenger.

Beneath the skin, the technical package closely paralleled the GT4's. Suspension was by double wishbones and coil springs front and rear, with hefty anti-roll bars at both ends in order to keep it all in check. The 3-litre quad-cam V8 retained its transverse layout and, as before, drive was through a five-speed gearbox with a limited-slip differential.

There were some detail changes from GT4 to GTB and, although the power output remained 255bhp at 7700rpm, the newer variation had a larger dry-sump unit. Given that Ferrari was looking to take the 308GTB silhouette racing in subsequent years, this was considered an insurance against oil surge generated during hard cornering – as well as greatly enhancing cooling, reducing engine height and facilitating the potential fitment of a KKK turbocharger.

With an all-in kerbweight of 1050kg, the glassfibre-bodied car's power-to-weight was improved over the GT4's. Maximum speed was up to 154mph at 7050rpm, but the real gain was in acceleration. From a standing start the GTB was seriously quick, and up to 100mph it was knocking on the door of the big boys like the BB and Countach. The 0-60mph benchmark was dispatched in 6.5 seconds, while

0-100mph came in 17. The standing quarter was scorched in 14.8 seconds at 93mph.

To put that in context, the Porsche 911 Turbo 3.0 and De Tomaso Pantera offered more acceleration for similar money, but neither was capable of matching the GTB's excellent average fuel consumption of around 20mpg.

It wasn't perfect, though. Far from it. The all-independent suspension had minimal wheel travel, and that compromised the low-speed ride quality. But dial-in some speed and that crashiness was overcome by poise and balance. That feeling of wieldiness at speed wasn't reflected in the car park, however – steering of 3.3 turns lock-to-lock provided a turning circle of around 40ft.

In 1977 the glassfibre body was replaced by a steel version, yet the tubular chassis remained unchanged – as did the engine and gearbox. The range was further expanded with the arrival of the GTS, which featured spider bodywork by Pininfarina. It was this car that would be immortalised in later years thanks to repeated appearances in TV show *Magnum PI*. Whether that was a good or a bad thing is open to debate.

The GTB and GTS continued to evolve. In 1981 fuel injection replaced the quad-Weber set-up, and power took a tumble to 214bhp. Fitment of fuel injection may have secured the GTB's continued place in markets such as the USA and Switzerland, but the 40bhp drop in power damaged the car's reputation. Happily, the GTBi and GTSi were replaced the following year by the more red-blooded Quattrovalvole.

As the name implied, the classic V8 engine received a pair of four-valve heads, raising the compression ratio to 9.2:1 and boosting power to a more Ferrari-like 240bhp at 7000rpm. Once again, the junior Ferrari was a 150mph car.

The 308GTB and GTS were easily the marque's best-sellers to this point (helped by being Ferrari's only official offering in the USA for many years): 712 fibreglass cars, 2185 GTBs, 3219 GTSs, 494 GTBis, 1743 GTSis, 748 GTB QVs and 3042 GTS QVs. If there were doubts that the firm was on the right track with its junior supercar before the GTB was launched, they would soon be put to bed – and the model has set a template that remains in place today with the stunning 458 Italia.

By the mid-1980s Ferrari's opposition looked rather different than it had done a decade previously: Lamborghini staggered on with the Jalpa, a rapidly ageing Urraco variation with Lego build quality; while Maserati had given up its supercar ambitions completely to concentrate instead on the Biturbo range. Lotus continued with the Esprit, which thanks to forced induction could punch much harder than its moderate engine capacity entitled it to – but overall Ferrari pretty much had the sector to itself.

Despite that, the marque refused to rest on its laurels,

1975 FERRARI 308GTB
SPECIFICATIONS

Engine
2927cc Ferrari F106AL mid-mounted transverse V8, DOHC, 16 valves, four Weber 40DCNF carburettors

Power
255bhp @ 7700rpm

Torque
210lb ft @ 5000rpm

Transmission
Five-speed manual, rear-wheel drive

Suspension
Front and rear: independent by coils and double wishbones, anti-roll bars, telescopic dampers

Brakes
Discs all round

Weight
1090kg (glassfibre car)

Performance
Top speed 155mph
0-60mph 6.5sec

Below right
308GTB was a fine return to form for Ferrari, with beautifully balanced styling and scorching performance.

'Leonardo Fioravanti was responsible for the shape
of the GTB and, as expected from the man whose portfolio includes
the Daytona and Berlinetta Boxer, it looked absolutely right'

'The 328 continued in production for four years, and in Thatcher's decade it proved consistently popular until its replacement in the autumn of 1989'

Below left
External changes
that turned 308 into
328 were minimal:
most obvious were
integrated bumpers
and bigger wheels.

1985 FERRARI 328GTB
SPECIFICATIONS

Engine
3185cc, mid-mounted
transverse V8, DOHC,
32 valves, Bosch
K-Jetronic
fuel injection

Power
270bhp @ 7000rpm

Torque
224lb ft @ 5500rpm

Transmission
Five-speed manual,
rear-wheel drive

Suspension
Front and rear:
independent by coils
and double wishbones,
anti-roll bars,
telescopic dampers

Brakes
Vented discs all round

Weight
1263kg

Performance
Top speed 163mph
0-60mph 6.3sec

ensuring that its entry-level model remained a force in the junior supercar market. Surprisingly, given the company's F1 experience with turbocharging, forced induction was restricted to the Italian market-only 208GTB/GTS models, launched in 1982. Instead, when it came to upgrading the 308, Ferrari stuck to what it knew. Despite this being a substantially new car, the 328GTB/GTS was a very familiar product, thus minimising the possibility of lessening the appeal of the firm's biggest-seller.

Pininfarina was entrusted with modernising the basic design, and made significant though subtle changes to update the looks, paying close attention to improving aerodynamic efficiency. The 328 might have looked superficially similar but many of the older car's sharp edges were smoothed off, giving the appearance of a longer, lower design. In fact, the 328 was almost half an inch taller.

In a decade where performance across all market sectors took a massive leap forward, and the average family car was now capable of 125mph, maintaining the junior Ferrari's lead was more important than ever. The answer was to give the V8 more power, and the way to do this was to enlarge it to 3185cc by boring and stroking to 83x73.6mm.

Like its predecessor the 328 boasted a Bosch K-Jetronic fuel-injection system, but it was improved through the fitment of Marelli MED 806A electronic ignition, resulting in improved long-term reliability. The upshot was a maximum power output of 270bhp at 7000rpm and, more importantly, 224lb ft at 5500rpm.

When it was launched at the Frankfurt Motor Show in 1985, the 328 GTB/GTS met with a positive reception from the press and public. After the previous year's Testarossa it was a clear indicator that Ferrari was keeping faith with the classically beautiful Fioravanti shape, even if the 328 lacked the visual drama of its new big brother.

On the road, the additional power and torque immediately made themselves evident, translating into serious thrust. That all-important 0-60mph dash now took a mere six seconds, helped by a shorter first gear ratio, and the top speed was 163mph – recalling the glory days of the original GTB's launch, when it outdragged the opposition.

To ensure the driver could exploit it all, the 328's all-independent suspension was honed to further improve handling – and ride, too. Uprated Koni dampers did their bit but, more importantly, the modernisation of the wheel and tyre package transformed the handling. The 328 ditched the 308QV's oddly-sized Michelin TRXs, settling for lower-profile Goodyear NCTs in 205/55VR 16 (front) and 225/50VR 16 (rear) sizes. It was here, probably more than anywhere else, where the biggest advance was made.

The 328GTB/GTS was the final flowering of the line that falteringly began with the GT4, back in 1973. Although that car promised much, the unpalatable styling hampered its appeal. Once the Fioravanti-designed model hit the market, there was no stopping Ferrari's junior supercar. The 328 continued in production for four years, and in the boom years of Thatcher's decade it proved consistently popular, right through until its replacement in the autumn of 1989.

Some 6068 examples were built, and the later cars proved the most dynamically complete and reliable of all. Tellingly, when a replacement became due, the 348tb and ts continued where the 328 left off, while the slow-selling four-seat family versions, kicked off with the GT4 and maintained by the Mondial, ended here.

And the Modenese design and engineering teams succeeded in their aims in replacing the 206/246 in style, even if it took customers years to appreciate the fact. Since then, the 308 has become the definitive first Ferrari for many; now that it finally has a chance of emerging from the shadow of the original Dino.

Thanks to car owners David Cooke, Ross Hamilton and David Byers, and to Ferrari specialist DK Engineering, +44 (0)1923 287687, www.dkeng.co.uk, for sourcing all three cars and for its general assistance with the article.

WANT TO BUY ONE?

The 308 and 328 are an obvious gateway to prancing horse ownership, but they have much more to offer than just their relatively low prices
Words: Keith Adams Photography: Paul Harmer

There can't be many enthusiasts out there who haven't considered owning a Ferrari at some point in their lives. And no doubt, if you've considered it without taking the plunge, then you'll have watched – with some regret – values of anything with a prancing horse on its snout climb ever upwards. Following the economic unpleasantness of recent years, and taking on board the consensus that classic cars are perhaps the wisest investments in the world right now, buying a 308 has never looked so tempting.

Financially, there's only one way they can go. The starting point for a 308GT4 or Mondial is £10,000, but such examples are few and far between, and will probably need serious investment to get back into prime condition. Decent GTBs realistically start at £25,000, with GTSs commanding a premium. The more desirable Pininfarina two-seaters are always going to be worth more. Because they're relatively plentiful you can take your time and choose the perfect car for you – the Ferrari Owners' Club is a good starting point for privately sold models. Buying a car from a dealer is straightforward: just look for a lavish history file.

Probably it's best to look at £25,000 for a GTB or £20,000 for a GT4 (early Dino-badged cars are worth more, apparently) as the *real* starting point on your depreciation-free Ferrari odyssey. At this level 308 ownership looks tempting when one considers that the 246GT can sit well north of £100,000. The 308 must start to follow soon.

Although 308s have a huge following, don't think you can jump into buying one without doing your homework. Later 308s and 328s (as well as Mondials, which overlapped the 348tb and ts long enough to be offered with its 3.4 engine) are well built by classic Ferrari standards. They're far from being the maintenance nightmare doomsayers would have you think, yet they are not without their foibles – especially the cheaper ones that haven't been lovingly looked after.

Of course, the idea of buying and running a £10,000 project Mondial or 308GT4 isn't without appeal, but bear in mind that it will be rusty. More so if it's a pre-1982 car, which didn't have zinc-coated steel panels. The good news is that if you're on the look-out for rust, these cars don't hide their corrosion in inaccessible places – the tubular chassis is pretty much bulletproof. Just keep a keen eye on all panels.

The engine is long-lived, with the proviso that it's been serviced correctly. If you're looking at a car with over 50,000 miles on the clock, check for evidence that it's been serviced annually, or at least every 3000 miles. A yearly service will cost upwards of £500, and for the less sympathetic owner it's tempting to skip it once in a while. You'll soon know if an engine's been abused – listen for piston slap, look for blue smoke, leaky camshaft seals and low oil pressure.

If you end up needing to rebuild that lovely V8, you'll be looking at the thick end of £15,000, with a top-end overhaul coming in at around half of that. You'll find your 'cheap' Ferrari is no longer a bargain.

The gearbox is tough and durable, but clutch wear is appalling on

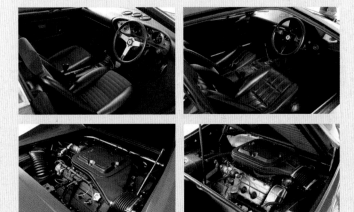

'These cars don't hide their corrosion in inaccessible places – the tubular chassis is pretty much bulletproof and shouldn't hold any horrors. The engine is long-lived, with the proviso that it's been serviced correctly'

the original 'plate. Don't expect more than 40,000 miles from the OE-spec plate and much less if the car has lived its life in town. But cost-wise it's a relatively inexpensive job, typically between £750-1000 at a specialist.

Other than that, there may be electrical issues to deal with, most often caused by a moody fusebox. Yet again the parts you need for replacement aren't too dear at £150, and repair isn't impossible if you're handy with a soldering iron.

And that's about it. There are pitfalls to trap you when buying any Ferrari, but they should be fairly evident when checking one out. The main thing is not to let your heart rule your head into buying the first car you see – a really straight body or tidy interior is a good starting point. Most people who own 308s and 328s are passionate about their motors and treat them with all the love they would their first-born.

Yet it's good to know that, if you plan to really *use* your first Ferrari, then it's more than capable of serving you well. Maintenance bills aren't out of order – unless you go for that 'bargain' rusty example with a care-worn interior – and depreciation simply isn't a factor.

Who says Ferraris can't be sensible?

The vagaries of fashion

have been followed, laughed at and questioned over the decades. Fashion affects the automobile world as much as it does design in general and clothing in particular. Take the two motor cars we have here. Both have evolved out of previous models: the 1981 Ferrari 512BB ('Berlinetta Boxer') from the 365BB first seen in 1973, while the 1987 Aston Martin Vantage is even further along the evolutionary path from the original DBS V8 that was unveiled in 1969. And both protagonists were affected by the whims of fashion at launch.

Ferrari, always conservative with its engineering under the eye of Enzo, came late to the mid-engined sports car layout. Its first mid-engined sports racer, the 250LM of 1964, was not really a road model and only 32 examples were produced. So Ferrari's first road car with its engine amidships was the 365BB. Yet the fashion for

mid-engined road machinery had been established eight years earlier when Ferruccio Lamborghini launched the Miura – the like of which had never been seen before. It was a styling and engineering sensation, and lays claim to the title of The First Supercar. Ferrari's rival was the 356GTB/4 Daytona: sensational to drive but lacking the all-important visual edge that playboys of the time were drawn to. The Daytona simply had no answer to the Miura's wow factor.

So by the time the Pininfarina-designed 365BB was launched, the mid-engine layout was no longer perceived as cutting-edge – to the *fashionisti*, anyway. The Miura held the high ground and was regarded as a bit of an animal, even though it couldn't actually fulfil Lamborghini's claimed acceleration and top speed. But it came first, so the later 365BB – and its replacement 512BB – were seen as 'me too'. Ferrari made the mistake of wild »

England takes on Italy

Two completely different approaches to the supercar
theme clash head-to-head on neutral Swiss ground.
Which one does it best?

Words: Robert Coucher   Photography: Paul Harmer

'The Aston Martin Vantage
was almost the opposite of
Ferrari's 512BB. Where better
now to enjoy both than
through the Swiss Alps?'

performance claims *à la* Lambo (0-60mph in 6.5sec; 176mph) and, when the BB failed to match these figures, it was panned by the press. Then the later 512BB was criticised for being *too* civilised and well-mannered, never mind that its nemesis, the Miura, is such hard work to drive.

The Aston Martin Vantage was almost the opposite of the 512BB. Its gestation period was far longer because the six-cylinder DBS was first seen in 1967, when the planned V8 engine wasn't quite ready for insertion. The American-looking DBS, styled by William Towns, was heavier than the previous DB6, the upshot being that it was slower than the older car. Not the most auspicious of starts. But the arrival of the V8 in '69 saw the big Aston's performance advantage restored. Troubled times meant the DBS V8 soldiered on until '72, when the restyled V8 saloon took over, but the reinvigorated 438bhp Vantage wasn't unleashed until 1977. Britain's first supercar had arrived.

Aston got its timing just right. Britain was booming and the 'loadsamoney!' City high-flyers of the 1980s really liked the look of the thumping Vantage. Big, powerful and flash, it was just the sort of he-man machine for blasting down to the country for shooting weekends or parking outside the casinos of Mayfair, where the doormen would pretend to acknowledge the driver was old money, especially when his Aston was finished in Prince of Wales specification. A starring role in the James Bond film *The Living Daylights* added pizzazz but the crushing performance (0-60mph in 5.4sec and a *real* top speed of 165mph) gave the Aston absolute street cred. It was faster than anything from Italy or Germany, and the Bulldog breed really liked that!

WHERE BETTER NOW to enjoy these fast and powerful supercars than through the Swiss Alps? From deep within the mountains outside Geneva we collect the Aston Martin Vantage

from an innocuous-looking modern garage, forgetting the driving for a while as we marvel at the race and rally weaponry stashed within.

But with time pressing, the Aston is fired up and eases out. And fired-up is the only way to describe the wallop of sound as the engine catches. This Vantage is a very special example of a special breed. One of just 43 left-hand-drive Vantages, it's a rare X-Pack model with additional suspension, mechanical and power upgrades. Upon hearing that still further upgrades were available from Aston Works Service in the early 1990s, the owner sent the car back to Newport Pagnell for the full package. This included a 465bhp 6.3-litre engine shoving out a staggering 460lb ft of torque, plus a six-speed manual gearbox, a big-bore, free-flow exhaust system, beefed-up brakes and suspension, and 16in alloys shod with wide 255/50 tyres. The total *additional* bill for this bespoke work came to a tad over £75,000... in 1992. Maybe that's why only five Vantages were afforded the treatment.

Finished in metallic blue with a cream piped Connolly leather interior and sitting on the wider rims with flared wheelarches, the Vantage certainly looks powerful. Slide in through the large door and the interior is wide but snug. The lashings of wood and the suppleness of the leather seats provide the ambience of typically British coachbuilt quality, even if things are slightly let down by some proprietary fixtures and fittings.

The driving position is commanding and the driving seat is comfortable rather than gripping. The long gearlever is prominent and an ample cigar ashtray is a pleasant throwback to the days when you would light up the colossal V8 in concert with a fat Cohiba. It starts easily and settles to a solid but high idle that belies the quartet of 48mm Weber carburettor chokes. Aston had problems with fuel injection fitted to the V8 saloon prior to the Vantage, but the way these carbs react to minute throttle inputs indicates that AML took the correct decision to »

Right and below
Snug yet comfortable in here, the leather and walnut trim adding a refined edge to brutal acceleration on tap.

Right
Aston 5.3-litre V8 engine was boosted to 438bhp for the Vantage. This 6.3-litre version, by Aston Works Service, pumps out 465bhp.

1987 ASTON MARTIN VANTAGE X-PACK

SPECIFICATIONS

Engine
6300cc V8, DOHC per bank, four Weber carburettors

Power
465bhp @ 5500rpm

Torque
460lb ft @ 4000rpm

Transmission
Six-speed manual, rear-wheel drive
Steering
Rack and pinion, power-assisted

Suspension
Front: unequal wishbones, coil springs, telescopic dampers, anti-roll bar.
Rear: de Dion axle, parallel trailing arms, transverse Watts linkage, coil springs, telescopic dampers, anti-roll bar

Brakes
Vented discs front and rear

Weight
1971kg

Performance
Top speed 175mph
0-60mph 5.0sec

retro-fit old-tech carburettors again. So let's see how it reacts to rather larger throttle inputs...

The Vantage's clutch is light but long in travel. The gearshift – this is the only known six-speed car in existence – is rubbery and moves about the wide H-pattern without objection. Twist the unusually small steering wheel and lots of power assistance is at your fingertips; let the clutch out and the Aston steps off the mark without hesitation even though first gear is high. You are immediately aware of the car's girth, but the visibility and squareness of it all make it easy to place on these narrow mountain roads. As we trundle down the valley, the Aston comes up to temperature, the suspension limbers up and the brakes start to bite.

At the bottom of the mountain you turn onto an open and clear dual carriageway, check that all's clear, allow the revs to climb gently in first gear, slip it into second in a straight line (I'm not naive enough to try this in first gear out of a 90° turn!), then mash your double-welted brogue down to the thick Wilton pile carpeting. In a split-second the once contentedly burbling V8 emits an almighty bellow, the Vantage hunkers down, the steering wheel starts to writhe in your hands, and the rear tyres spin as the power easily overcomes their prodigious grip. Almost immediately you need third gear, where the force is unleashed again, the tyres spinning ever more demonically, the V8 continuing to roar as you dive for fourth gear. The big car is now really shifting and the long dual carriageway has been gobbled up and spat out with impunity.

Think of the throttle pedal as a sharp assegai and the Aston as a wild African buffalo. A sharp prod elicits a furious display of animal power and aggression. You cannot conceive of something so sizeable being so explosively reactive. But the Aston's aggression is controlled: the awesome thrust is effectively harnessed by the capable chassis with its planted de Dion rear end and limited-slip differential. Like an animal evolved to suit its natural habitat, the

'In a split-second the V8 emits an almighty bellow and the rear tyres spin as the power overcomes their grip'

Vantage does exactly what it exists to do – to lunge down a ribbon of tarmac at almost unimaginable pace.

Recovering from the car's accelerative onslaught (just five seconds to 60mph!), you begin to explore its wider capabilities through the twisting Alpine roads. Here the Aston requires more concentration and learning. It is heavy at 1971kg and the power steering seems a little over-assisted. You need to commit the car to a corner, allow the steering to gather up the cornering forces, then power on through. Once you get used to the non-linear reaction from the steering wheel, the big Aston can be cornered fast but a heavier, less-assisted rack would be preferable to counter the lateral lurching and to match the other meaty controls.

Also, the suspension seems to have to work hard on less-than-perfect surfaces. On the mostly mirror-smooth Swiss roads the Aston is sure-footed, but on rougher sections it seems to jump around a degree too much, which is surprising considering it has the X-Pack and additional upgrades. A word with Kingsley Riding-Felce at the Works Service department suggests that the geometry might need adjustment because these Vantages are very sensitive to this set-up. Or it could be that the Vantage is just so damn powerful and needs a better driver than me to tame it.

Having shredded expensive rubber in the mountains, it's time to roar back down the A1 motorway into Geneva to collect the Ferrari. Through the numerous tunnels the Aston's massive engine sound is amplified to a cacophonic degree even when you're loafing along in the tall overdrive sixth. Soon a young driver in his »

Below
Only two seats in the BB's
intimate cabin,
and they're mounted low
and close together.
View out is pure Le Mans;
view inside is very '80s.

Above
Four-carb flat-12 sits
longitudinally behind
cabin; makes a fantastic
racket. Not as powerful
as the Vantage's V8, but
shoves a lot less weight.

**1981
FERRARI
512BB**

SPECIFICATIONS

Engine
4942cc flat-12, DOHC
per bank, four valves
per cylinder, four
Weber carburettors,
dry sump

power
360bhp @ 6500rpm

Torque
332lb ft @ 5000rpm

Transmission
Five-speed manual,
rear-wheel drive
Steering Rack
and pinion

suspension
Front: double
wishbones, coil
springs, telescopic
dampers, anti-roll bar.
Rear: double
wishbones, coil
springs, telescopic
dampers

Brakes
Vented discs front
and rear

Weight
1597kg

Performance
Top speed 155mph.
0-60mph 6.0sec

hotted-up Peugeot latches onto the rear of the Vantage and his passenger seemingly climbs out of the car to get some action shots on his camera phone. The whole thunderous adventure is enlivened by dropping a gear in the Aston, sluicing in plenty of juice, then lifting off sharply to allow the exhaust to pop explosively, accompanied by huge flames shooting out from the tailpipes. This has to be the most outrageous tunnel car in existence.

SOMEWHERE BEHIND a block of suburban flats in Geneva there is a drab grey door let discreetly into the hillside. A man responds to the buzzer and the electric door whirrs quietly back into the concrete. Atmospheric lighting flicks on and reveals a black-carpeted interior, while pinpoint spotlamps highlight a collection of immaculate classic Ferraris, all painted in matching scarlet. It is an astonishing sight, straight out of a thriller.

The Ferrari 512BB is driven out of its lair and, next to the bluff Aston, it looks low and pointy. It's more obviously a sports car, with its red paint and black leather trim. Observing the Pininfarina form with today's eye, you realise that the Ferrari is actually very beautiful. The long nose and forward cockpit spell speed, while the fat rear haunches wrapped voluptuously around the mid-mounted, horizontally opposed 12-cylinder engine indicate power. The classic Ferrari alloys, round rear lights and signature large yellow front indicator lenses lend real road presence, so why is it that more of us have not coveted this beautiful BB like some of Maranello's other models? The whole fashion thing comes back to mind, but today that is no longer

of consequence because this Ferrari looks so right. Bigger and more commanding than the smaller Dino and 308, this is a proper man-sized 4.9-litre car with an F1 race-derived 360bhp at a dizzy 6800rpm. And in today's market it costs less than a third of the price of the fractious Miura.

You drop down into the low-slung cockpit, where headroom is spare and the seating position almost fully reclined. The seats are firmer than the Aston's and you are met with the sight of red illuminated instruments – very discothèque – and that classically turned alloy gearshifter with its exposed gate. The clutch requires a shove (still an improvement over the 365BB's) and the cold gearbox oil makes the lever recalcitrant and sticky. So, slide it back into second, then ease it forward into first and add some revs.

Also Weber-caburettored, the BB moves off without fuss but initially feels a bit stiff and unwilling. But within the first few yards you savour the unassisted yet pin-sharp steering. Everything about this car is sharp. It has that typical Ferrari mechanical tingle, and no control has any slop whatsoever.

Onto the motorway the Ferrari strains at the leash. Allow the big 12 to rev and it does so with turbine smoothness, howling as you close in on the red line. It proves to be nowhere near as hard-hitting as the Vantage's brutal V8 and it really needs to be kept on the boil, but the spinning mill works superbly in this chassis. Relaxing, you allow the BB to motor down the carriageway in fifth gear and are amazed at how quiet and refined it is. The suspension proves more absorbent and better damped than the

»

Aston's. In the mountains the BB responds with precision. It spears into corners, seeming to pivot about your hips, and you can place it with absolute accuracy thanks to the superlative steering. The set-up is inclined towards initial understeer, yet it answers so quickly to throttle inputs that it hardly matters.

Gaining confidence and speed, you start to attack the bends with more commitment and allow the pliant, high-walled 215/70x15 Michelins to find their envelope of grip. When new, the BB's engine position – it's mid-mounted high in the chassis over the box – was criticised for creating a degree of polar movement in extremis. In the real world, driven and enjoyed as a classic car, even a classic Ferrari, this is not an issue – buy a four-wheel-drive Subaru if you are after computer game levels of grip.

Here, you turn the BB into an uphill corner, hear the tyres squeal as you get on the power, and enjoy the sensation of it squatting, with the rear end breaking grip for a little oversteer play. Wonderfully

tactile stuff. Coming down the steep passes is a little more tricky, as that rear-end weight is more forthcoming and the disc brakes get hot hauling down 1597kg from considerable speed. The Ferrari is not as powerful, torquey or fast as the rumbustious Aston, but it is quicker through the mountains thanks to its thoroughbred chassis, willing engine and razor-sharp steering.

Unexpectedly, the overtly sporting Ferrari BB512 is significantly more refined and quieter than the Aston Martin with its open exhausts and firm suspension. As you might expect, the Vantage is blisteringly fast on open roads, the BB quicker through twists and turns. The Aston Martin turns out to be a beautifully hewn tool of immense power. But the Ferrari 512BB is a precision instrument of deep ability, a supercar you can drive every day. Swap the paint jobs and I'd take the Ferrari.

Thanks to Kidston SA of Geneva for arranging this road test (www.kidston.com).

'The Vantage is blisteringly fast on open roads, the BB quicker through twists and turns'

RED
ROUTE

The Mille Miglia was Italy's greatest
road race and a key part of Ferrari's heritage.
Richard Meaden recalls the final event,
and drives part of the classic route
in the fabulous Ferrari 360 Spider

Pictures: Gus Gregory and Klemantaski Collection

Edward Eves

There has never been

anything quite like the Mille Miglia. One thousand miles of flat-out racing through towns and open country, it was motorsport on a massive scale. Open to a vast array of machinery, from 750cc bubble-cars to hugely powerful V8 and V12 road-racers based on the Grand Prix cars of the day, the Mille Miglia brought drama, danger and heart-pounding spectacle to the doorsteps of five million Italians.

Starting from Brescia in the far north of the country, the route twisted its way to the Adriatic coastline. From here it hammered down through Rimini and Ancona, then across the Appenine mountains to Rome, up along the backbone of Italy through Tuscany, over the Futa and Raticosa passes, before descending into Bologna, Modena and eventually back to Brescia. It was a race that consumed an entire country.

Last run as a competitive event in 1957, the Mille Miglia is still a source of fascination for many enthusiasts. Not only was it the scene of some of the most Herculean drives in motor-racing history, but as the vast majority of the

route is still used as public road today, it is possible to follow in the tyre-tracks of Moss, Fangio and other heroes from a bygone age.

It's this promise that brings us to the Piazza Vittoria in the heart of Brescia, home of the Mille Miglia and the starting point for our story. We're privileged to be behind the wheel of Ferrari's 360 Spider; the ideal car for such a challenging drive as it shares technology and takes inspiration from today's F1 cars, just as the quickest Mille Miglia racers did in 1957.

Some of you might be of the opinion that a drop-top Ferrari is a soft option, the purer driver's car being the coupé. That has often been the case in the past, but the 360 was designed with a barchetta version in mind from the start, giving it the best possible chance of matching the dynamics of its berlinetta brother.

The result is, without any shadow of doubt, the world's most savage soft-top: all-aluminium construction, 400 searing horsepower, six-speed Formula 1-style paddleshift transmission, acceleration from 0-60mph in under 5sec, 100mph in a shade over 10sec, top speed of »

Above
Brescia, May 1957, just before the start of the final, fateful Mille Miglia; the crowd in the Piazza Vittoria press in on the cars during scrutineering.

'400 searing horsepower, six-speed Formula 1-style paddleshift, 0-60mph in under 5sec, top speed of 185mph, and an engine note that makes your ears bleed'

MILLE MIGLIA
Km. 1564

From left
The route of the Mille Miglia
(Thousand Miles). Actually, it's
972 miles long – but what's 28 miles
between friends? The Piazza Vittoria
on a quiet Sunday morning. Collins
and Klemantaski roar out of Brescia
and into the dawn. Closeness of
crowds made the event special
– and ultimately deadly.

185mph and an engine note that makes your
ears bleed. If this isn't in keeping with the spirit
of the Mille Miglia, then I don't know what is.

On race day in 1957, the piazza would have
been a seething mass of exuberant Brescian
spectators, race officials, bustling mechanics
and impatient drivers. But now, at 7am on a
peaceful mid-summer Sunday morning, the
town has sensibly elected to stay in bed.

It's a fittingly dramatic starting point for such
an enormously gruelling race. The imposing
Post Office building towers above us, making us
feel very small and insignificant as we fire off a
few static shots of the Spider.

Hood down, the car is a wonderful sight – a
combination of sharp, pointy 21st century
edginess and classic Ferrari curvaceousness. It's
the twin humps behind the head restraints that
do it for me, harking back to racing forebears
that still haunt this historic civic square.

Fittingly, Ferrari was race favourite in '57,
although previous winners Stirling Moss and

trusty co-driver (and journalist) Denis Jenkinson were much fancied in their fearsome 400bhp Maserati 4.5. The fastest cars started last, the final few leaving Brescia at around 5.30am, their exact start time being their race number.

Car number 534, Ferrari's best hope of victory, was driven by Brit ace Peter Collins, accompanied by Louis Klemantaski. The latter was the finest motoring photographer of his day, and would act as Collins's co-driver and document the race from the passenger seat of the 4.1-litre V12 Ferrari. It's mostly his amazing work that you can see in this feature, alongside that of renowned photographer Gus Gregory, a man after Klemantaski's heart if ever there was one.

Static shots completed, we leave the town square and complete the short blast along cobbled backstreets to the start ramp at Via Rubuffone. The 360 Spider ambles across the uneven surface, its Pirelli tyres slapping a knobbly, staccato beat on the road, while its electronic dampers coolly isolate the washboard **»**

Left and below
The Ferrari of Wolfgang von Trips is pushed towards the starting ramp. The number signified the start time (5.32am). Piero Taruffi accelerates away from the Rome Control.

Above and above right
A typically eye-popping stretch of road. The Collins/Klemantaski 335S moves in on two slower cars.

bumps. Pedestrians and cyclists whistle and wave as we pass, their passion for fast, fabulous cars still wide awake even at this ungodly hour. The sun is low but warm, the atmosphere already sticky – a precursor to another scorching Italian summer's day.

From Brescia, the route heads first for Verona. Running pretty much straight, and flanked by elegant, proudly shuttered town houses and tall horse chestnut trees, the road out of Brescia is nothing short of a suburban drag strip. Almost immediately you're struck by the fierce challenge that lies ahead. Given the freedom (and courage) that Collins and Klemantaski had in 1957, we too could quite easily be topping 160mph within

Peter Coltrin

the first few miles; instead, the 360 is chomping at the bit as we burble through traffic.

When gaps do appear, the car's razor-keen throttle response and flip-shift gearbox whip us to indecent velocities. But to avoid a night or two's stay at the pleasure of the local carabinieri, we reluctantly settle for enjoying the excellent low-speed ride quality, incredible tractability and short but fabulous stabs of engine noise bouncing off the buildings and trees.

After a quick cappuccino stop in Verona, it's clear that even a modern, bright red Ferrari is going to struggle to cut through the dawdling ranks of Fiats and Alfas, so we decide to hit the autostrada to make up some time on our journey to Ravenna on the Adriatic coast. The 360 Spider is a sublime companion. We've had the roof down from the start, the air-conditioning taking the sting out of the sun and the clever aerodynamics eradicating any buffeting, even when cruising at over 100mph.

From Ravenna the road is eerily straight, and it is nothing short of awe-inspiring to think that even if we could travel back some 43 years, to May 1957, our state-of-the-art, 400bhp, all-aluminium, all-singing, all-dancing 360 Spider would struggle to keep pace with Ferrari's Mille Miglia racers. Imagine the Mulsanne Straight running from Calais to Paris, and you'll have some idea of what the coastal run is like.

It's hard to imagine the noise, heat and fierce concentration that would have filled the Collins/Klemantaski Ferrari as they hammered flat-out towards Ancona in excess of 170mph, peering into the shimmering heat-haze in an attempt to pick out fast-approaching and potentially lethal S-bends. For a more graphic illustration of how fast they were travelling, take a look at a map of Italy and imagine driving from Brescia to Rome via Verona, Ferrara, Ravenna, Rimini and Ancona in just five hours, including pit stops and the tight mountain run inland. That's an average speed of 107mph, in case you were wondering. We almost feel embarrassed to be driving on the same piece of road. »

'For the first time, the 360
feels like it's working hard, the
engine note hard and insistent'

It's the first week of the Italian holidays, and judging by the number of mopeds and cars on the road, all of Italy has decided to have a day at the seaside. By now it's clear that there's no way we'll be able to do the whole route and complete all the photography we need, so rather than slog all the way down the coast and then across the mountains to Rome, we high-tail it west for an overnight stop in Tuscany. It's a wise decision, as tomorrow we'll be tackling the toughest section of the Mille Miglia, over the hills of Radicofani towards Siena, Florence and the switchback-laden Futa and Raticosa passes.

Fascinating though it was to experience the wide-open coast roads, they didn't tell us much about the Spider. But the breathtakingly quick SS2 that slices through the wonderful Tuscan scenery of the Val D'Orcia is a far sterner test. The climb to Radicofani is the most memorable, the road cresting and falling like a bitumen rollercoaster. For the first time, the 360 feels like it's working hard, the engine note remaining hard and insistent, the cornering and braking loads more severe.

Increased engine and wind noise apart, there's no other indication that you're in a convertible. The steering and turn-in are as sharp and instantaneous as in the berlinetta, and the suspension is just as taut and tolerant of mid-corner bumps. It feels together, cohesive, tight as a drum. Without pushing beyond eight-tenths, we're still chomping through this fabulous stretch of road, but the proximity of trees, not to mention walled bridges positioned on tight bends, means

it's an unforgiving playground for journalists, and a potentially lethal test for 1957's race drivers.

With close to the same power as our 360, but with narrow tyres and no seatbelts, let alone traction control or ABS, it is no wonder drivers described competing in the Mille Miglia as like walking a high wire without a safety net. Nevertheless, it was a challenge the very best drivers relished, and a perfect backdrop on which to display their dazzling talent.

By this stage, Collins and Klemantaski were romping away from the opposition. Not only were they ahead of all their Ferrari team-mates, but such was their pace that Moss and Jenkinson's 1955 record time was seriously under threat. One of the fastest drivers in the world at the time, Collins was looking forward to the tortuous

Right
Classic Klemantaski study of Collins's hands on the 335S's wheel. With its 4-litre V12 producing around 400bhp, it was capable of over 180mph.

Above left and above right
360 Spider retraces the Ferraris' tracks across the Futa Pass. Alfonso de Portago and co-driver Edmund Nelson leave their last stop. A tragic end to the race awaits.

mountain stages of Futa and Raticosa, just north of Florence. Despite having been driving solidly for more than seven hours, he was confident of stretching his lead even further. If only he knew what really lay ahead – for, as Klemantaski described in his report for *Motor* magazine, it would be a far sterner test than they imagined.

'Every corner of note had a crowd on it, all waving us on excitedly, for they knew we were winning. This was second-gear work all the time, with a drop down to first gear for the hairpins. The steering ratio was such that on the hairpins, using the wheel and the throttle, Peter could get around without having to take another bite at the wheel. As we reached the top the sky to the north of us, towards Bologna, was black, and soon a physically welcome but morally distressing

rain began to come down.

'Goggles misted up, faces were stung by the raindrops, and then, worst of all, we began having difficulty in getting around right-hand corners. Almost simultaneously a slight crunching noise was occasionally heard, coming from the region of the back axle, on left-hand bends, and I tried to think of a connection between the two. The rain stopped, leaving the roads terribly slippery, then it turned to sleet...'

Quite where Collins got his stamina from is beyond us. It really is an incredible run, the seemingly endless SS65 twisting and turning first over the Futa and then, almost immediately after, the Raticosa pass. From wide-open sweeps and fresh-air corners, the character of the road can change in an instant as trees close in, casting

deceptive shadows across the tarmac.

The prospect of man-handling Collins's fearsome car along this stretch on streaming tarmac sends a shiver down our spine, but now, just as you'd hope, the 360 is absolutely in its element. The feelsome power steering and darty front end carve into the tightest turns with utter confidence. You begin to push yourself harder and harder, relying more and more on the Spider's reserves of grip and poise.

Having the latest generation F1 shift is a massive help too, as it allows you to grab a lower gear as soon as you see the corner tightening. Seemingly no matter how late you flip down a gear the Spider remains planted to the road, and the shifts are absolutely flawless, with perfectly judged heel-and-toe-style blips every time. The »

'Most corners are second-gear,
the fastest straights topping out in
the shrieking upper reaches of third'

upshifts are now smoother too, proving conclusively that the second-generation F1 system is much more satisfying than it used to be. Personally, I've always been a bit of a Luddite when it comes to self-shifting transmissions, but now even I have to concede that it frees you to concentrate more on the road ahead. And you need to if you're to stay one step ahead of the SS65, for it seems to take great pleasure in reeling you in with its hypnotic, rhythmic sequences of second- and third-gear corners, only to pitch a savagely tightening switchback into your path.

Any mistake, no matter how small, punches your pounding heart into the back of your parched throat. To be a passenger here, as

Klemantaski was in the leading car, must have been like being caught in the eye of a storm, pitched and tossed from corner to corner, his life held in Collins's whirling hands.

If the brain-out missile-run down the coast from Rimini to Ancona was an almost sadistic test of the driver's courage, and the true domain of those with the tallest final drive and the biggest balls, then the relentless tarmac bobsled run from Florence to Bologna was for the artists. Only those with sensitivity, exquisite car control and an almost telepathic ability to read the road ahead could balance their over-powered machines on a knife-edge for hours at a time.

The great masters of the Mille Miglia could

cope with the monstrous demands of both sections, but for us this is by far the most exciting, largely because it is immeasurably less daunting. Most of the corners are second gear, with the fastest straights topping out in the shrieking upper reaches of third. There's less time to think here – you simply become immersed in your own world, concentrating on each and every bend, revelling in the acceleration, noise and fierce braking forces. For the drivers of 1957, making a mistake over the Futa or Raticosa was one of the few occasions where it would simply mean an exit from the motor race rather than the human race.

It would still have hurt though. Wicked concrete fences line the valley side of the road,

Above
One of the great motor
racing photographs.
The Collins/Klemantaski
Ferrari leads the race
as it charges through the
mountains on the approach
to Rome. The record time
set by Moss and Jenkinson
in 1955 appears under threat.

while equally unyielding rock, trees or stone walls run close to the left-hand side of the car. In the Mille Miglia heyday much of this would have also been lined with people, drunk on the spectacle, not to mention the odd swig of Chianti. Today we share the SS65 with a constant stream of noisy, hard-ridden Ducatis. Mixing it amongst them is fun, and gives us some idea of what it must have been like for Collins and the

other Scuderia Ferrari drivers dicing amongst themselves and dispatching slower traffic.

The corners come at such a pace it is almost impossible to watch your mirrors and the road ahead, but the 360 has so much in reserve that it is laughably easy to empty our mirrors of distractions. None of the bikes can live with the combination of 400 prancing horses and the adhesive qualities of four Pirelli P Zero tyres. It

takes no more than three corners to leave them in our venturi-tunnelled wake. On tight, tricky roads like this, the 360 rules supreme.

The 360 Modena has been criticised for washing into understeer prematurely, then snapping into oversteer when you inevitably back off. On these hill-roads, the corners either seem to be tight unsighted second-gear bends or fast sequences that you can straightline with confidence hard in third or fourth. At high speeds, understeer isn't a problem, and you can feel the underbody aerodynamics start to draw the Ferrari closer to the tarmac. In the thick of the tight stuff, the fact that the front end gives in before the rear conditions you to focus all your concentration on your braking points and turn-in speed. There simply isn't the scope for gathering up an excess 5 or 10mph's worth of scrabbly understeer, so you don't push into the last 10 per cent or so of the Spider's ultimate ability. With Armco, stone walls, trees or – worse still – a fresh-air drop waiting to embrace us, it just isn't worth it.

Besides, the 360 has another weakness. The brakes, though fade-free and feelsome, have a spookily unpredictable habit of what feels like prematurely triggering the ABS when really pressing on. They can be fantastic for five or six corners, then for no apparent reason the pedal hardens, pulses at a higher frequency than you'd get by triggering the ABS, and halves the

Left, far right and top right
The Ferrari team cars being prepared in the courtyard at Maranello – which is where, more than 50 years later, our man Meaden reluctantly hands back the keys to the 360. Collins/Klemantaski about to take the lead: mechanical woes would end their race just 100 miles from the finish.

effectiveness of the brakes for a heart-stopping moment. It's impossible to drive around, and can happen when the brakes are very hot or stone cold. Weird.

Collins and Klemantaski had more to worry about. After surviving the sleet-covered mountain roads, their ailing Ferrari deteriorated rapidly, the battered transmission finally failing just 100 miles from an historic victory.

As the knotted tarmac starts to untangle its way towards Modena, we decide to peel off the Mille Miglia route and head to some of our favourite roads in the hills above Maranello for one last blast before taking the car back and reluctantly handing over the keys.

We knew it already, but this last thrash just goes to underline the 360's magnificence and addictive spirit. Far from being the poor relation, the Spider feels more immediate and involving than the berlinetta, if only because with the roof down you genuinely fear for your hearing every time the revs pass 6000. It's the sort of car for which you'd set your alarm for 4am to drive to Scotland and back just for the hell of it.

Collins and Klemantaski's misfortune opened the door for fellow Ferrari driver Piero Taruffi to win the Mille Miglia after failing to finish more than a dozen times. In fact, Ferrari would fill the next two places as well, but celebrations were short-lived when news filtered through of a massive accident involving another Ferrari driver, the King of Spain's nephew, the Marquis de Portago. Witnesses reported his Ferrari careering off the road at well over 160mph having suffered a puncture or possibly a wheel or transmission failure. Completely out of control,

the car was launched into the air by a granite mile marker and snapped a telegraph pole in half before spearing into the crowd with hideous consequences. The Marquis and his co-driver were killed instantly, along with nine spectators. Inevitably the Mille Miglia died with them. They were less than 30 miles from the finish.

The speed and power of the cars (the factory teams were talking of racers hitting 200mph in 1958), and the huge uncontrolled crowds lining the streets finally became too lethal a combination, leaving the Italian authorities with

no option but to abandon any future events.

There's no doubt the Mille Miglia was a brutal race, an anachronism – but it was also an intrinsic part of Italian culture, and formed a major thread that runs through Ferrari's genetic code. The 360 Spider might be a million miles safer and more refined than the racers of 1957, but you only need drive it on the Mille Miglia route to discover that the same raw passion which powered them to victory more than 50 years ago still burns inside every one of Maranello's red cars. Peter Collins would have approved. △

SN05 NHL

S O L A R
P O W E R

We go chasing the sun with two of the most
desirable convertibles money can buy: Ferrari's
F430 Spider and Lamborghini's Gallardo Spyder

Words: Richard Meaden Photography: Andy Morgan

Below
Gallardo's wedgy shape loses none of its aggression in decapitated form, helped by a profile that, with the roof folded away, is uninterrupted by protrusions, from wing mirror to tail-light.

The VW Touareg driver

never saw it coming. Mesmerised by the receding sight and sound of the slate-grey Gallardo Spyder burbling through the bustling Highland town of Glen Coe, his eyes are glued to his rear-view mirror rather than the road ahead.

Watching incredulous from the Ferrari, it's clear that the Corsa innocently parked in his path doesn't stand a chance. Nailed by two-and-a-half tons of wayward SUV with a grimace-inducing *crump-thump-skrrssch*, the hapless Vauxhall hatchback buckles under the force of the collision, while the distracted Touareg driver wears the expression of a man who's just swallowed his own tongue, snapped from blissful daydream to waking nightmare in one sickening thud.

It's an unexpectedly dramatic end to a fabulous two days in which we've enjoyed these Modenese roadsters to the full amongst the towering peaks and tranquil lochs of the Scottish Highlands. It's also a timely reminder of just what a spectacle these cars make amongst ordinary traffic. They certainly made an impression on the Corsa...

Rewind 48 hours, and John Hayman and I have just emerged from the Gallardo after a five-hour haul from Northamptonshire to Livingston, on the outskirts of Edinburgh. We've not lowered the roof once, which feels a bit fraudulent, especially when the sun's out, but when you've got big miles to cover you stick to the motorways, at which point the appeal of open-top driving is torn to shreds in the conversation-killing slipstream.

Better, we think, to keep our powder dry until tomorrow, when we're due to collect the Ferrari F430 Spider and make for the roads that lie between Fort William and Mallaig, on the west coast. Not only are they a fittingly epic stage on which to drive these two towering supercars, but the endless Highland days see the sun rise at just after 4am and darkness held at bay until almost 11pm. Short of driving to Scandinavia, nowhere packs more sunshine into a summer's day. Let's just hope Mother Nature doesn't rain on our parade.

We arrive bright and early at Rio Prestige (the supercar hire company) to collect the Ferrari which it has kindly made available to us for this test. The car is finished in the classic combination of Rosso Corsa paint and Crema leather, and looks quite a sight. More of a surprise is that it's also fitted with an equally 'classic' manual gearbox and steel brakes, rather than the optional F1 paddle-shift transmission and carbon stoppers ❯❯

Right
Ferrari looks slightly
ungainly in drop-head
form, particularly with the
hood up and parked next
to the Lambo.

'The Lambo is more pleasingly proportioned than the Ferrari'

that the vast majority of F430 customers are reported to select. It's fortunate in a way, because the Gallardo has three pedals and a stick, too, so we'll be comparing old-school like with like.

For the most part, the drive up to Fort William isn't a memorable one, thanks largely to a sat-nav system that seems determined to take us through every unremarkable, traffic-choked town between Edinburgh and the Highlands. Things pick up once we get to Crianlarich, from which point the roads open, the traffic abates and Hayman decides to stretch the Lambo's legs.

It's quite something to follow, even when you're chasing it in a Ferrari. Emitting a ground-shaking soundtrack, the chiselled Gallardo, with its broad, square shoulders, looks just as cohesive as the coupé from which it's derived, and is more convincingly sculpted and pleasingly proportioned than the slightly awkward-looking Ferrari.

The reason becomes apparent when we decide to drop the roofs. The complexity on show in both is jaw-dropping, even if the assorted whirring, clunking and straining of electric motors is ultimately a bit of a palaver compared with the simplicity of, say, a BMW Z4. But while the entire engine deck of the Lambo tilts skywards to allow the tightly folded hood to

contort itself into the small rectangular compartment close to the rear scuttle, the Ferrari's mechanism is confined to the small humps that surround each roll-hoop, thereby preserving the beautiful 'display case' engine cover.

While it's wonderful to see the red crackle-finish of the Ferrari's 4.3-litre V8 on show, the roll-hoops, roof cover and humps interrupt the F430's sharp lines. The Lamborghini's design is tidier and less disruptive, even if it does deny you any glimpse of the equally impressive V10. The flat, vented deck runs in one unbroken line from cockpit to tail-lights, creating a beautifully clean, lean profile. It also incorporates a brilliant glass anti-buffeting screen, which raises and lowers like an electric window from the bulkhead behind the seats. It's a neat touch.

With our pace increasing and the road punctuated by some wicked crests, dips and smooth sequences of corners, both cars are finding a fast rhythm. The F430 has that distinctive, pointy-steering feel of the Berlinetta, with very keen front-end responses, and it's an easy, satisfying model to thread along these unfamiliar highways at a brisk pace.

I have to confess to inadvertently pulling at the indicator stalk a few times and wondering why the transmission wasn't delivering a punchy shift, before remembering, somewhat embarrassed, that I should be stirring that quaint alloy stick ▶▶

GALLARDO SPYDER
SPECIFICATIONS

Engine
4961cc V10, dohc per bank, aluminium alloy head and block, dry sump

Power
513bhp @ 8000rpm

Torque
376lb ft @ 4500rpm

Transmission
Six-speed manual, four-wheel drive, rear lsd, ESP, ASR

Suspension
Front and rear: double wishbones, coil springs, dampers, anti-roll bar

Brakes
Ventilated discs, 365mm fr, 335mm rear, ABS, EDB

Weight
1570kg

Performance
0-62mph 4.1sec (claimed)
Top speed 195mph (claimed)

Basic price
£131,000

down by my left knee. It feels odd in a car I normally associate with fingertip immediacy, but the action of the clutch and lever are light and positive, and the evocative ball-topped stick is soon clacking between the fingers of the hallowed open gate in satisfying style.

We power through the humbling beauty of Glen Coe, two raucous wedges of aluminium darting through the holiday traffic, in pursuit of possibly the only car-and-driver combination capable of upstaging us: a Hertz rental Ford Focus driven by photographer Andy Morgan. By the time we pass Fort William, it's well into the afternoon, and Morgan's shutter finger is clearly getting itchy.

While he and Hayman busy themselves with some shots of the Lambo, I make off with the Ferrari for a solo drive. It's a sharp, dashing blade, the F430. Quick-witted and hungry for revs, it thrives on the fast, flowing roads that characterise this remote region of Scotland. You need to work at it, though, for while tractable, the V8 really hits its stride – and finds its voice – above 5000rpm. Below this, the engine emits an intrusive but not especially pleasant blare. Stay above it, however, and the Spider builds to a shrieking crescendo that ricochets off the craggy outcrops at the road's edge, filling the open cockpit with echoes of Fiorano.

There's tremendous feel to the brakes, and excellent stopping power, too. In fact, for all but the most extreme road

and track use they seem plenty strong enough, even if they do look a bit weedy behind the five-spoke alloys. It's delightful to brake hard into a corner, roll your ankle across to execute a heel-and-toe downshift and find the brake and throttle pedals perfectly placed.

Less satisfying is the scuttle-shake that shivers through the structure over major road imperfections. It's not catastrophic, but it is noticeable, and it does diminish the sense of precision you feel compared with the Berlinetta. Worse is the pronounced kick-back through the steering wheel when you hit a mid-corner drain cover or pothole with the inside front wheel. It really does jar, especially when the flow of information is otherwise detailed and delicate. The impact wrong-foots the car for a moment or two. If you've experienced the rock-solid integrity of the Berlinetta, it comes as quite a shock.

Inherently, though, the F430 Spider's chassis balance remains exciting, exploitable and minutely adjustable. Entering one of the countless tightening corners a shade too fast, I'm forced to brake deeper than ideal, and wind-on another quarter-turn of lock. It's one of those moments that makes you catch your breath, but the Ferrari is with me all the way, tightening its line without complaint, the mildest hint of understeer the only outward sign of my misjudgment. For an agile, prickly, mid-engined car, it's

F430 SPIDER
SPECIFICATIONS
Engine
4308cc V8, dohc per bank, aluminium alloy head and block, dry sump
Power
483bhp @ 8500rpm
Torque
343lb ft @ 5250rpm
Transmission
Six-speed manual, rear-wheel drive, E-diff, CST
Suspension
Front and rear: double wishbones, coil springs, 'Skyhook' adaptive damping, anti-roll bar
Brakes
Ventilated and cross-drilled 330mm discs front and rear, ABS, EBD
Weight
1505kg
Performance
0-62mph 4.1sec (claimed)
Top speed 193mph+ (claimed)
Basic price
£127,050

'The F430 is a sharp, dashing blade,
quick-witted and hungry for revs'

Right:
Quiet, open roads of the
Highlands provide the perfect
territory for enjoying cars with
this level of performance. An
11pm sunset is an added bonus.
Gallardo's raucous exhaust note
emphasised when you have the
top down (and a towering
rockface close by).

'The Gallardo is astonishingly sure-footed and surreally rapid'

impressively forgiving. By the time I return to Morgan's photographic base on the shores of Loch Shiel, he's done with the Gallardo. Having got really dialled in to the F430's responses, the contrast between it and the Lamborghini is immediate and startling: where the Ferrari is all about lightness of touch, the Gallardo is a chunky heavyweight that demands a much more muscular approach.

The clutch, gearbox and steering are all significantly weightier than the Ferrari's. The engine brims with bombast from the moment

you fire it up, and the chassis feels beefier, all four tyres planted squarely on their treadblocks where the Ferrari always seems light on its feet. It's a more physical, all-encompassing car. You drive it with your forearms rather than your wrists, and while you don't have to bully it, you do have to assert yourself before the Lamborghini gels.

If there's one element that dominates the Gallardo experience, it's the engine. Moments when the Ferrari can be caught off the boil simply don't exist in the Lambo, for the big-capacity V10 has grunt to spare. It pulls with conviction from nothing and even manages an inspiring second wind between 7000 and 8000rpm, its note hardening, the sense of acceleration intensifying just when you think things are about to tail off. At full rev with the roof down is a cataclysmic experience, the brutal, tortured howl surely ranking as the most visceral cry since Chewbacca did his flies up too quickly.

The gearshift isn't as quick as the Ferrari's, thanks to the extra effort required and also because of a slight gristly feel as the lever passes the neutral plane of the gate. It's not obstructive;

in fact, if you like to get stuck in, the shift's meaty quality can be particularly satisfying. However, for sheer speed and purity, the Ferrari 'box is best, although I can't help thinking that the superb F1 system better suits the F430's character. Heresy I know, but...

Wearing Pirelli P Zero Corsas the Gallardo is a gripfest on these smooth, well-surfaced roads, long swooping corners highlighting its high-g abilities to perfection. Coupled with weighty steering that increases in effort and feel as you pile on the speed and cornering force, it's astonishingly sure-footed and surreally rapid. The one fly (or should that be midge?) in the ointment is a pronounced self-centre effect that tries to pull the car straight when you relax your grip on the suede-rimmed wheel as you see a corner begin to open out. You can drive around the trait, but you're forced to steer straight rather than let the wheel flow through your hands, which compounds the physicality of hustling the Lamborghini.

As ever with the Gallardo, the brakes come in for criticism. Not for their lack of staying power, as the roads here are fast and flowing rather than tight and twisty, but for the initial lack of feel and pedal travel, making smooth driving, not to mention effective heel and toeing, less than intuitive. Again, you do learn to compensate with time and familiarity, but it could be better.

It's been a memorable day's driving, but it's not over yet, for we have an appointment with a sunset on the shores of the Sound of Arisaig. Keen to get prepared in plenty of time, Andy leads us back to our hotel, the amusingly named Cnoc-na-Faire in the equally chucklesome Back of Keppoch. The plan is to check in, dump our bags and head back out, but as we assemble outside at 7pm the sun's still beating down as though it's mid-afternoon. As photographers are as fickle as farmers when it comes to the prevailing weather conditions, we return inside 'to let the light soften', whatever that means...

Three fine courses and two hours later, it's still broad daylight, but with Hayman twitching every time a resident orders a pint of lager, we decide to head back out, finally running out of light at 11pm. The nights really are short this far north.

Next morning, we have a few more shots to do before heading back to Edinburgh. It's an opportunity to let thoughts and feelings crystallise – and hopefully find a way of picking a winner.

As we've established, faults are few and far between. The Ferrari's biggest failing is the mild but noticeable scuttle-shake and serious steering kick-back, while the Lambo suffers from clumsy brake feel and a lack of delicacy. Neither model, it has to be said, is as pure or precise as its tin-roofed relative, but hasn't that always been the case?

After many memorable miles, deciding between them is virtually impossible. Both deliver a rare sense of occasion and connect you with the world you're driving through like few other cars, their speed, sound and involvement all top-drawer. In all honesty, when two machines are this closely matched, aesthetics are as good an arbiter as any.

Forced with making a choice, we'd go for the Lamborghini. While its ham-fisted brake response and the steering's over-keenness to self-centre are annoying, with time you learn to drive around them, but the Ferrari's steering grates more. Perhaps the surgical precision of the Berlinetta means the F430 has more to lose in the transition to Spider. That to our eyes the Gallardo also gets the styling nod seals the win for Sant'Agata, but by the slimmest of margins.

If you fancy following in our tyre-tracks and recreating this test, Rio Prestige now has both a Gallardo Spyder and an F430 Spider. For more information on these and other cars in Rio's impressive fleet, visit www.rioprestige.com or call Edward Legge on 01506 466911.

'After many memorable miles, deciding between them is almost impossible'

POWER TO THE PEOPLE

Capitalism meets communism as we drive a
Ferrari 612 through the People's Republic of
China. Driving adventures don't come any bigger
Words: Richard Meaden Pictures: Andy Morgan

阜康妆

服务

ئەمدىلىلە شتورۇپ، سوتسىالستىك بارپا قىلايلى!
落实科学发展观，构建社会主

15 000 RED MILES

PIRELLI

CT·250ND

PIRELLI

00032

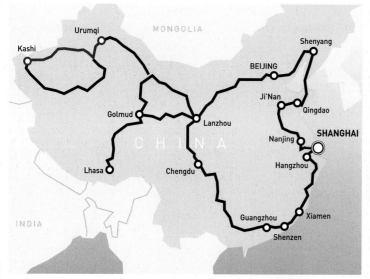

The sign says

'Urumqi', but it might as well say 'Centre of the Earth', for the gritty, grimy, smog-cloaked Chinese industrial city in which we've just arrived is, according to the Guinness Book of Records, further from the ocean than any other major city on the planet. So why are we here, some 1400 miles from the sea and, seemingly, a million miles from home? Why, to drive a Ferrari 612 Scaglietti of course! Surprised you had to ask.

We've been invited to take part in Ferrari's '15,000 Red Miles' tour of China, an incredibly ambitious stunt that must surely rank as the most significant Italian foray into the Far East since Marco Polo decided he'd pack in his job making mints with holes and do a bit of travelling.

On August 29, a pair of Maranello's finest 2+2 supercars (one red with a silver nose, the other silver with a red nose) set off on a record-breaking journey around this vast country, from the vibrant city of Shanghai on the east coast to

Shenzen in the south, then to the mystical Tibetan city of Lhasa, high in the Himalayas, and then to Urumqi in the far north – which is where we come in.

The mammoth tour has been split into 11 sections, with a fresh pairing of journalist and photographer put into each car at the beginning of every leg. Our portion of the journey promises to be a corker, requiring us to drive from the middle of nowhere, sorry, Urumqi, to Kashgar, westernmost outpost of the People's Republic of China and age-old cultural and commercial crossroads on the ancient Silk Road. All that stands between us and there are 850 miles of tarmac and gravel roads that will take us over mountains that make the Alps look like molehills, and through arid deserts that stretch as far as the eye can see. Drive stories don't come much bigger.

While Ferrari wanted to keep the Scagliettis as close to standard as possible, certain essential modifications have been made to protect them

Opposite: toll booth on road out of Urumqi (we saw lots of booths but rarely anyone collecting money).
Top left: route of '15,000 Red Miles', with our leg in red.
Top: plenty of carts but very few cars in Urumqi.
Above left: first fuel stop (petrol is around 30p a litre).
Above: everywhere you go there are men in uniforms; this one's at the entrance to a national park.

from the rigours of China and its rugged terrain. First and most obvious is the increased ride height, upped by an inch or two to stand a chance of coping on loose, uneven surfaces, and a set of Pirelli SottoZero winter tyres to find some grip and resist punctures. A pair of funky mesh grilles cover the headlights, while sturdy underbody protection plates guard the sump and other vulnerable components from rocks.

The boot space is occupied largely by an auxiliary fuel tank, which boosts the 612's capacity to a huge 150 litres for a dawn-till-dusk driving range. With their flamboyant liveries, they look like refugees from the Paris-Dakar Rally Raid. Essentially, though, each Scaglietti's core »

hardware remains, from the 540bhp dry-sumped V12 and its assorted management systems to the six-speed H-pattern gearbox (silver car) and F1 paddle-shift transmission (red car).

Only a fool would embark on such a trip without back-up, and in support of the two Ferraris are two Fiat Palio estate cars, two Iveco minibuses carrying luggage and spares, and a very cool camouflaged military-spec Iveco 4x4 for what eventuality we're not quite sure but, to be honest, we hope we don't find out. There are nine full-time expedition members – three Italian technicians from Maranello, led by Gigi Barp, an official photographer, a video crew and a friendly gaggle of Chinese interpreters and fixers. Together the convoy makes quite a sight.

A surprise late addition to the group is Ferrari's esteemed and charismatic head of PR, Antonio Ghini. That he has chosen to participate in our section of the drive is the best hint yet that of the 11 legs we could have landed, Urumqi to Kashgar promises to be particularly special. Naturally, Ghini is as excited and fascinated as we are at the prospect of exploring the breathtaking terrain and experiencing the ancient cultures of this far-flung

corner of China, but he's also keen to explain the purpose of the '15,000 Red Miles' expedition, and Ferrari's aims for the emerging Chinese market.

'We didn't want simply to import our cars to China, build showrooms and offer them for sale,' he says. 'We know it's a complicated market and that it's not going to be easy to sell Ferrari in China. Driving for pleasure is firmly established in the West, but over here you drive only to get from A to B. Driving just for the sake of it is an alien concept. People aspire not to drive themselves but to be driven, in a large saloon or SUV. This is a sign of status for wealthy, successful Chinese. As for two-seater sports cars, well, the feeling is often, "Why would I want one of those? What am I going to do with that?"

'Of course, the first Chinese GP was a big step towards introducing the Western passion for cars. We had a great race that year, too, so our red cars made a big impression, but it's important to us that we show to China that there is more to Ferrari than racing. This 15,000-mile adventure

is our opportunity to do that – and by driving around China we aim to show that we've taken the time and made the effort to get to know the country and its people, to explore its culture and experience the spectacular scenery. You could say we've come to pay our respects to China.'

After an eventful night in Urumqi, where your intrepid journo and snapper manage to sidestep Chinese culinary delicacies such as ox penis and Turtle's Rim (whatever that is), not to mention escaping the over-friendly attentions of numerous 'professional' women stalking the hotel's Romance Bar – I know, the clue's in the name, but we were very jet-lagged – we're pleased and

'Through the chaotic traffic we adopt the local technique of hooting first, asking questions later'

Above: These policemen strolled up and took turns to have their photos taken with the Scaglietti. Speeding isn't really an issue in China, but the official limit is 80kph on the highway, 40kph in towns. Though most people we met had no idea what a Ferrari was, they recognised that it was something special.
Opposite top: early-morning street scene in Urumqi – vast junctions like this are typical and, when they're heaving with traffic, crossing them is an adventure in itself. **Below left:** farmer's truck had sheep on upper deck, cows underneath. **Bottom left:** nomadic shepherd had found a riverside pitch for his tent. **Bottom right:** boulders block our path.

relieved to be leaving next morning.

By night, Urumqi is a sprawling, neon-splashed melting pot of large Western-style hotels, vast, shadowy industrial areas and shambolic, decaying slums. By day the city is robbed of the neon's rose-tint, leaving your eyes to cast across a grubby skyline torn asunder by fast-growing ultra-modern skyscrapers, fume-belching brick chimneys reminiscent of our own industrial city-scapes of the 1800s, and, as though making a last stand against the march of Westernisation, traditional Chinese temples perched on distant hilltops. This strange scene is crowned by a thick blanket of smog, and the air is heavy with the sooty tang of coal smoke. Welcome to China.

We take no prisoners as we break free of

Urumqi, tucking the nose of our 612 into the wake of the Chinese-driven Iveco van, cutting through the chaotic traffic as though protected by some unseen forcefield and adopting the local technique of hooting first and asking questions later. Braking or any kind of steering-based avoidance manoeuvre is regarded strictly as a last resort, but by some miracle the traffic flows not only freely but with good humour.

It is already clear that while the average Urumqian on the street doesn't fully grasp what the Ferraris are, let alone what they are doing cutting and thrusting through the Xinjang province's capital city, they know that they are something special – particularly when a gap in the traffic allows us to unleash a healthy lunge of

second gear. However, it's also obvious that while the Scagliettis have immense curiosity value, the 5m-long supercars are but chocolate fireguards to many of the down-to-earth Chinese, who appear to reserve genuinely lustful looks for the more practical charms of the Iveco vans and rugged off-roader.

Once clear of the tumultuous city centre, Urumqi's high-rise zone soon sinks to low-rise slums that hug the muddy fringes of the road. Cars and buses are scarce, their number replaced by lorries, tractors and donkey-carts. The people are dirt-poor but industrious, and while they all have clothes on their backs and food in their bellies, it surely won't be long before they begin to wonder when China's burgeoning economy will benefit them. One thing's for sure: the gulf between the outskirts of Urumqi and the manicured, high-gloss image of China that's beamed into our living rooms from F1's Shanghai finale extends beyond simple geography. Even our Chinese guides refer to what we're seeing as 'the real China', and I for one believe them.

We stop to brim the convoy, not the work of a moment with two cavernous Scaglietti fuel tanks to fill, but with a bootful of PetroChina's finest we climb back into our silver 612S and watch as

Urumqi shrinks in our mirrors. Despite the modifications, and the gruelling 6000 miles or so that have already passed beneath the Ferrari's wheels, our Scaglietti feels remarkably together. The ride is softer and the initial steering response has been dulled, thanks to the lateral give and squirm of the chunkier tyres' open treadblocks, but the 612 retains much of its commanding, imperious manner and makes effortless progress as we head into the open countryside. Bumps in the road trigger assorted rattles from the suspension yet there's nothing to suggest it's anything to worry about, and we soon settle into a steady, satisfying rhythm, rural China gliding past our windows.

In fact, although the signs say we're in China,

the scenery's more like northern France, with long avenues of plane trees lining the road and broad pastoral countryside rolling away on each side. Only the growing spikes of the distant mountain ranges hint at what's to come. We've been climbing almost since leaving Urumqi, imperceptibly at first, but now, as we begin to look down on, rather than across, the fields of crops it's clear we're driving into the foothills of the Tian Shan range.

The sky is increasingly overcast and the edges of the road are closing in, jagged banks of rock getting closer to the side window and casting a shadow over the car. The impression of being funnelled into a confined space is profound as we enter a deep and dizzying gorge that cuts its

way through a series of peaks known as the Flaming Mountains. With a sheer drop into the river on our left, sheer rock face climbing to unseen heights on our right, and nothing but a series of red and white painted posts standing between us and oblivion, this road certainly focuses the mind.

The gorge winds on for miles, each corner revealing ever-more-spectacular views. In what will become a recurring game during our journey, the changing scenery prompts photographer Andy Morgan and I to think of where it reminds us of – and we decide that the gorge, complete with tumbling river, abundant pine trees and humbling scale is like the wilds of British Columbia or Yosemite National Park. The sense of solitude is marked as our incongruous string of red dots winds its way through this giant landscape, with only the occasional encounter with sheep-herders or impatient drivers of coal-laden trucks to break the sense of isolation.

As if to remind us of our vulnerability, the road appears blocked by a landslide. Rocks the size of small cars litter our path and we're forced to take to a diversion onto a makeshift road built of scree and boulders. The red Ferrari is ahead of us, straddling the deepest ruts with aplomb, but

Above: compacted snow, sometimes with a glossy coating of ice, and a sheer drop on one side – the journey suddenly gets more interesting. Highest point is 4280 metres up. **Opposite page:** lorry has been stuck on this hillside for a couple of days; cement factory pumps dust into air already polluted by coal power stations. **Opposite below:** the Iveco back-up vehicle, nicknamed Shaggy, and some shaggy locals.

then one wheel slips off the high ground and with a graunch the car is beached. We can hear the grinding and scraping on the undertray from our distant vantage point, but with some gentle fore-and-aft shunting the Ferrari frees itself and continues unharmed.

You could be forgiven for thinking that such remote, tranquil and beautiful mountains would be out of China's dirty, industrial reach, but no. Tucked away in this bleak, isolated place is a ❯❯

'You have to concentrate intently on

coal-fired power station. Smoke stacks pump clouds of fumes into the innocent mountain air, and all that's unfortunate enough to find itself downwind (including the grimmest town you've ever seen, and a school playground teeming with kids) is shrouded in a noxious fug of God-knows what. A few miles further on, a dust-caked cement works adds to the filth. I take some solace from the fact that we're doing our bit to improve the local environment, for thanks to its pollutant-scrubbing catalytic converters, the gasses coming out of the Ferrari's exhausts are surely cleaner and less harmful than the air which entered its combustion chambers.

Whether it's due to the epic pollution or, as is more likely, the increasing altitude and rapidly decreasing temperature, the pine trees have

long gone and the road now cuts through rocky snowfields, its surface a glistening, slushy grey-black emulsion of mud and stones. Ahead of us is a towering wall of white, topped with menacing crags. We can't seriously be driving up there, can we? Yes is the short answer, for as we get closer to the impossibly sheer face, a thin, zig-zagging road can be seen clinging to the mountainside by its fingernails. Look harder and it's possible to see lorries clawing their way towards the summit, inch by perilous inch. And we are next.

Although levels of tension have risen appreciably inside our Ferrari, the car itself is untroubled by the situation, Pirelli tyres finding reliable, consistent grip, V12 lugging heartily despite the gruel-thin air, traction-control system

blissfully inactive, even when the sludgy gravel cedes to packed snow and then patchy ice. And so it's with buttocks clenched tight that we press on, rounding hairpin after treacherous hairpin, slowly making progress as the outside temperature gauge sheds degrees C. Then, just as the wind whips up and the temperature hits zero, our convoy stops. We all climb out, clinging to our cars for stability, and crane our necks to the heavens. Three tiers up we spot the problem: two, no, three lorries, stationary in the snow. Great.

From what our interpreters can gather, there was a heavy snowfall a couple of days ago and the trucks have been stuck ever since. Stuck? For a couple of days! What the hell are we going to do now? Keep driving, of course. So we climb slowly towards the stranded lorries, then teeter

the road, avoiding the bigger rocks'

around them on the edge of the abyss before finally, triumphantly, cresting the 4280m summit. It might be small beer compared with the 5200m the team reached on their run to Lhasa, but for Morgan and I this is our own personal Everest and we savour the moment.

What goes up must come down, and if we thought the icy ascent was a bit hairy, the view that greets us as we begin our descent makes our mouths go dry. Despite the sunshine and blue skies the downward run is just as snowy. In fact, thanks to the combination of sun and a cold wind, the surface has melted then frozen, turning the road into a 1-in-3 ice rink. It's a challenge none of us is really all that keen on facing, but short of reversing back down from whence we came, radioing in a rescue helicopter

or adopting the foetal position and crying for our mothers, there's nothing for it but taking a deep breath and pointing the Scagliettis down the mountain.

The trick, apart from making sure that each vehicle is separated by a healthy margin, is to build minimal momentum: just enough to keep going but not enough to have to rely too heavily on braking, for you get the feeling that should the car begin to run away with you, things would get very ugly very quickly. Amazingly the Scaglietti manages to find some front-end grip, which means we could steer away from the drop and into the rockface if all else fails, but apart from a few faint zizzes of ABS and the occasional slither, the steepest section of ice passes without incident. And r-e-l-a-x.

After the initially scalp-prickling icy descent, the gravelly section that follows, though still steep, is more like fun. We get up some speed, and by quietly dropping back, away from Barp's eagle-eyed gaze, manage a few tentative slides on the loose surface. As the snow fades, bleak, fractured rock faces are revealed, and as the view opens out a little, barren boulder-fields stretch out before us. It's stark but less oppressive than the gorge, with a real sense of ever-expanding space and optimism. Eventually the rocky tundra is replaced by smoother, more habitable terrain, the highlight of which is a breathtakingly beautiful plain, lush with swaying, corn-coloured grass and fenced by majestic, snow-dusted peaks. A freight train hoves into view, seemingly from nowhere, and » runs parallel to us for a time before arcing gracefully in front of us as we approach a level crossing. Our surroundings look more like Mongolia – no surprise, as we're relatively close to the border – and just as we think the scene couldn't get any better we catch sight of a herdsman on horseback with his flock of sheep, silhouetted against the velvety hillsides. It's a magic moment and a welcome distraction from the ragged gravel track on which we're attempting to make progress.

Pounded by the infrequent passage of overloaded coal lorries, it's a constantly shifting bed of crushed stone and semi-submerged boulders. The surface has two distinct lanes, the centreline and fringes marked by ridges of loose material that clatters and scrapes along the Scaglietti's belly every time we steer around parked lorries or herds of sheep. It's energy-sapping driving, for you have to concentrate intently on the surface, avoiding the biggest rocks, straddling ruts and slowing for dips and hollows that threaten to smack the Scaglietti's precious alloy nose. Dust from the lead car is

choking and thick enough to mask oncoming trucks. Only a barked alert over the walkie-talkie prevents a sickening head-on impact.

Trucks aren't the only hazard, nor indeed are they the worst. That honour goes to the sinister motorcades of blacked-out Land Cruisers that overtake us, showering the Ferraris with stones and gravel as they pass. Police? Government officials? We never find out who they are, but if he spots them in time, Barp implores us to pull over and let them pass. It's a largely vain effort to protect the vulnerable bodywork and avoid a broken windscreen; by and large, even such evasive driving fails to save the Ferraris from a pebble-dashing.

Our progress is excruciatingly slow. At one point I make the mistake of looking at my watch and cross-referencing it with the odometer. Half an hour later I look again: we've done five miles. Another 30 minutes pass and I groan as the odometer confirms we've managed another 10 miles, bringing our tally to little more than 150 miles in just over seven hours. Right now I'm beginning to wonder if we'll ever

get to our overnight halt at Korla.

And then, like a geological full-stop, the mountains and grassy, snow-dusted pastures cease without warning, the lush Alpine surroundings brutally butt-jointed to a vast, arid plain of near-lunar nothingness. It's as though God simply ran out of rock and inspiration. Squinting into the void, it becomes clear that the dustbowl is bisected by an arrow-straight strip of tarmac that pricks the shimmering, far-flung horizon. After a gruelling non-stop day-long slog that's seen us wind through wooded valleys, ascend perilous icy switchbacks and crest the snowy peaks of the Tian Shan mountain range, the parched, sandy fringes of the Taklamakan Desert are a new and menacing challenge. Our journey, it seems, has only just begun.

Opposite, top right: you can travel through mile after mile of deserted landscape and then come across a town heaving with people. **Middle left:** Meaden at the wheel. **Middle right:** tarmac roads occasionally peter out and you have to work out which side of an approaching truck to pass. **Bottom right:** big, Western-style hotels are among first signs of a changing culture.

'Sinister motorcades of blacked-out Land Cruisers overtake us...'

RED
LEADER?

Ferrari says the 430 Scuderia is as quick
as an Enzo. We put the car through a full
performance test to find out if this is true
Words: John Barker Pictures: Matt Howell

It's said that

Enzo Ferrari built road cars simply to fund his passion for racing, and it seems something of that spirit lives on at Maranello today in the way that the company has no qualms about using its supercar back-catalogue to reference the performance of its latest road cars. The 599 GTB Fiorano took as its benchmark the iconic F40, and gave it a drubbing. Now the Enzo, Ferrari's most potent and fastest road car of all time, finds itself used to illustrate the pace of the 430 Scuderia.

The Scuderia is the feistiest mid-engined V8 road car the marque has built, but even with 503bhp – 20bhp more than the stock F430 – it's way down on the Enzo's 650bhp. Yet while it can't hope to attain the Enzo's top speed, Ferrari says the Scuderia can match its 0-60mph time and, far more significantly, replicate its lap time around the Fiorano race track.

It sounds extraordinary when you consider that the Enzo predates the Scuderia by barely five years and back then represented Ferrari's take on the ultimate supercar. Yet while the Enzo has a carbonfibre tub and panels, the all-aluminium Scuderia is 15kg lighter. At a claimed 1350kg it weighs 85kg less than the

regular F430 thanks to a wide-ranging weight-reduction programme that includes hollow anti-roll bars and titanium road springs, lightweight bumpers, a Lexan rear screen and, inside, reduced sound-deadening and extensive use of carbonfibre, notably for the door casings and seat shells.

Then there are standard-fit carbon-ceramic brakes and sticky Pirelli P Zero Corsa tyres, both of which offer the benefits of five years' extra development over the Enzo's carbon brakes and bespoke Bridgestones. All these details add up, but if you're looking for the technology that helps the Scuderia nail the same lap time as the Enzo despite a 150bhp shortfall, it's the chassis. Specifically, it's the combined effect of the Scuderia's E-diff, its electronically controlled locking differential, and F1-Trac, the advanced stability control developed originally for the 599 GTB. Working together, they maximise the drive the 430 Scuderia finds out of corners and enhance stability going into them, too. Michael Schumacher is said to have been instrumental in the development of this system.

What we want to know is, will the Scuderia

deliver on the West Circuit at England's Bedford Autodrome as convincingly as it does at Fiorano? We'll soon see. Normally we'd get the performance figures in the bag before pounding around the track, but today circumstances compel us to do the laps first and visit nearby Millbrook Proving Ground second. This will be followed the next day by an early-morning call at the Thorney Motorsport rolling road in Milton Keynes.

It's as we're signing in at the Autodrome that we get a call from the Ferrari GB press manager telling us he's in the canteen – and that he has a surprise. When we test any other car, it is delivered to the office and gets collected a few days later. Not a Ferrari. Its cars come from the factory with a support crew, which today includes an engineer, a technician and a test driver to check that the car is as it should be and offer advice on how to get the best out of it. The surprise is that today the test driver is a bloke called Marc Gene. Yup, Ferrari's F1 test driver will do a couple of laps of the West Circuit before handing over to me. No pressure, then. Thank goodness Schuey was busy...

As usual, Ferrari has a target – in this instance

'The Scuderia is unquestionably the feistiest mid-engined V8 road car that Ferrari has built'

Above, centre: Barker attaches the VBOX timing gear.
Right: Ferrari F1 test driver Marc Gene is on hand to offer tips on getting the most out of the Scuderia, which he and Michael Schumacher helped develop.

the big-hitting Porsches that have already been around the recently revised West Circuit: the 523bhp 997 GT2 and 604bhp Carrera GT, which recorded 1:23.5sec and 1:23.3sec respectively. The Enzo lapped the old circuit, which was a bit quicker, in 1:21.3sec, so if the Scuderia gets close to that, it'll be on the money.

Gene reckons the fastest times will come with the steering wheel manettino set in the 'Race' position, which slackens the traction and stability systems but still allows them to optimise corner speed. A couple of laps alongside the hugely likeable and, of course, effortlessly rapid Gene reveal a few things: first that the Scuderia can carry huge speed to the apex under braking, second that there's a bit of understeer in the quick turns, and third that he can't stop himself cutting across the odd kerb.

Back in the pits, Gene delivers his verdict. 'In Race it was definitely helping out of the hairpin and other slow corners,' he says, 'but it was perhaps a little conservative in the very fast turns. Try it in the next setting up, CT-off, for a couple of laps.' New for the Scuderia, CT-off retains stability control but disables traction control, thus allowing wheelspin.

There's a lightness, an athleticism about the »

Above: F1-Trac stability control system keeps the Scuderia in check on track. **Right:** intake and exhaust system improvements have contributed to Scuderia's extra 20bhp over the standard F430.

Left: checking the Scuderia's weight.
Below: a Ferrari technician interrogates the car's on-board computer in an attempt to discover why it refuses to rev to peak power on the rolling road.

Scuderia that you notice right from the off. The steering has good weight but relays clearly that the nose is light, and you quickly appreciate that the key to a fast lap is keeping things tidy. It's as if you have to guide it along a narrow path, not allowing either understeer or oversteer to get beyond a quarter turn. Imagine a bigger, more potent, more feelsome Lotus Exige, and you're not far off.

Even with traction control assisting in Race mode, it pays to feather the throttle out of the Bank hairpin so as not to get the tail out and excite stability control into throttle-cutting action. Perhaps unusually for a 500bhp car, the Scuderia is more awesome into the corners than out of them, the highlight of the lap being the entry to the new Pif-Paf sequence. You brake with confidence from over 110mph and peel in still hard on the brakes, anti-lock resisting triggering, the grip of the Pirellis divided between braking and cornering, while the E-diff and stability-control system ensure rock-solid composure.

This corner also shows off the superb 'F1-SuperFast2' paddleshift to best effect. Not only can you be lunging deep into turns hard on the brakes but you can pop in a downshift too, the changes so smooth that there's no suggestion of the balance being compromised.

The fastest laps are with Race mode selected, although there's just a couple of tenths in it – 1:22.5sec with versus 1:22.7 without. It feels

like it'd go a bit faster with less understeer, and reducing the front tyre pressures to match the rears (we normally stick with the maker's recommendations) does the trick.

It feels like the rear is taking more of the cornering load, which makes things a bit serious in CT-off in the faster turns (and no quicker overall), but in Race mode the Scuderia seems to balance right on the edge. It's there in the lap time, too – 1:21.7, which takes its advantage over the Porsches out from around 1sec to over 1.5sec. Allowing for the changes to the circuit, that also puts it on a par with the Enzo we tested on the old layout, and there's no question that the Enzo, with simple traction control and a purely mechanical limited-slip diff, was looser and much scarier.

A COUPLE OF HOURS later, we're lined up on the mile straight at Millbrook. First it's the in-gear acceleration tests. From a little over tickover, this 4.3-litre, flat-plane-crank V8 feels and sounds like one of the sweetest and fruitiest twin-cam in-line fours you've ever heard. There's a sense, especially in the higher gears, that it is not 100 per cent happy paddling in the shallows of its rev range, but

that might be because of the way it snaps to attention at 3250rpm. In an instant, the delivery changes as valving inside the exhaust system directs exiting gases onto a more free-flowing route. It's as if corks plugging the Scuderia's tailpipes have been yanked out – the V8's note hardens to a raw blare and the car kicks forward with serious intent.

At around 7000rpm there's another uplift that marks a wailing and even more urgent push to peak power at 8500rpm. By this point, less than 200rpm short of the limiter,

'The acceleration feels like a single uninterrupted lunge from zero to over 160mph' all five lights in the steering wheel rim are aglow. Ignore them in Race mode and the V8 will stutter against the limiter at 8640rpm precisely. It's a limiter that, incidentally, is more saw-toothed in the first three gears.

As well as delivering 20bhp more than in the F430, the Scuderia's V8 pumps up the torque curve too, and certainly the delivery is more consistent than you'd imagine from the way the engine note changes. Third gear offers serious punch from 20mph to a whisker over 100mph and, once it's into its stride, the kick in the back never lets up: 40-60mph takes a mere 2.1sec and 80-100mph 2.3sec.

As with the 599 we'd previously tested, to execute a standing start with the aim of nailing the best time rather than the most drama, you won't be needing the launch control button (marked LC) on the centre console. Marc Gene talks us through it. Twist the manettino fully clockwise to switch off everything apart from anti-lock, press the brake and select first with the right-hand paddle, then pull and hold the left-hand paddle for about three seconds. There'll follow a long beep and the digital gear indicator will blink 'L' and '1' alternately to let you know that the Scuderia is primed for launch.

All you have to do now is snap the throttle open. The first start feels almost perfect. We hit the throttle, the revs rise rapidly to around 6000rpm and after a moment the Scuderia brings the clutch in and takes off. It feels like there's no slip at all, yet the revs don't die; indeed they stay almost constant and the Ferrari snaps forward, driving us into our seats. You get a 'free' limiter-brushing auto upshift from first to second gear, but from there on it's up to you – using your skill and judgement, Spot-the-Ball style, you use the shift lights and rev-counter to judge when it's time to request the upshifts.

There's a lovely, soft ba-boom on each change but essentially the acceleration feels like a single uninterrupted lunge from zero to over 160mph. At the Autodrome there was the feeling that slivers of time were being saved on upshifts, and analysis of the standing-start acceleration trace shows this to be the case. Whereas the 599 (shift speed 100ms) felt very good, its trace clearly showed the first three upshifts as steps. In contrast, that of the lighter Scuderia (60ms) shows a small step from first to second gear, but thereafter the curve is virtually smooth.

Normally we'd alternate runs in either direction, but the *real* launch control of the Scuderia needs to 'learn' the surface for the first couple of runs and delivers the best times on run four or five. We are impressed with the clean lunges; there's not a whiff of burnt clutch as the E-diff and electronic clutch management conspire to deliver the best take-off.

Now, we consider 3.9sec to 60mph and 100mph in the low eights to be pretty sensational. However, the Scuderia is not delivering what Ferrari claims. We can't see it bettering 3.9sec by four-tenths, but that's what the engineer says it should be doing. Suspicion falls on the tyres, which still look roughed from the Autodrome, so they are replaced with another set that are 10 per cent worn. We line up again and, to our surprise, »

less than half a dozen runs later we've bagged an Enzo-matching 3.5sec to 60 in each direction and an average of 7.7sec to 100mph. Not much else we've tested has gone quicker.

The Scuderia's performance versus that of the 599 we tested makes interesting reading. Fully fuelled, this Scuderia weighs 1374kg (against a claimed 1350kg), giving a power-to-weight ratio of 372bhp/ton. Our 599 was 1733kg, giving 364bhp/ton. Despite this, the front-engined V12 berlinetta just has the edge over the mid-engined V8, getting to 100mph three tenths of a second faster and growing the advantage to almost 2sec by 160mph. And although the 599 is 359kg heavier, it has a

superior torque-to-weight ratio, which shows in the in-gear times, especially in the higher gears: 50-70mph in fifth and sixth takes 3.9 and 5.8sec in the 599 compared with 4.4 and 6.8sec in the Scuderia.

IT WOULD HAVE BEEN good to confirm the Scuderia's power, but despite the best efforts of Thorney Motorsport, two hours on the rollers and half a tank of Shell V-Power, the Ferrari refused to play ball. Some cars don't like their rear wheels doing 140mph when the fronts are static, and the Scuderia refused to rev out. However, Ferrari had dyno-tested the engine and the output we saw on the rollers at 7000rpm matched almost exactly what had been seen on the dyno on the way to 501bhp.

There's nothing about the way the 430 Scuderia performed to suggest it has anything less than 500bhp; it nailed an excellent time around the West Circuit and bagged a very impressive set of figures at Millbrook. Indeed, the closer you get to the Scuderia, the harder you push it, the more impressive it is. It showcases Ferrari's F1-derived technology – particularly its F1-SuperFast2 automated manual 'box and E-diff and F1-Trac stability

'The harder you push it, the more impressive it is…'

control – better than any other Ferrari we've tried. And even a sceptic of such technology transfer must concede that the Scuderia's abilities are exceptional and uniquely inspired. All-time great status is surely a certainty.

Specification

Engine	V8
Location	Mid, longitudinal
Displacement	4308cc
Bore x stroke	92 x 81mm
Cylinder block	Aluminium alloy, dry sumped
Cylinder head	Aluminium alloy, dohc per bank, 4v per cylinder, variable valve timing
Fuel and ignition	Electronic engine management, sequential multipoint injection
Max power	503bhp @ 8500rpm
Max torque	347lb ft @ 5250rpm
Transmission	Six-speed 'F1-SuperFast2' automated manual gearbox, rear-wheel drive, E-diff, F1-Trac
Front suspension	Double wishbones, coil springs, adaptive dampers, anti-roll bar
Rear suspension	Double wishbones, coil springs, adaptive dampers, anti-roll bar
Brakes	Cross-drilled and vented carbon-ceramic discs, 398mm front, 350mm rear, ABS, EBD
Wheels	19in front and rear, aluminium alloy
Tyres	235/35 ZR19 front, 285/35 ZR19 rear, Pirelli P Zero Corsa
Weight (kerb)	1350kg (test car 1374kg)
Power-to-weight	378bhp/ton (test car 372bhp/ton)
0-62mph	3.6sec (claimed) (see table, right)
Top speed	198mph (claimed)
Basic price	£172,625
On sale	Now

RATING ★★★★★

PERFORMANCE

ACCELERATION TIMES

0-30	1.5
0-40	2.1
0-50	2.8
0-60	
0-70	4.3
0-80	5.4
0-90	6.5
0-100	
0-110	9.2
0-120	10.8
0-130	12.7
0-140	15.1
0-150	17.8
0-160	21.2

1/4 MILE

sec	11.6
mph	125.0

IN-GEAR TIMES

20-40	1.8	3.0	3.8	-	-
30-50	1.5	2.5	3.2	5.3	-
40-60	1.6	2.1	2.7	5.2	6.8
50-70	1.6	2.1	2.7	4.4	6.8
60-80	-	2.1	2.7	3.6	6.5
70-90	-	2.2	2.8	3.6	5.6
80-100	-	2.3	3.0	3.8	5.0
90-110	-	-	3.2	3.8	5.3
100-120	-	-	-	4.0	5.6
110-130	-	-	-	4.4	5.8
120-140	-	-	-	4.8	6.3
130-150	-	-	-	5.4	-
140-160	-	-	-	-	-

BRAKING

dist. ft	297

MAX SPEED

198mph (claimed)

AVERAGE g

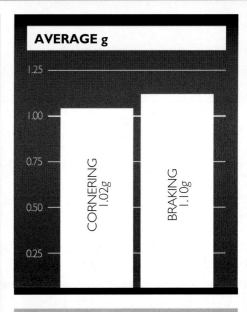

CORNERING 1.02g
BRAKING 1.10g

■ TOTAL WEIGHT – 1374kg

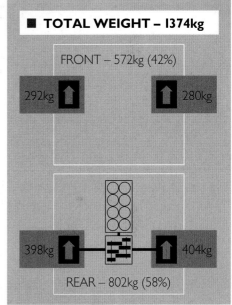

FRONT – 572kg (42%)

292kg 280kg

398kg 404kg

REAR – 802kg (58%)

0-100-0 (Including reaction time)

FERRARI 430 SCUDERIA 12.6sec

0 1 2 3 4 5 6 7 8 9 10 11 12 13 14

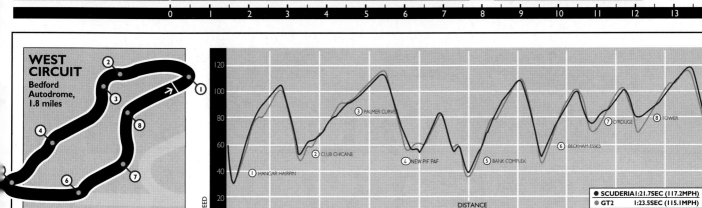

WEST CIRCUIT
Bedford Autodrome, 1.8 miles

① HANGAR HAIRPIN
② CLUB CHICANE
③ PALMER CURVE
④ NEW PIF PAF
⑤ BANK COMPLEX
⑥ BECKHAM ESSES
⑦ O'ROUGE
⑧ TOWER

● SCUDERIA 1:21.7SEC (117.2MPH)
● GT2 1:23.5SEC (115.1MPH)

▲ Scuderia (red) is faster than the 997 GT2 (grey) just about everywhere, with superior minimum corner speeds that are worth a stack of time. Slight understeer of the Ferrari is preferable to Porsche's tail-heavy oversteer in this respect, while its seamless upshifts save time too – look at the big steps in the GT2's trace as it accelerates.

THE ULTIMATE TEST

Words: Mark Hales
Photography: Charlie McGee

The F40 has been the ultimate pin-sharp, aggressive supercar since 1987. Can the Enzo match it? Until now, no-one has been able to compare the two directly

There is an argument

that says supercars are a profligate irrelevance whose extra capability can't be researched on today's roads. That their layout is unforgiving and gives a driver no clue as to where the limit lies, denying them the confidence to press on. That ownership is a quick way to lose large sums of money – along with your licence...

There's more, and it would be a skilled lawyer who could mount a genuine defence to any of it. But given the number of different examples popping up all over the world, there are obviously plenty of people with the necessary means who are willing to take the risks. The two Ferraris in the pictures here are both numbers in limited-production runs, all of which were sold before manufacture, and both are owned by the same man – amiable property investor and accomplished racer Grahame Bryant. Cars built as ultimates whether relevant or not.

The idea was to see if and how the breed has evolved in the last two decades, and for me there is no better starting point than the Ferrari F40. I've driven a fair few miles in the early example owned by Nick Mason and, on a dry road, it was always massively, hugely exciting, a raw and brutally visceral experience, intoxicating for its sheer energy and the more so because it remained unpredictable. It became a

huge favourite as much for its capacity to thrill as the fact that it never pretended to be anything it wasn't.

The Enzo – the new millennium's F40 – I knew little about. Grahame's was the first example I had seen in the flesh and there is no denying it's a striking sight. The red paint, which saturates the schnozzle-heavy shape, has a kind of chromed allure that richens the hue and only adds to the controversy over the styling – those who like the blend of space-age insect front and chunky kit car back and those who don't seem to inhabit equal-sized camps. Both cars, though, have angular lines, each a composite carapace apparently hewn from blocks of ice rather than a skin pulled tight over smooth sinew. For the F40, folded paper was simply the style of the mid-1980s; the Enzo, you get the impression, is that way for a more specific purpose – the square edges defining channels to direct the passage of air over and through its body.

It also features an engine twice the size of the F40's – six litres – with half as many cylinders again (12 in a vee) and a claimed output of 650bhp at 7800rpm. It's a big lump of metal and, together with the computer-controlled semi-automatic six-speed gearbox, fills half the Enzo's dimensions, pushing the cockpit space forwards because there's no other choice. The F40's more conventional five-speed transaxle

Below: mid-corner, pushing hard, and the turbos cut in. Suddenly the F40's rear is pushing sideways. It's not as friendly as an Enzo...

'The muted hum turns to a harsh buzzing, the whoosh becomes a bellowing roar. The car rocks from one rear corner to the other as the tyres scrabble'

'The F40 is a more
stripped-down, sweaty and
intimate experience and,
whether you like it or not,
you are always involved
with a chassis that is
beautifully balanced'

and compact 2.9-litre V8 are smaller in every respect, and the
claimed 478bhp at 7000rpm is mainly thanks to a pair of
Japanese turbochargers. These, we will sample first.

The F40's door is ample but it's still a scramble across a wide
sill latticed with signature carbon-fibre weave. Sink into the
thinly padded bucket seat and survey the dash ahead, trimmed
by afterthought in grey suede cloth and speckled with dials and
switches borrowed from the Fiat parts bin. Push the button
and there comes not the offbeat rattle of a traditional V8 but a
muted wheezy hum, more like a low-revving four than a fire-
breathing eight. The footwell seems too crowded for a pair of
size 12s and the clutch is heavy. Pull the round black knob and
glinting wand of a gearlever (which pokes up from the
traditional slotted gate) towards you and back, into the first
slot. The engine seems benign and you drive off as you would
in any volume model.

The concrete road at Leicestershire's Bruntingthorpe Proving
Ground sends a rumble and boom through the bare plastic,
mixed with such a clatter from the stones pinging off the
wheelarches that, had Grahame not already mentioned it,
you'd fear for the structure. Meanwhile, the car jiggles over the
ruts but rides rather than reacts to the bumps – a sense of
control which immediately feels good – while all the time the
wheel writhes gently in your hands.

This, I remember, was one of the car's defining features.
A wonderfully sensitive instrument which feels out the road
surface and sends the report back to your fingertips – take
your hands off and watch the rim gently shuffling this way and

Above: the F40's
ahead, with turbos
spinning hard, but
there's no chance for
it – the Enzo will be
able to overtake.

that while the nose of the car gently follows suit. I remember, too, that it's a means of feeling out puddles and changes in grip, things that can never quite find their way past the numbing of power assistance and a tactile asset unknown to so many drivers of modern cars.

As the revs rise, the gentle hum takes a harder edge overlaid by a breathy whoosh as the turbos start to spin up, accompanied by a gentle but insistent push in the back. Thus far I don't let it run much beyond 4000rpm, which leaves time to deal with the Ferrari gearshift, a device whose details and foibles could almost fill a chapter on their own. The synchros are tough and instead of a nice metallic snick they feel oddly rubbery; you push against them and they give a little, apparently trying to spit your effort out, then they give in and let the lever clack against the gate.

This and the heavy clutch make a smooth and elegant shift something to be savoured – especially when changing down. Trying to match the revs seems to make little difference to the feel of things, and inevitably your efforts to align an engine that spins up at the touch of the accelerator with a gearshift that seems to need both guidance through the gate and a wait for the synchros means a learner's jerk every time. Timing rather than force is the way forward and although it does get easier, it's hard to say why. You just find yourself grinning and saying to yourself, 'that was a good one…'

Time, then, to up the effort. Leave the long, straight road

and turn off to the right, lift the revs and push the lever against the slot for second, wait what seems an age for it to slip home, then instead of tickling the accelerator, give it a proper push. The result is like flicking a switch halfway through the turn. At first there's nothing but a gentle surge, but suddenly, like a feline alerted from slumber, the lazy loaf morphs into a predatory ball of energy. The muted hum turns to a harsh buzzing, the whoosh becomes a bellowing roar. As the tyres scrabble the car rocks from one rear corner to the other, and instinctively you must catch the tail slinging off to the left with a quarter turn of reverse lock. The body corkscrews as the car responds and weight shifts between tyres already struggling for grip, then as you straighten up, the rump squats, digs in and launches you down the following straight. Seven thousand-five comes up in an instant. The tug for third seems easier. Another savage fist in the back lasts only an instant longer than the last. It's time for fourth.

Folklore says that the 478bhp claim is rather modest and the real figure is much more. It certainly feels like it because there's but a moment to contemplate the long sweep to the left which is fast-forwarding at an unfeasible rate. Ease the car in, use the feel of the wheel, take note of the gentle tugging that says there's grip to point the nose, then follow it through with the power. About the mid-point, the tail gently but firmly steps to the right as the revs rise. The tyres

Below: could there be two more distinctive body shapes? The F40 is pure mid-1980s, while the Enzo's cab-forward style is dictated by the huge engine and semi-auto transmission.

'I'd heard how Schumacher had the rear tyres permanently on fire and how even his freakish talent couldn't make the car quicker than it was with traction control switched on'

have lost the battle again despite the higher gear and you still couldn't feel it coming. The reaction still has to be instinctive. It's not so much the amount of acceleration – although 500bhp in 1100kg is always likely to be exciting – it's the suddenness of it all.

You notice too that your ears are ringing and that the brakes are not remotely up to the performance. They grumble and judder, the car slows rather than stops, and there's no reassuring bite. Maybe it was the technology of the time, but it still seems a surprising oversight given the rest and it makes you realise more than ever that this style of performance really can't be fully unleashed on the public road. In which case, what of the Enzo, which promises to be faster still?

Hook the fingers under the sunken door catch and click it open, let the massive structure swing up, propelled by hissing gas struts and supported on a huge, forged central crank. Notice the similar lack of trim in the cabin, the weave of carbon fibre, the rubber mats fixed to the floor. Spot that the seats, which look more substantial than the older car's, tilt forward to reveal a small hammock where you can stow your toothbrush and spare underpants. See that there are only two pedals, brake and accelerator, and there's no gearlever – shifting is by two paddles, right/up, left/down, each a fingertip's distance from the computer-game steering wheel. You begin to realise more and more how the layout has influenced, if not defined, the styling.

Sliding in is easy with half the sill missing, then haul the

Above: this is much more difficult to induce. With traction control on, it just won't happen, and even with it off the front initially pushes out. But if you try hard enough, eventually the rear loses its grip...

door down and feel the solid clunk as it closes. The simple circular crank handle at the front turns out to be the window winder, and you see why the glass is smaller than you might like – there has to be room for the side pocket below it, which in turn creates room for the left elbow. The driving position, though, is perfect. Deep, grippy seat, good view through the bowl of a screen, sensibly sized wing mirrors, wheel straight ahead and well clear of the legs, feet straight ahead, big footrest for the left one, padded shin rest for the right leg... The designers have thought about this.

Now survey the rows of buttons and strings of lights. The only ones we need today are those marked 'R' for reverse, 'ASR' to turn off the traction control, and 'RACE', which hands back most of the gearshifting decisions that the normal mode assumes for you or, as Grahame put it, 'will let you get the wrong one and make an arse of it...' Pull back on both paddles to bring up 'N' for neutral on the screen next to the red and white speedo and tacho, and press the starter. A proper V12 rasp comes swiftly from behind, hook the right paddle for first, lift up and release the handbrake and press the right pedal. The car eases forward and, without any more effort than it takes to tell, you are soon trundling down the straight wondering how much louder the road roar drumming at the fibre and the thump and bang as the 35-section tyres slap the gaps in the concrete can get.

Meanwhile, it's hard to resist the schoolboy delight of hooking the right paddle just to see whether it will produce the »

same result every time... And every time the engine holds its rpm while the note changes from a rasp to a metallic clatter before the electronics thump the clutch back in. Not exactly quick and not as smooth as a conventional auto, but impressive in the way it revises the process to suit the power you use and the speed you go. Hook the left paddle to go down and the system blips up the big, rasping engine to match the road speed. This is even more fun, especially if you are coming down from an illegal rate, because the blips are bigger.

All this control at your fingertips is very seductive, but it does take its time – it has to because the gaps between the six gears in a 200mph-plus car are necessarily wide, so you can't zip through them like you can in a Touring Car. Within a mile, though, you realise that anyone could drive an Enzo, and do so with three digits. A finger and thumb to hold the power-assisted wheel and one more to hook the paddles. No-one need ever fluff a shift or stall the engine.

Which also releases you to look at the road. You realise how much concentration is involved dealing with basics like getting the F40's gears selected smoothly and in time, and how tense it makes you. You also notice things like the Enzo's ride, which is stiffer over the bumps, massively taut but not uncomfortable, and how the car tracks dead straight towards the first corner, wheel inert in your hands. Nothing like the living thing in the F40, and composure which only makes the way the nose points as you ease the wheel to the right even more surprising.

You get used to a bit of lag while a car's body takes up an attitude and the wheel settles at whatever slip angle the tyres

FERRARI F40

SPECIFICATIONS

Engine
2936cc V8, twin turbos, double overhead cams, four valves per cylinder, Weber-Marelli engine management and fuel injection

Power
478bhp @ 7000rpm

Torque
425lb ft @ 4000rpm

Transmission
Five-speed manual gearbox, rear-wheel drive, limited-slip differential

Suspension
Front and rear: double wishbones, coil springs, dampers, anti-roll bar

Brakes
Ventilated 330mm discs front and rear

Weight
1100kg

Performance
0-60mph 3.7sec (claimed)
Top speed 201mph (claimed)

Value
Cost £193,000 new
Value now £130,000-£200,000

dictate, and you also know the alternative is often a sudden lunge, which upsets everything. Here it's more a feeling of authority that never makes itself felt until summoned. The possibility it might do the same at high speed is then an exciting prospect normally exclusive to race cars equipped with downforce...

Head towards the long sweepers and aim the nose to find out. It points in as expected but... then there's a hint of push from the front, which if you try and balance with the power only summons the traction control. By that time you are going mighty fast and although, unlike the F40, the car remains completely composed, somehow it wasn't what you expected. Only afterwards in a reflective moment, when you crouch down and look at the Enzo's side view, does it make sense. The gap under the car necessary to make it usable over speed bumps and cambers cannot help but allow air underneath, and keeping this out is the first law of formula car aerodynamics. The flow over the top and through the channels does make some difference, but air below is what lifts the body at speed, so the Enzo's initially pointy front must come more from a stiff chassis and clever dampers. Not a disappointment exactly, just a reminder that this is, after all, a road car.

The Enzo skips and jitters, rocks from one corner to the other in traditional mid-engined style through the bumpy loop that heads back to the straight, where, without the slightest effort, 140mph comes up on the screen. You really would have to be very, very careful in this car... Idly, I prod the pedal further and, just for devilment, hook the left ❯❯

'Sink into the thinly padded bucket seat and survey the dash ahead, trimmed by afterthought in grey suede cloth and speckled with dials and switches borrowed from the Fiat parts bin'

'The driving position is perfect: deep, grippy seat, good view through the bowl of a screen, wheel straight ahead and clear of the legs, feet straight ahead... the designers thought about this'

paddle. The car hesitates while the gear slips in then, as the massive engine comes back, the Enzo doesn't suddenly explode like the F40, instead it surges forward with massive, seamless ease. Leave the foot hard down, let the needle climb round the rev counter, anticipate the limiter, and tweak the right paddle with a forefinger. The shift is quicker now and the thump as the clutch goes home sends young Ollie Bryant's head rocking back. Halfway along the long straight and 180mph is already showing. The book says 217.5mph, and, maybe because 180-and-counting was so easy, you believe it.

When the time comes to shed all this energy, the response to a gentle push on the left pedal is truly astonishing and, like the initially pointy nose, it's the kind you'd expect from a formula car. The bite from the four enormous 13.5in carbon-ceramic discs is massive and consummate without being sharp and jagged, and the car just stops without dipping its nose or weaving. Back up to speed again, just to lean on them harder, but they just bite harder back. The Enzo, it seems, takes care of everything for you; the shifting, the braking, the steering, everything... even the potential to sling the tail like the F40. There are no turbos, the power delivery is much, much more progressive and there's more grip from the 345-section rears, but the Enzo's 650bhp is still a mighty lot of power and you can feel the traction control cutting it again and again. It's very subtle.

Pressing the button to turn it off could therefore be the eventual chink in the Enzo's so-far seamless armour. The kind of electronic cut that renders an F16 unflyable, or the difference between the Enzo's composure and the F40's barely containable exuberance. I've heard how Michael Schumacher

FERRARI ENZO

SPECIFICATIONS

Engine
5998cc V12, double overhead cams, four valves per cylinder, Bosch Motronic engine management and fuel injection

Power
650bhp @ 7800rpm

Torque
585lb ft @ 5500rpm

Transmission
Six-speed sequential paddle-shift gearbox, rear-wheel drive, limited-slip differential, traction and stability control

Suspension
Double wishbones, pushrods and horizontal coil spring/damper units

Brakes
Ventilated 380mm diameter carbon-ceramic discs front and rear, ABS

Weight
1365kg

Performance
0-60mph 3.5sec (claimed)
Top speed 217.5mph (claimed)

Value
£450,000

had the rear tyres permanently on fire at Fiorano and how even his freakish talent couldn't make the car quicker round the lap than it was with the ASR switched on... Maybe so, but there is no hideous transformation to trap mere mortals. On the slow corners and in second gear, at first the extra power just picks up the front and makes the car push on. Then, as you try harder, it gently breaks the traction and sways the tail, then promptly hits the rev limiter, which acts as a form of traction control.

Third gear takes a little more time to push the tail out of line but once there it drives obligingly through the corner like some vintage two-wheel-drive rally car. The power steering weights up at odd moments – as it does over the sharper bumps round the top loop – but apart from the fact my thumbs keep hitting the horn buttons it is so very much easier to manage while out of shape than the F40, and almost entirely because there is no wheelspin spiking out of control the moment the turbos get a sniff of freedom.

So is the Enzo the perfect supercar, and is it light years ahead of the F40? Well, that depends. It is extraordinarily impressive. Ferrari has done a wonderful job of packing and balancing all the basic ingredients, and at last has found a set of brakes to equal its engine. It has used electronics to manage the more challenging tasks, but let them take the strain only where it felt this was necessary. The result is a carefully integrated whole, not so much sanitised but sensible and, as far as anything like that can be, safe. Turn off the only bit you can and the Enzo behaves like any other powerful, well-sorted car. Push it hard enough and it will push its nose into the »

'The Enzo, it seems, takes care of everything for you; the shifting, the braking, the steering, everything... even the potential to sling the tail like the F40'

corner then, when you light up the rears, slew the tail on the way out. This is how it should be, but the stiff platform, big tyres and what aerodynamics they could contrive means the threshold has been shifted way above the norm. Few will find an opportunity to experience it.

The F40 is a much more stripped-down, sweaty and intimate experience, and whether you like it or not, you are always involved with a chassis which is beautifully balanced in its own right – not least because it has a relatively small engine sited close to the middle. The means by which Ferrari persuaded that engine to develop supercar power, though, dominates the car and the driving experience, and although the turbos make it so very exciting, it will never be easy or predictable. In that respect, the Enzo is definitely progress, because it provides more of everything without the drama. Whether that makes it everyday usable or not, is another matter entirely…

evo

TRACKDAYS

MERCHANDISE

evo TRACK EVENINGS AT BEDFORD

LAST ONE!
FRIDAY 2ND SEPTEMBER 2011

PRICE £125

BOOK NOW! Visit www.evo.co.uk and click on 'shop'

EVO PRESCOTT HILL CLIMB
WEDNESDAY 6TH JULY, £175

EVO RUN WHAT YA BRUNG
SATURDAY 15TH OCTOBER, £10 ENTRY

Entry fee applies to drivers and spectators. Registration for unlimited runs on track costs £25. See www.RWYB.co.uk for full information

CLICK ON 'SHOP'
@ WWW.EVO.CO.UK

EVO T-SHIRT
HIGH-QUALITY T-SHIRT, LIMITED-RUN DESIGN
£17.99

LIMITED-EDITION EVO PRINTS
GIANT A2 PRINTS, LIMITED TO 150 OF EACH IMAGE
£4.99 each

EVO MAGBOOKS
IN-DEPTH PERFORMANCE TESTS, DETAILED BUYING ADVICE AND LAVISH PHOTOGRAPHY
From £6.99

EVO BOX FILE
THE PERFECT WAY TO KEEP YOUR EVOS SAFE AND ORGANISED **£12.99**

ORDER NOW! Visit www.evo.co.uk and click 'shop'
For more information visit www.evo.co.uk/trackdays

Spirito di Enzo

With a 611bhp version of the Enzo's V12, the Ferrari 599 promised to take GT-supercar performance to a new level. We drove it back-to-back with a 550 Maranello to find out

Words: Richard Meaden Photography: Gus Gregory

The literal journey

from Maranello to Fiorano is a short one. Out through the famous factory gates, past the celebrated Cavallino restaurant, and on, through a warren of side-streets packed with workshops, engineering companies and souvenir shops, until you reach the guarded entrance to the hallowed test track itself.

The metaphorical journey takes rather longer – a decade, to be precise. It's hard to believe that, at time of writing, ten years have passed since the introduction of the 550 Maranello. Back then, supercars were wide, unwieldy mid-engined monsters, just as they had been since the '70s. When Ferrari decided to replace the flamboyant, side-straked F512M with the useable and comparatively understated front-engined 550, it was almost considered sacrilege.

Time, of course, has proved the ultimate arbiter, the burgeoning vogue for front-mid-engined designs vindicating Ferrari's move to a front-engined GT supercar. It's this fact, coupled with the measured process of evolution from 550 to 575M, that has made the Maranello one of

those rare cars which has stayed on top of its game. When in 2004 **evo** magazine rated the ten greatest cars of the previous ten years, the 550 was our champ.

Harry Metcalfe, our editorial director, even bought one. His blood-red 550 was built a couple of years after the model's '96 debut, but thanks to its standard, option-free spec, it's totally representative of the earliest cars, providing a perfect snapshot of what the 550 Maranello was like at launch.

When we received our invitation to try the new 599GTB Fiorano, both on the Modenese roads we know and love, and on the test track with which it shares its name, driving Harry's 550 out to Italy to meet it was too good an opportunity to miss. This is undoubtedly the best yardstick by which to measure the 599.

Even if you're not in the fortunate position of having an all-time-great Italian supercar at your disposal, the 1000 miles from the UK to Modena remain one of the classic European road trips. Admittedly, the vigilant British and French police have denied us much of the flat-to-the-boards »

Above: despite its advancing years, 550 is still an impressive supercar and a wonderful long-distance partner. The 599 (right) has its work cut out to move the game on significantly.

drama so redolent of supercar drive stories of the '70s, but there's still a tremendous sense of freedom and anticipation as you emerge from the Eurotunnel and head out onto the wide, open French autoroutes.

The 550 is a magnificent partner, loping through France at an effortless, unobtrusive 100mph, its turbine-like V12 providing endless urge and emphatic sixth-gear response. Displacing some 5.5 litres and developing 485bhp and 415lb ft of torque, the Maranello's stats remain compelling. Short-shifting away from the péage barriers, slotting sixth and gently squeezing the throttle to its stop becomes something of a 550 party piece, for feeling the elastic, velvet-smooth surge of its big-capacity V12 hauling hard from low revs is highly addictive. The subdued but softly simmering soundtrack fits the sensation to

a tee. Aside from its epic engine and tremendous reach, what makes the 550 such a terrific long-distance machine is its fuel range. A tank capacity of 115 litres means you can take great chunks out of your journey between fuel stops, magnifying the sense of relentless progress. It's also extremely comfortable, the 'Daytona' seats offering plenty of support, enabling three- or four-hour stints at the wheel without fatigue or discomfort. Only the constant rustle of wind noise around the mirrors and door seals, along with a weak stereo, hint at the Maranello's advancing years.

Luggage space is more than acceptable, but the boot aperture was clearly designed around the legendary 'squashy bag', for it is restrictive and

forces us to stow photographer Gus's rigid Pelican case on the useful rear luggage shelf. The lack of interior storage space is more irksome, especially for small, slippery items like mobile phones. I lose count of the times I have to fish my Motorola out from under the seat after bursts of spirited acceleration.

An unusually generous schedule means we don't have to drive through the night to compensate for our afternoon departure from the UK, but nevertheless it's still dark by the time we approach our overnight halt in Strasbourg. The Maranello's interior takes on a new and even more soothing ambience by night, the pleasing array of round, analogue instruments illuminated with a soft, green-tinged glow. The absence of a sat-nav screen and other ugly technology completes the 550's modern-classic feel.

We start early the next morning, crossing the Rhine into Germany. As is increasingly the case, the autobahnen are choked with traffic and roadworks, but given a fleeting glimpse of open carriageway, the Maranello still breezes to 130mph with the ease that normal cars hit 90.

Crossing the frontier into Switzerland always feels a bit James Bond to me. Perhaps it's the uniformed border guards, brandishing side-arms and a licence to bill. Whatever, 40 euros lighter and windscreen wearing a Swiss road-tax sticker, we head through the grim, industrial city of Basel before picking up signs for St Gotthard and the Italian border beyond.

It's great to feel the mountains close in around you: snow-capped peaks flaring against an azure sky, the 550's scarlet profile spearing through the scenery like a dart. Peeling off the lorry-beaten track, away from the St Gotthard tunnel and up into the web of the Susten, Furka, Oberalp and Gotthard passes is a truly liberating experience, offering so much more than basic expedience.

Empty roads, a smooth surface and some fantastic sequences of hairpins are too good to miss, as they provide our first opportunity to taste the Maranello's dynamics. The steering is heavier than I remember, but direct enough to cope with the switchbacks, and we're soon finding a rhythm, each up- and down-shift accompanied by a delicious *schlick-schlick* as the ball-topped gearlever slides weightily between the open gate's alloy fingers. The clutch shares the steering's

'It's hard to believe that ten years have passed since the introduction of the 550'

'On a challenging, twisty road
it's an absolute riot, the car up on tiptoes
through quick direction changes

'The Enzo-derived engine has lost none of its aural ferocity'

meaty weight, and there's great satisfaction when you time a downshift perfectly, with engine speed, road speed and gears meshing with sweet precision. It doesn't happen every time, but often enough to keep you absorbed in the process of consistently finding that sweet spot.

By the time we crest the climb and power out onto the fast, open sweeps and straights across the Gotthard's snowy plateau, there's no doubt that the Maranello has abiding appeal, not just through its sheer breadth of ability but also in the unshakable confidence of its delivery. Seemingly, however fast you want to go, it always feels like there's something in reserve.

Once in Italy we're increasingly swept along, not just by the fast-moving traffic and our proximity to Modena, but also by blind faith in the carabinieri taking a charitable view of a red Ferrari making rapid progress down the autostrada, just as Enzo intended. Naïve or not, it's a nice thought, so we keep the beautiful cast-alloy throttle pedal pinned to its stop for a little longer, until we're regularly nudging 160mph. It's a final rousing demonstration of the 550's

supercar credentials before we head into downtown Maranello, peel off the Via Abetone, drive through the factory gates, and park beneath the hallowed entrance to the old factory courtyard. Stationary at last, the 550's sleek snout is spattered with bugs and road grime, the hallmarks of a classic **evo** commute to Modena. What a great car.

NEXT MORNING, OUR FIRST sight of the 599GTB Fiorano is, appropriately, in the test track's courtyard. We've bagged a red car with a black interior, just like Harry's 550. It's also fitted with the optional Brembo carbon-ceramic brakes and 'Challenge' alloy wheels (20in front and rear, as opposed to the standard 20in rears and 19in fronts). From experience with the 575 HGTC, Ferrari is confident that more than half of all 599 customers will tick these boxes.

Upwards of 90 per cent are expected to opt for the F1 transmission, as fitted to this car, with only a tiny minority of customers – possibly fewer than 50 per year – choosing the traditional H-pattern manual. It hardly seems worth the effort of offering a stick-shift, until you realise

that the overwhelmingly popular F1 'box remains a £10K option. Multiplied by the 500 or so Fioranos that'll be built every year, that equates to around £5million additional revenue per annum...

The 599's interior is spacious, the boot more useable (swallowing the dreaded 'Peli' with ease) and the detailing immaculately executed. Carbon fibre is used extensively, while aluminium is also employed to create a sporting, high-quality feel. The instruments are very like those in the Enzo, combining a big rev-counter with a complex LCD panel. This panel now works in conjunction with the manettino to display clearly which dynamic setting you've selected. In Race and CST-off modes you also get a lap-timing facility, triggered by a button on the back of the steering wheel.

The seats are excellent multi-adjustable items developed by Recaro, and come with additional, adjustable support around your hips and ribs thanks to pneumatic bladders that squeeze you tight for high-speed road or circuit driving. It's a more effective and less disconcerting solution than the aggressive 'active' seats fitted to the BMW M5 and M6, and certain AMG Mercedes.

Twist the key, step on the brake and press the big red 'Engine Start' button on the steering wheel, and the 6-litre V12 wakes with a boom. Bypass valves take the edge off the decibel level soon after, but a blip of the throttle confirms that the Enzo-derived engine has lost none of its aural ferocity, sounding every inch the 611bhp, 448lb ft hyper-GT.

From start-up the transmission defaults into automatic mode. Normally I would immediately engage the manual setting, as F1 transmissions

Right: new 'F1-Trac' stability and traction-control system enables 599 to lap Fiorano test track 1.5sec quicker than with just traditional ASR.

FERRARI 550
SPECIFICATIONS

Engine
V12

Location
Front, longitudinal

Displacement
5474cc

Bore x stroke
88 x 75mm

Cylinder block
Aluminium alloy

Cylinder head
Aluminium alloy, dohc per
bank, four valves per cylinder

Fuel and ignition
Electronic engine
management,
multi-point fuel injection

Max power
485bhp @ 7000rpm

Max torque
415lb ft @ 5000rpm

Transmission
Six-speed manual, rear-wheel
drive, traction control

Front suspension
Double wishbones,
coil springs, adjustable
dampers, anti-roll bar

Rear suspension
Double wishbones,
coil springs, adjustable
dampers, anti-roll bar

Brakes
Vented and cross-drilled
discs, 330mm front,
310mm rear, ABS

Weight (kerb)
1716kg

Power-to-weight
287bhp/ton

0-62mph
4.4sec (claimed)

Max speed
199mph (claimed)

Basic price
£143,685 (1997)

Above: shift-lights mounted in the top edge of the steering wheel; rev-counter takes centre stage in binnacle, supported by an LCD 'multidisplay' (bottom left) which shows different info depending on which mode is selected on the manettino.

are generally hopeless when it comes to self-shifting. Not so in the 599, which makes an impressive fist of it, neither short-shifting excessively nor stubbornly hanging on to a low gear. It also manages clean starts, and with a button rather than a fiddly T-bar to engage reverse, low-speed manoeuvring isn't the trauma it once was.

Early impressions are of light steering, quick responses and a very rigid structure. The ride is hard but not unyielding, and you're immediately aware of the magnetorheological dampers' minimal reaction time and uniquely clipped action. Shunning gas or oil-filled dampers with electronically-altered valving, the new Delphi-developed items are filled with a special fluid

which alters in viscosity when subjected to an electronically controlled magnetic field. The result is a damper that reacts four times faster than previous designs, can be infinitely adjusted, and yet contains fewer moving parts.

The suspension is just the start of the Fiorano's groundbreaking technological content. F1-Trac is Ferrari's latest take on controlling stability and traction, and it employs ideas and software developed for the Scuderia's Formula 1 cars. Using a vehicle dynamics model stored in the 599's control systems, F1-Trac is a predictive system that estimates optimal grip by continually monitoring the speed of both front and rear wheels. By comparing this real-time data with that stored in the model, F1-Trac is able to

modulate power delivery for optimal acceleration, and the result (according to Ferrari's comparative test data) is a 20 per cent increase in longitudinal acceleration out of a corner, which translates to a 1.5sec reduction in lap time at Fiorano compared with a car relying on conventional ASR.

Central to this system is the now-familiar manettino, located on the steering wheel. First seen in the F430, this tactile little switch is the key to unlocking the 599's potential and revealing each layer of its personality, from open-handed friendship to clenched-fist aggression. It's an uncanny system, its five stages – ranging from low grip to brain out – each accompanied by damper settings, throttle mapping and F1-Trac sensitivity tailored to suit the conditions or your mood. I say mood because, although the first two stages are Ice and Low Grip, I can imagine, after a long drive or a hard day, that the added security and compliance of the Low Grip setting would make perfect sense, especially if you also opted to let the 599 handle the gearchanges in its much-improved auto mode.

On warm, dry Italian asphalt, Sport (the third of the five settings) is really your base setting, for traction isn't an issue through fast, smooth corners, and the Fiorano finds plenty of drive out of tight hairpins. If you do manage to wake the stability systems, you soon appreciate that they are only as intrusive as you are clumsy. Turn in too sharply, attempt to carry too much speed, or get greedy with the throttle, and you get that treacly feeling as the car momentarily bogs down. It's quick to react, though, and as you begin to wind off the lock, the steering sensors talk to the throttle and engine-management systems and the V12's taps are opened, feeding as much torque as your steering angle permits.

This is also true in Race mode, but because the thresholds have been upped, the 599 is allowed to dance that bit closer to the limit, even letting its rear wheels spin a little and its tail slide under

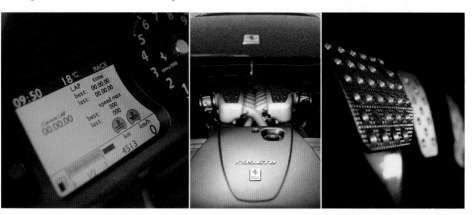

SPECIFICATIONS

Engine
V12

Location
Front, longitudinal

Displacement
5999cc

Bore x stroke
92 x 75.2mm

Cylinder block
Aluminium alloy

Cylinder head
Aluminium alloy, dohc per
bank, four valves per cylinder

Fuel and ignition
Electronic engine
management, multi-point
fuel injection

Max power
611bhp @ 7600rpm

Max torque
448lb ft @ 5600rpm

Transmission
Six-speed manual or F1
SuperFast paddle-shift
gearbox, rear-wheel drive,
ASR, F1-Trac

Front suspension
Double wishbones,
coil springs, SCM
adaptive dampers

Rear suspension
Double wishbones,
coil springs, SCM
adaptive dampers

Brakes
Vented and cross-drilled
discs, 353mm front,
328mm rear, ABS, EBD

Weight (kerb)
1688kg

Power-to-weight
367bhp/ton

0-62mph
3.7sec (claimed)

Max speed
205mph (claimed)

Basic price
£171,825

'Driven as fast as you dare, it devours the road and corrupts your soul'

power. On a challenging, twisty road it's an absolute riot, the car up on tiptoes through quick direction changes, sliding enough to need correction but not enough to slow your progress or give you too much of a scare. It's like those special days when you know you're driving out of your skin: very fast, but smooth, precise and controlled. The wonderful (or sobering) thing is that often you don't know where your talent ends and the Fiorano's electronic magic begins.

Until you try the CST-off mode. Now you realise that the manettino is also an honesty switch. The Race setting's latitude means you've already had to think carefully about your abilities before engaging it on the road, but another twist to the right means you're exploring wild and uncharted territory. No traction or stability control can come and save you here; you're on your own.

Initially you are more circumspect with the throttle, waiting longer before you explore the second half of its travel on the exit of a corner,

but after the first twitch of oversteer you know that the 599 is with you all the way. The speed-sensitive steering is perfectly weighted and geared for quick corrections, and the engine is so strong and responsive, even from low revs, that you have plenty of control. It's also clear that the 599 doesn't wag its tail readily, even with the stability and traction systems deactivated. Some provocation is needed to get it out of shape, but once you have there's more than enough poke to keep the rear Pirellis spinning. So long as you're dialled in to the zero-inertia responses of the chassis and the quick-witted reactions of the steering, the Fiorano responds to analogue inputs just as sweetly and readily as it accepts computer control. However, you do need to have your wits about you.

Whether you choose to fly by wire or by the seat of your pants, the time comes when you feel sufficiently buoyed to take a deep breath and truly unleash the Fiorano's full force. When you do, and the shift-lights across the top of the

steering wheel begin to illuminate, your whole world streams into fast-forward. Flat-out in the 599 is an all-encompassing experience, each gear delivering a more intense hit than the last: first-bang-second-bang-third-bang... By the time you pull fourth everything seems hotter, brighter, more vivid, all your senses heightened by the frenzied ferocity of the acceleration and the guttural, malevolent engine note that penetrates your very core.

The Bugatti Veyron may post fiercer figures, but it surely can't match the Fiorano's naturally aspirated immediacy on give-and-take roads. You could shave with this car's throttle and chassis responses, while the F1-SuperFast transmission punches upshifts like a fully sequential racing car, with barely an interruption in acceleration. Downshifts are equally emphatic, a three-gear downchange from fifth to second executed in an instant, exhausts emitting a rolling barrage of thunderous pops and bangs. Driven as fast as you dare, it devours the road and corrupts your soul.

Hands and legs quivering with adrenalin, swapping back into the 550 for a drive along the same stretch of road is an education. It feels soft, with plenty of pitch under acceleration and dive under braking. Hard cornering generates noticeable body roll, and you can sense the Maranello hunkering down on its outside corner. Steeply cambered hairpins, where the apex falls away from the inside wheel, set the unloaded wheel chirruping, and you begin to feel the 550 working hard. Ultimately, you're often waiting for the car to settle, its conventional dampers slow to recover from the last bump or crest. Of course, 'slow' is a relative concept, but once you've driven the road at Fiorano pace, the Maranello's best efforts are clearly from a bygone era.

Proof of this can be found when changing gear. Indeed, charging into one hairpin I catch myself frustratedly pulling back on the wiper stalk and wondering why I'm not getting any downshifts...

Working the clutch and stick is tremendously tactile, and the 550's gearbox is a good one, but it feels appropriate only because of the V12's mellow delivery. Specifying a 599 with a manual gearbox makes as much sense as Wayne Rooney playing football with his bootlaces tied together.

The Maranello's steering feels heavy after the delicately-assisted Fiorano, especially if you need to apply some corrective lock, but it's still easy to appreciate the fluidity with which the 550 tackles a road. Its limits are lower, and it breaks away nice and progressively, but where the 599 slides, reacts to your inputs and comes neatly back into line without hesitation, the 550 is slightly lazy in its responses. Predictably, the brakes are a weak point, the initially firm pedal softening a little as the drilled and vented cast-iron discs begin to lose their bite. Towards the end of a spirited charge up our hill route they are grumbling for mercy, and it's also noticeable that the engine's oil and water temperature gauges have registered the effort required to keep pace with its younger, fitter sibling.

Don't misunderstand me, the 550 has shown its class, but ultimately the fight was even more one-sided than we imagined. Roomier, more comfortable and better equipped to isolate you from the rigours of urban and long-distance driving, the 599 is the consummate GT. And yet, when you tap into its latent ability, it delivers spectacular performance coupled with unprecedented exploitability, while exploring its prodigious limits unaided presents as fierce and absorbing a challenge as you could wish for. It is, quite simply, the most enthralling, concentrated, mind-altering supercar I've ever driven. ⚠

This page: after a stint in the 599, the still-impressive 550 starts to show its age. New car's optional carbon brakes (top) particularly impressive.

Left: the beginning of one of the best days of his life: FXX owner unveils his new trackday toy in a Fiorano pit garage. He'll soon be lapping the test circuit as a 'Client Test Driver'.

TOY STORY

The 1.5million-euro Ferrari FXX is the ultimate track car. We join an owner as he drives his for the very first time

Words: Richard Meaden Pictures: Gus Gregory

Even when you've

seen it you can't quite believe it. No, not the Ferrari FXX – although now that you've asked, yes, it's every inch the sensational, heart-pounding projectile you'd hope – but the pantomime that surrounds it.

We're at Fiorano for a behind-the-scenes glimpse of what it's like when an FXX owner sees and drives their car for the first time. There are two FXXs being handed over today, but only one of the customers is happy to deal with the media. In the moments before he arrives, it's pandemonium. Like an A-list celebrity encircled by flunkies, minders, managers and assorted hangers-on, the FXX is swamped by Ferrari personnel, an island of calm surrounded by a choppy sea of scarlet that fusses and fettles and fiddles with anything that looks like it needs fussing, fettling or fiddling with.

Right now there must be more than 40 people crammed into the plush but hardly spacious confines of Fiorano's famous pit garage. Half are FXX programme technicians, the other half an assorted gaggle of edgy managers and PR

»

Far left: Ferrari racing boss Jean Todt takes a close interest in the FXX programme. **Left:** owner training includes lapping Fiorano in a 360 Challenge race car. **Right:** each FXX enjoys the full support of Corse Clienti department.

bods, furtive journalists, scurrying photographers and, lest we forget, the bloke who, bluntly, has paid for this bunfight: the FXX's new owner. Small, fit, tanned and surprisingly unassuming, our man is a middle-aged Italian American. Friendly, but preferring anonymity, we'll call him Mr X – or better still, Mr FXX.

The crowd gathers closely around his car, which was swathed in a scarlet cover moments before he entered the pit garage. Giuseppe Petrotta, the FXX project manager, makes a short speech then

beckons our man to pull back the cover. The silken sheet slips away, revealing the red, bestriped machine, and there's a moment's awed silence before spontaneous applause spreads around the pit. Suffice to say, Mr FXX looks chuffed, if a little nervous. But then so would you given the surroundings, the circumstances and the scale of the challenge (and invoice) that awaits him.

It's a scene that could happen only at Ferrari. But then, the FXX is a car that only Ferrari could make, and perhaps a car only Ferrari could sell.

There's genius at work here, but not all of it has been channelled into the engineering. How else do you explain the audacious concept of 'inviting' 29 hand-picked clients to shell out a cool one and a half million euros – plus local taxes, naturally – on a car they can only drive on a race track, but can't actually race?

The core of the FXX's appeal, at least to those in a sufficiently privileged position to be approached by Ferrari in the first place, isn't its extreme performance or even its rarity. Rather, it's the fantasy being sold along with it: the dream of becoming part of Ferrari's test team.

According to Giuseppe Petrotta, these 'Client Test Drivers' will be a valuable source of

'The FXX is every inch the sensational, heart-pounding projectile that you'd hope'

information. 'How much is too much?' he asks rhetorically. 'Can we continue to offer more and more performance in our ultimate cars? And if the answer is yes, where do we define the limit? How do we make them exploitable and accessible to our customers? These are the kinds of questions we believe the FXX programme will enable us to understand.'

It's a reasonable enough quest given the rapidly escalating performance of series production supercars like the 599GTB. But an 800bhp, 1155kg super-Enzo? That's quite some starting point. For those at the less able end of the 29-person spectrum, you can't help but fear that the FXX dream could rapidly turn into a carbonfibre-splintering nightmare with one ill-timed flex of their right foot.

Of course, that's something Ferrari desperately wants to avoid, which is why every FXX customer

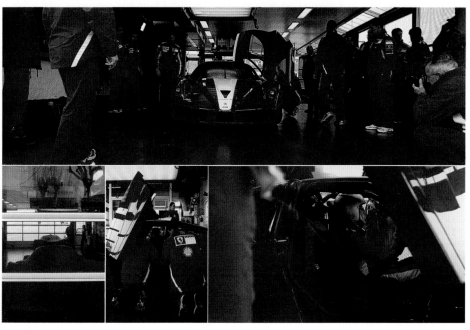

»

a specific output of some 128bhp per litre, arriving at a cataclysmic-sounding 8500rpm – while an impressively muscular 506lb ft of torque makes its presence felt at 5750rpm, up 250rpm and 21lb ft over the Enzo. Crucially, the FXX is 100kg lighter, tipping the scales at 1155kg (dry). In fact, it would be lighter still were it not for the added weight of a roll-cage, fire-extinguisher system and other equipment that befits the FXX's role as a track-based development car.

Brembo and Bridgestone, two of Ferrari's closest technical partners in Formula 1, have worked hard to provide the FXX with the very best brakes and rubber. Ceramic composite discs, measuring 398x36mm up front and 380x34mm at the rear, are clamped by six-piston calipers and supported by ABS and ASR systems recalibrated to work with the grip levels provided by the bespoke slick tyres. While that translates into awesome dry performance and security, it also means that the FXX will be a far more malevolent beast for novice hands to control in the wet, which perhaps accounts for the Ferrari crew's nervous skyward glances towards the threatening, steel-grey clouds.

As you'd expect, the firm has also reduced the shift speed of the F1 paddle-shift transmission for the FXX. It now takes just 80 milliseconds to swap cogs – amazing, but still more than twice as long-winded as the F1 car.

Yet perhaps the most impressive aspect of the new machine is its revolutionary aerodynamics. Along with under-floor aero and a three-stage in-car-adjustable wing, it also employs something called 'base bleed' aerodynamics. It's a concept that stems from aerodynamic techniques applied to artillery shells, where it was discovered that reducing the area of low pressure behind the base of a shell results in a reduction in drag.

The same principle has been applied to the FXX, using a speed-related system that can cunningly redirect the air that ordinarily flows through the front air intakes, to the radiators and back out via the venturi tunnels that lead to the tail. When required, those hungry front intakes can be automatically blanked off via a series of electro-mechanical flaps. This redirects the airflow along the car's flanks into the side intakes, where the air then passes through carbonfibre ducts that run through the engine compartment and emerge as pancaked pipes in the rear bodywork.

Ferrari has established that the engine can do without this cooling airflow for 40 seconds without harm – long enough to dispatch most straights on most circuits around the world. Beyond 40 seconds, the frontal intakes are opened once more to resume flow through the

goes through a full day's intensive familiarisation and training – both in their new toy and a 360 Challenge race car – around the technical twists and turns of Fiorano. One-to-one tuition with a professional test and race driver is the best way to negotiate such a steep learning curve, and it's all backed up with a detailed classroom session tackling the specific demands of Fiorano as well as providing a refresher of basic trackcraft.

Mr FXX has changed out of his civvies and into his Client Test Driver uniform: a shimmering red race suit with FXX emblazoned across the shoulders. There's no doubt he looks the part. In a quiet moment I ask him if he managed to get any sleep last night, adding that if I knew I was driving my own FXX for the first time, and at Ferrari's holiest of holies, Fiorano, I'd have been bouncing off the walls.

Mr FXX smiles. 'Well, of course it's a very big day for me, but I flew in from the States only last night, so to be honest I was feeling pretty jetlagged. The last thing I wanted to do was spend all night staring at the ceiling, so I had a glass of wine and a sleeping pill! Now I'm fine.'

Each FXX takes to the track alternately, so that each customer has the circuit to themselves and, presumably, to avoid any potentially embarrassing tangles. Helmet on and harness pulled down tight, Mr FXX is ready to go. A shrill whirr from

the starter prepares us for the explosion to come, and as the 12 cylinders catch, the assembled crowd flinches in unison as the FXX roars into life, filling the pit garage with a soundtrack straight from the Targa Florio, accompanied by a rich, eye-watering haze of exhaust fumes.

As it heads off down to Fiorano's distant Turn 1, the FXX looks like a Le Mans racer, bobbling stiffly on its suspension, coughing and crackling with impatience as its driver short-shifts through the gearbox on the first lap while checking all the systems are functioning.

When you appreciate what Ferrari has done to create the FXX, it's no wonder that it makes the Enzo on which it is (loosely) based seem tame. At its heart is a thoroughly re-engineered 6262cc version of the Enzo's 6-litre V12. The cylinder heads, pistons, cams, crankcase and combustion chambers have all been reworked and redesigned, while the exhaust system has lower back-pressure, doubtless thanks to the fact that it makes only the smallest of token gestures towards silencing the screaming motor.

As a result, power is up from 650 to 800bhp –

'The FXX is devastatingly quick around Fiorano, lapping six seconds faster than the Enzo'

Above: taking to Fiorano's hallowed tarmac. Revised aerodynamics mean FXX has 40 per cent more downforce than Enzo – and less drag at high speed. **Far left:** Meaden straps in for a passenger ride to remember.

'The explosive rush is momentarily sense-scrambling, redefining in an instant what constitutes top-end power'

Left: as befits a dedicated track car, the FXX is fitted with a full roll-cage and a fire-extinguisher system. **Bottom:** Enzo V12's been reworked to give 800bhp.

radiators. It's a beautifully executed idea that's just one of a number of aerodynamic revisions for the FXX which result in a 40 per cent increase in downforce over the Enzo.

The combination of more power, less weight, vastly increased grip and race-car levels of downforce means the FXX is devastatingly quick around Fiorano, lapping a whole six seconds faster than the Enzo. In fact, the only thing quicker on this hallowed loop is the Scuderia's Grand Prix car. The FXX is a monstrous machine for the customers to even begin to get their heads around, but it's to the instructors and Mr FXX's eternal credit that every session passes without incident, the red and white car's pace building appreciably with every lap, the driver's right foot remaining planted for longer down the straight and being applied earlier on the exit of each corner. Mr FXX is looking confident but

Below: Note the absence of rear-view mirrors – instead, the pod on the roof contains a rear-facing camera that relays action from behind the FXX to a TFT display on the dash.

FERRARI FXX SPECIFICATIONS

Engine	65deg V12
Location	Mid, longitudinal
Displacement	6262cc
Cylinder block	Aluminium alloy
Cylinder head	Aluminium alloy, dohc per bank, four valves per cylinder
Max power	800bhp @ 8500rpm
Max torque	506lb ft @ 5750rpm
Transmission	Six-speed sequential manual gearbox, rear drive, ASR
Suspension	Front and rear: double wishbones, pushrod links, coil springs, gas dampers
Tyres	245/35 ZR19 front, 345/35 ZR19 rear
Weight (kerb)	1265kg
Power-to-weight	642bhp per ton
0-62mph	sub-3sec (estimated)
Top speed	217mph+ (estimated)

The eBay FXX

NOT ONE OF THE 29 ELITE customers selected by Ferrari? Well don't despair – just keep an eye on eBay.

Shortly after the ultra-exclusive, invitation-only FXX was launched, Exotic Motorcars of Boynton Beach, Florida, offered one for sale on the ubiquitous Internet company's US auction website.

Some 46 bids were received before the car was eventually sold for a cool $3,000,100. However, there's some doubt as to whether the buyer was genuine or just some spotty kid having a laugh, as the successful bidder's eBay log reveals no other purchases anywhere near as significant.

Urban myth or awesome truth, the eBay FXX has registered on Ferrari's radar. When I mention it to an insider, he's quick to say that whoever has bought the auctioned FXX will have no involvement in the Client Test Driver programme, nor be invited to the international FXX driving events or receive technical support from the factory.

I think it's also safe to assume that the vendor himself is no longer on Messrs Montezemolo and Todt's Christmas card list.

---

considered, obviously keen to explore the otherworldly performance, but mindful to keep his aspirations firmly in check.

Which is all terrific news as far as I'm concerned, for while the original schedule for the day states that I'll be treated to a passenger ride in Mr FXX's FXX alongside Ferrari test driver Dario Benuzzi, we've been informed that Mr FXX is having so much fun that he's decided to play taxi driver himself. Fair enough, but the last time I sat next to a Ferrari owner on a test track, the ride ended somewhat abruptly in an F50-shattering crash that did irreparable damage to my faith in Ferrari owners and, it has to be said, my underwear.

This time, though, it's different. Mr FXX is completely dialled in, and from the moment we drive out of the garage I know I'm in safe hands. He is building speed gradually, working temperature into the tyres, brakes and fluids, girding himself for another three laps in what must rank as the world's ultimate trackday car.

Our first flyer is like opening a window on another world. The power is all-encompassing, pushing and pulling and squeezing me in ways accelerative g hasn't managed since I rode in the back of an Arrows F1 car. My neck's stinging with the effort of keeping my chin down, and as we plunge into the braking area for Turn 1, those hard-worked muscles burn once more as my chin smacks into my breastbone. The brakes are like a brick wall, but you can feel and hear the ABS working its subtle magic, waiting until the onset of lock-up and a whispered chirrup from the Bridgestone slicks before bleeding the faintest amount of pressure from the most lightly loaded front wheel.

My favourite sensation comes at a section of the lap where Mr FXX holds fourth gear, slowly and smoothly increasing the throttle opening through the early phase of a long right-hander. The combined result of downforce and slick grip pulls hard on my neck, then he spots the exit and cracks through the remaining throttle travel while straightening the steering wheel. It's this explosive rush, from 7000 to 8500rpm, that is momentarily sense-scrambling, redefining in an instant what constitutes throttle response and top-end power. Those FXX customers who also own Enzos will never look upon their road cars with quite the same awe again.

On our cool-down lap, I ask Mr FXX if the car is everything he hoped it would be. I get a predictable but reassuringly adrenalin-soaked answer. 'Honestly, it has completely exceeded even my wildest expectations. I've got an F430 at the moment, and it's an incredible car, so much better than the 360 in every respect.

'But this, this is incredible. The power is amazing, the braking totally beyond anything I have ever experienced. And yet it's so tractable, so friendly to drive. Of course, it takes great concentration to drive it, but that's the speed rather than the car itself, if you know what I mean. Apart from the birth of my children, I would have to say that today has been the best day of my life.'

GET 3 ISSUES OF evo FOR £1

Experience the thrill of driving with **evo**, *the monthly magazine devoted exclusively to the greatest cars in the world. If you're passionate about performance cars then* **evo** *is your ultimate monthly read.*

WHY NOT TRY evo FOR YOURSELF?

Claim 3 issues of evo for just £1 today, and you'll receive the best performance car features hot-off-the-press for 3 months with **NO OBLIGATION**. If you enjoy reading it after the introductory period your subscription will automatically continue at the low rate of just £23.75 every 6 issues – saving you 12% on the shop price, so order yours today!

SUPER

CALI

Fresh from the factory, we drive a California out onto the roads around Maranello.
Be in no doubt, this is a great Ferrari

Words: David Vivian Pictures: Gus Gregory

Right: exterior has some gorgeous details, even if the overall shape isn't one of Ferrari's very best. Below: multi-function touchscreen works well but looks clunky compared with the rest of the beautifully detailed cockpit (below right).

When the California

debuted at the 2008 Paris show, it was greeted with more than a little scepticism. Purity of purpose is what people expect from a Ferrari, so it was perhaps unsurprising that news of a multi-tasking, all-things-to-all-men (and women), sportscar-cum-GT-cum-retractable-hardtop-convertible with retro leanings and a recycled name was met with suspicion.

Some people claimed that being a front-engined V8 – unprecedented in Ferrari's 63-year history – the California started out as a Maserati project that became too expensive but was too far advanced to can. Some said that with its portly kerbweight and refined double-clutch trans it was a shameless sop to the US market, and that 453bhp (30 fewer than in the F430) wasn't enough. Some, perhaps unwisely, suggested that a Ferrari designed to attract women drivers (a projected 50 per cent of sales) was simply an oxymoron that should have been strangled at birth. And some called it Ugly Betty.

But all that was before they got up close and personal. I'm standing more or less beneath the window of Enzo Ferrari's old office in the car park of his factory's iconic main entrance, from where he could keep an eye on the gatehouse activity and would have been able to see our Ferrari for the day. Wonder what he'd have thought. This is the first time I've had a really good look at the California, and while there's no refuting the charges that the rear is bulky and the Coke-bottle-kick swage-line on the doors is corny and overdone, the result is almost inexplicably great: cinematically cool, Ferrari to the core.

Inside, the subtle retro theming is just as evocative, especially the optional Daytona-style seats, lavishly cowled instrument binnacle and circular face-level vents. A classy flourish is the big yellow centre-display rev-counter and, just to be sure all your senses get a workout, the beautifully tactile fillet of aluminium on the centre console that houses the buttons for the launch control, the transmission's auto mode, the electronic handbrake and the electric windows is unnecessarily gorgeous. The big multi-function touchscreen display bang in the middle of the dash isn't, however – even if its aluminium framing has more or less the same hue and sheen as the steering wheel boss flanges that put the engine start button and simplified manettino (just three drive modes – comfort, sport and stability control off) within easy reach. In fact, the cabin is pretty wonderful: chamois-glove snug, extremely comfortable, easy to see out of and blessed with a terrific driving position.

Hardtop retracted (fast, slick, oddly Germanic), the California sounds much more masculine than it looks. The double-speed whirr of the starter ignites an instant bark of high-compression, light-flywheeled combustion, followed by a few seconds of drain-pipey resonance calming to that uniquely clean, flat, baritone idle you only get with a flat-plane-cranked V8.

»

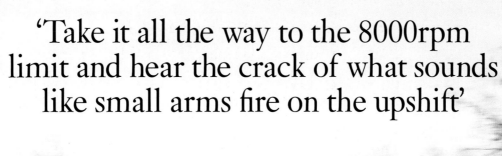

'Take it all the way to the 8000rpm limit and hear the crack of what sounds like small arms fire on the upshift'

FERRARI CALIFORNIA

SPECIFICATIONS

Engine
V8, Front-mid, longitudinal, 4297cc

Power
453bhp @ 7750rpm

Torque
358lb ft @ 5000rpm

Transmission
Seven-speed dual-clutch gearbox with paddleshift, rear-wheel drive. F1-trac traction control

Suspension
Front: Double wishbones, coil springs and dampers (magnetic optional). Rear: Multi-link, coil springs and dampers

Steering
Power-assisted

Brakes
Ventilated carbon-ceramic discs, 390mm front, 360mm rear, ABS

Weight
1735kg

Performance
0-62mph sub-4.0sec (claimed). Top speed 193mph (claimed)

Left: cockpit is a brilliant combination of sportscar and GT. Note the paddles for the DCT dual-clutch transmission and the steering wheel-mounted starter button and manettino for the three-mode stability system.

'It settles to that uniquely clean, flat, baritone idle you only get with a flat-plane-cranked V8'

Opposite: 4.3-litre V8 sits well back in the chassis.
Above left: all Californias get cross-drilled and ventilated carbon-ceramic discs as standard.
Compact light units feature LEDs. Paddleshift dual-clutch gearbox works so well
it makes even Ferrari's F1 system feel slow.

No, it isn't quite the same engine as the F430's. The basic architecture is very similar, but the California's direct injection allows a higher compression ratio and it has a wider bore and shorter stroke, displacing 4297cc rather than the 4308cc of the F430. What people couldn't work out at the California's launch was how Ferrari could claim a sub-4 second 0-62mph time for the 275kg heavier, front-engined car, making it slightly quicker over the benchmark sprint than its mid-engined stablemate.

While at the time of writing these claims have yet to be substantiated, you swiftly sense that the combination of the engine's extra torque and the dazzling speed and responsiveness of the seven-speed double-clutch transmission – a Scuderia's

F1 paddleshift truly seems slightly tardy by comparison – just might do the business. Added to which, the California has a launch control. Whatever the truth, it feels assertively rapid and would well and truly put an M5 in its place.

In fact, if the factory claims stack up, the Ferrari accelerates with a sustained intensity to which few cars would be able to find an honest answer, covering the standing quarter-mile in a fraction over 12 seconds on the way to its 193mph top speed. No chance of that today, but just playing the engine via the paddles is addictive enough, especially when you take it all the way to the 8000rpm limit and hear the crack of what sounds like small arms fire on the upshift. Few motors sound as lean, hard and malicious as this

one when stoked.

In the beginning it's all about noise. Noise that makes the small hairs on the back of your neck tingle. Noise that gives onlookers their initial close encounter with cars of the fast kind. And, in the case of the California, the sonic signature is more heart-stopping than the shape that owns it. In the best cases, sight and sound meld perfectly (as in the case of the 430 Scuderia and the 360 Challenge Stradale before it). But the California sounds a lot tougher than it looks. People turn round when they hear it coming, then stare straight through it, unable to match the bone-crunching feral howl with the comparatively demure presence from the front.

As well as being faster than it has any real right »

to be, the California is also the owner of a formidably well-sorted chassis and extremely stiff body structure that doesn't flex, shimmy or shake, however rough the road surface. With the suspension on its comfort setting, the ride is remarkably pliant and forgiving, smothering ruts and dips with unprecedented equanimity for a Ferrari. The handling is fluent and composed, but with noticeable body-roll and gently cushioned responses to the helm. It's more compatible with the GT side of the California's character, along with the impressively low levels of wind noise with the roof up (and lack of buffeting with it down) and the way the engine quietens to an ambient murmur on a light throttle load.

Engage the Sport button, though, and the California sharpens up its act significantly. The high cornering forces it's capable of are conducted by steering which, once it sheds its initial low-speed deadness, becomes beautifully weighted and scalpel-sharp. Although still quite softly sprung by F430 standards, there's something palpably correct about the chassis dynamics: the reassuring immediacy of its responses, the fine ride – firm yet unerringly supple – the way it feels lighter than it is and closely coupled to the road. And the standard ceramic brakes are every bit as mighty as you could hope and more progressive at the pedal than some rival systems.

True, the California never quite feels as nimble and lithe as an F430

'Fact is, the California is a

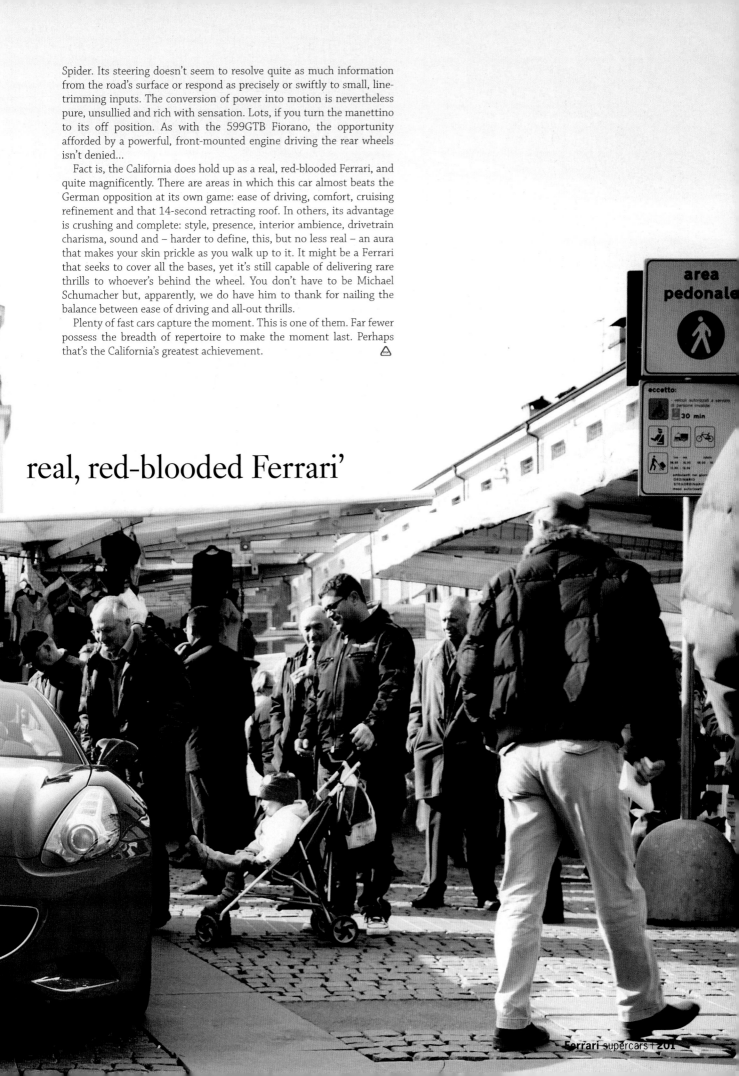

Spider. Its steering doesn't seem to resolve quite as much information from the road's surface or respond as precisely or swiftly to small, line-trimming inputs. The conversion of power into motion is nevertheless pure, unsullied and rich with sensation. Lots, if you turn the manettino to its off position. As with the 599GTB Fiorano, the opportunity afforded by a powerful, front-mounted engine driving the rear wheels isn't denied...

Fact is, the California does hold up as a real, red-blooded Ferrari, and quite magnificently. There are areas in which this car almost beats the German opposition at its own game: ease of driving, comfort, cruising refinement and that 14-second retracting roof. In others, its advantage is crushing and complete: style, presence, interior ambience, drivetrain charisma, sound and – harder to define, this, but no less real – an aura that makes your skin prickle as you walk up to it. It might be a Ferrari that seeks to cover all the bases, yet it's still capable of delivering rare thrills to whoever's behind the wheel. You don't have to be Michael Schumacher but, apparently, we do have him to thank for nailing the balance between ease of driving and all-out thrills.

Plenty of fast cars capture the moment. This is one of them. Far fewer possess the breadth of repertoire to make the moment last. Perhaps that's the California's greatest achievement.

real, red-blooded Ferrari'

area
pedonale

eccetto:

30 min

The 458 Italia is Ferrari's most technologically advanced road car...

❶ Paddles for twin-clutch gearbox
❷ Active suspension switch
❸ Driving dynamics mode selector
❹ Controls for information systems
❺ Twin TFT information screens
❻ The road that shaped the 458 Italia

...but is it any good?

After driving the 562bhp mid-engined V8
supercar in the hills of Modena and on
Ferrari's Fiorano test track, **Chris Harris** decides
Pictures: Gus Gregory

Everyday cars.

If only Ferraris were everyday cars. That's the lingering thought after my eight hours with the company's latest take on the mid-engined V8 Berlinetta. It is both a reason for celebration and, at the same time, no little frustration that the 458 is undoubtedly the finest all-round sportscar that Ferrari has ever made. The marque has produced such a useable, amenable machine that it's saddening to think so many 458s will never see everyday use, because it's only when you delve into the car's full dynamic vocabulary, covering everything from stop-start town driving to maximum-attack lapping, that you fully appreciate what Ferrari has achieved.

It's hard to know where to start with the 458. The numbers are so compelling, so difficult to digest that, like the chubby child in the tuck shop, it's difficult to concentrate on any single image or piece of information for longer than a fleeting second before darting to the next. I mean, I'm smirking just typing the power figure: 562bhp delivered at 9000rpm. The 'ickle Ferrari, the nipper of the family, now serves up over five-fifty horsepower. What a way to flick a single finger to the harbingers of sportscar oblivion. And this puppy runs direct injection and emits 37 fewer g/km of CO_2 than its predecessor.

Actually, it isn't hard to know where to start with the 458 – or any Ferrari for that matter. Gone are the days when Enzo would charge you handsomely for a majestic V12 then get old man Scaglietti to bash some aluminium with a lump hammer and bung it in for free, but the motor remains the centrepiece of these cars. It's a large-displacement unit now, a full 4499cc, which makes its ability to spin to 9000rpm (the engineers say it could go to 9300rpm) without using any titanium internals all the more

remarkable. It also accounts for the sizeable torque figure: 398lb ft is available at 6000rpm, but a quick check of the factory dyno readouts reveals over 270lb ft from just 2500rpm. On paper, the 458 doesn't have a powerband, it has a dizzying power crescendo that, in conjunction with a dual-clutch gearbox, results in a claimed zero to 124mph time that's 0.4sec faster than the absurdly rapid 599GTB.

What a disappointment, then, that as I thumb the large starter button on the steering wheel, the 458 fires with a slightly bilious parp, then settles to a glum, ordinary idle. These pesky flat-plane cranks may facilitate vast engine speeds, but they're pretty uninspiring at very low revs.

You sit low in this car, yet the view out is still impressively uncluttered. The scuttle is low and the driver-centric controls, clocks and digital displays create a busy area around the driver, but equally a sense of space in the rest of the cabin. Straight ahead of you is a 10,000rpm rev-counter, flanked either side by TFT screens that provide everything from lap times to an analogue speed display. The most commonly used controls are now located on the steering wheel: wipers, indicators and the wee jelly-bean 'manettino' that alters the suspension and chassis electronics. It's perhaps the most radical re-think of a sportscar's basic control surfaces in the past three decades – if Ferrari has got it wrong, the 458 will be badly hampered as a driving machine.

I want to tell you just how good this car is at low speed. That's unexciting, I know – you want Troy Queef tales of bitch-spankery in the Modenese hills – but you need to stay calm and hear about the 458 in town. We can spank later. Now, I'll stop short of saying that anyone can make a fast sportscar, and that the real genius of the trade lies with those who can make them

Left: first batch of 458s line up at Maranello, waiting to head out onto the surrounding roads. **Below left:** Jean-Jacques His, powertrain director, talks the gathered journalists through the model's underpinnings. **Far right:** 458's V8 powerplant is 191cc larger than the F430's, with an additional 79bhp.

'It's clear within the first few miles that Ferrari's decision to use a double-clutch gearbox was the correct one'

perform with decorum at low speeds, but there's a lot of truth in that statement. The 458 is possibly the best supercar below 30mph.

We roll out of Fiorano onto the freshly wetted roads of Supercar Valley and it's clear within the first few miles that Ferrari's decision to use a double-clutch gearbox was the correct one. Less than 50 milliseconds after you flick either paddle, the gear engages, and the fanatical level of calibration carried out by the development team leaves you struggling to find fault with the way the transmission operates. The real advantage is at low speed – you can dawdle in the 458 with no clanking actuators and no rancid clutch smell. The King's Road no longer constitutes a clear and present danger to untalented twits in this new Ferrari. Part of me thinks that's a shame.

It rides so well, too. Having learned lessons from the F430 and 599, you can now de-couple the damper setting from the chassis electronics as you can in the 430 Scuderia. On the road, I prefer it in Sport mode with the dampers set to soft. Like this, the 458 is extremely capable. The body structure is 20 per cent more rigid than the

430's in terms of dynamic torsional stiffness, lending a more solid platform to the front double-wishbone suspension and rear multi-link layout that it shares with the old car. Serious time has been invested improving both camber control and wheel centre rigidity for the rear wheels, and the result is a car that relies more on its spring and damper units and less on its anti-roll bars. You really feel this at low and medium speeds, the slacker bars allowing a greater degree of independence across each axle, bringing surprising ride comfort with the dampers on their softest setting.

Traction benefits hugely, too. Heading up into the hills, the roads are wet and the surface cratered with poor repairs – not a place you'd normally want to be in a 562bhp Ferrari – but the 458 is about as tame as this type of vehicle can be under such circumstances. Its electronic chassis armoury is now impregnable – F1-Trac melds with E-Diff3 to create an acronym orgy of unparalleled dynamic brilliance. Roughly translated, the 458 is knob-proof, even on crappy Italian roads. And the intervention is so calm, so polite. Where a ➤➤

430 would just shut the throttle with admonishing abruptness, the 458's brain can deploy varying degrees of throttle angle as requested by its garrison of sensors, regardless of what the idiot driver is doing up front. In Sport mode there's a few degrees of slip, whereas in Race there's enough slip for the incautious novice to pirouette, leaving some vestige of hope for those who would like to see a shunted Fandango down SW3.

I have to say I prefer the greater degree of nannying available in Sport because the feeling of invincibility is more consistent. If one enlists the help of the computer, best to use most of its considerable powers. Either have it all working, or not at all.

This is a brilliantly balanced road-car chassis, but it's also one that questions the conventions of sportscar interaction between driver and car rather more than I'd expected. You see, the 458 is no great communicator. Drive it fast and, at first, you'll be disappointed by how mute the steering is, how smooth the gearchanges are, how little information regarding road surface and grip levels appears to be available through the controls and the seat squab. Familiarity will dispel some of those fears, but after something

like a GT3, the 458's steering rack will always feel a touch arcade-game. There's a reason why: it's a very fast, very aggressive system with just two turns between the locks (the 458 really can be driven through tight hairpins by simply crossing your hands), so the hydraulic pump is a monster. For me, it doesn't detract from the experience whatsoever, but there will be those who expect greater levels of communication from a mid-engined Ferrari.

Does it feel as fast as the claimed figures? Perhaps not quite. I say that because the last 599 I drove felt unhealthily, slightly scarily rapid in a straight line, whereas this car never seems quite so intimidating under full throttle. Nevertheless, the 458 sets new standards for straight-line performance in this class. It pulls convincingly from 2000rpm and builds so strongly in the mid-range that by the time you're waiting for the final, frenzied attack on the rev-limiter you're left a little disappointed that you don't sustain some manner of neck injury. Don't worry, this is still an engine that rewards every last ounce of abuse, it's just that it would require rocket propulsion to inject a serious extra snap of acceleration beyond what's already occurring at 7000rpm.

The sound is pretty awe-inspiring by most road-car standards, but it's heavily synthesised – there's a disconnect between what your right foot tells you that you should be hearing and what erupts from the tail-pipes. At times it's irritating, especially in town in Race mode, where the exhaust valves open at very low revs and bombard everyone with noise.

Another criticism that creeps up on me during the day is the throttle response at low speed. Given how slick the transmission is at rationalising those vast numbers at a tootle, I find it hard to just tickle the accelerator and let the car coast, because there's absolutely no dead travel at the top of the pedal. As the day wears on, this becomes my biggest – but, in fairness, one of my few – irritations with the 458.

I had expected the steering-wheel buttons and general control locations to drive me mad, but they just don't. Okay, it takes some time to get used to the indicators, but their self-cancelling system works well, and while the amount of information available on the TFT screens could be bewildering, it's made much less so by being so easy to flick between displays. Ergonomically, it works well, but it would help if there was a digital speed readout in the

'This is a brilliantly balanced road-car chassis, but it's also one that questions conventions'

Left: there's no open-gate shifter between the 458's seats – a conventional manual gearbox is not being offered on this car. **Below left:** speedo is a computer-generated image. **Right:** gearshift paddles are longer than on previous Ferraris, in order to make them easier to operate mid-bend.

Above left: array of dials and buttons surrounding the driver can look overwhelming at first, but once familiar they all make sense. **Right:** brakes are similar to those on the F430 – which is no bad thing. **Below left:** our man Harris spots one of his favourite Ferraris on the wall at Maranello.

'Be in no doubt, this is not an expurgated supercar experience'

rev-counter clock face. There is one definite black mark, though: Ferrari is joining the ranks of car makers whose steering wheel rims are suitable only for the larger primates – of which, despite my nickname, Monkey, I am not one.

It'll be no surprise to you to learn that the 458 is altogether sensational at Ferrari's own Fiorano circuit. It was developed here, so it stands to reason that it should work rather well around the mixture of low- and medium-speed turns. Its 1min 25sec lap time is identical to the Scuderia's, yet it weighs 1485kg (135kg more) and runs a regular road tyre – albeit one that was developed especially for this car.

What appeals to me most about the 458 on track is the sheer breadth of driving experience it offers. I can't think of another car that serves up everything from computer-chamfered excellence to gratuitous, smoky sideways, and several variations in between. As on the road, the chassis electronics are superb. Traction is never an issue, even as the tyres get hot, but even greater improvements lurk in the earlier phases of each turn. That aggressive steering would count for nothing if the car couldn't sustain such abrupt direction changes, yet the added support from that rear suspension and some much firmer bushes means the 458 actually feels a good deal more

FERRARI 458 ITALIA
SPECIFICATIONS

Engine
V8, mid, longitudinal, 4499cc

Power
562bhp @ 9000rpm

Torque
398lb ft @ 6000rpm

Transmission
Seven-speed DCT gearbox, rear-wheel drive, E-Diff3, F1-Trac

Suspension
Front: double wishbones, coil springs, adaptive dampers, anti-roll bar
Rear: multi-link, coil springs, adaptive dampers, anti-roll bar

Brakes
Ventilated and cross-drilled carbon-ceramic discs, 398mm front, 360mm rear, ABS, EBD

Weight
1485kg

Performance
0-62mph 3.4sec (claimed)
Top speed 202mph (claimed)

alert than the lighter, shorter-wheelbased 430.

I'd like to tell you that I could feel the electronic differential doing its thing, but you realise how effective it is only when you switch everything off; a dollop of understeer appears from nowhere and you discover that the rear tyres do have their limitations. The brakes, the same size as the F430's but with fewer pistons in the front calipers (because of metallurgic improvements), don't fade at all in five fast laps, and the pedal feel is spot-on.

However, be in no doubt – this is not an expurgated supercar experience. The inner mentalist is always lurking, desperate to be unleashed by the manettino switch and paint black lines at will. Not that this is of any relevance, but the 458 has uncommon balance when it's in full-slide mode.

So, low-speed throttle response and steering aside, there is little to gripe about here and a whole load to celebrate – the 458 continues what must be the finest patch of road-car form Ferrari has ever enjoyed. Which leaves only the thorny issue of usage. So I'll end with a suggestion: if the manufacturer vetted each potential Enzo owner for suitability, perhaps it should make all 458 buyers agree to a minimum mileage condition? About seven thousand per annum would seem appropriate.

Under the skin of the Ferrari

Words: John Simister

Telaio, sospensioni e sterzo
Translation: Chassis, suspension and steering

What it does
The chassis is still made from aluminium, but it's 20 per cent stiffer in torsion and uses bonding where the new aerospace-spec alloys can't be welded. The rear suspension uses an extra toe-control link to keep the right alignment during steering inputs, which has allowed use of an ultra-quick steering rack (30 per cent quicker than the F430's) without making the response hyperactively twitchy. There's now more innate roll stiffness in the springs and less in the anti-roll bars, improving response time and the ride. The dampers are adaptive magnetorheological units as used in the 599 and, optionally, in the California.

How it feels
Remarkably supple ride for a car which leans so little in the corners. The steering is ultra-alert but it feels natural within the first few hundred yards, with a progressive response and no dartiness. You always flow with the 458, you never fight it.

Interfaccia uomo-macchina in chiave ergonomica
Translation: Ergonomic human-machine interface

What it does
The steering wheel includes switches for indicators, lights and wipers, and a button to alter the damping mode. The TFT screen to the right of the tacho shows a 'photographic' speedo, replaceable with sat-nav or ICE info; the screen on the left shows minor gauges, the trip computer or, in Race mode or above, a 458 plan view and whether the engine, brakes and tyres need to be warmed up, are ready for action or have become too hot. A further page can show the degree of electronic control of traction, stability and braking according to the manettino setting.

How it feels
The displays are a window into the 458's workings, the switches mean you hardly have to take your hands from the wheel. Finding the indicator button when about to exit a tight roundabout can be a problem, though.

Integrazione tra aerodinamica e stile
Translation: Integration of aerodynamics and design

What it does
Pininfarina styled the 458 but within tight aerodynamic constraints. The drag coefficient isn't great at Cd 0.33, but there's a massive 360kg of downforce at maximum speed. Radiator air exits next to the headlights, while air to cool the transmission and engine enters under the sills ahead of the rear wheels and exits in such a way as to narrow the low-pressure area behind the 458 and so reduce turbulence. The best bits are the winglets in the front air intakes, fixed at their inner ends, with the outer ends allowed to move down by 20mm as speed rises. This diverts air under the car into cleaner airflow, preventing an excess of air entering the radiators.

How it feels
Planted, the whole time. To feel such front-end bite when turning at big speeds is breathtaking.

458 Italia

Cambio a doppia frizione
Translation: Double-clutch gearbox

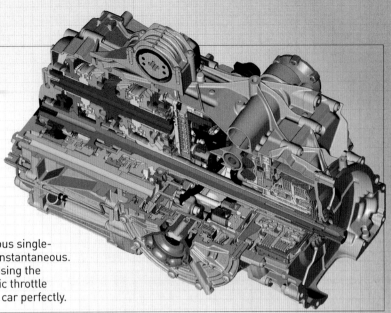

What it does
The internals of this seven-speed, Getrag-built double-clutch transmission are similar to the California's, but the ratios are shorter, the shift times are faster and the downshifts automatically get yet quicker when you're braking hard. A double-clutch gearbox can theoretically change gear with perfect smoothness and no torque interruption, but Ferrari has deliberately made the 458's interpretation a bit rougher round the edges to give a more 'mechanical' feel to the shifts.

How it feels
In auto mode, shifts are massively smoother than in the previous single-clutch gearbox. In auto Race mode, part-throttle kickdown is instantaneous. Manual upshifts have a perceptible jerk, smoothed away by easing the throttle, while downshifts are smoothed by a perfect, automatic throttle blip. Shift speed is lightning-fast. The calibration matches the car perfectly.

Differenziale elettronico integrate col F1-Trac
Translation: E-Diff combined with F1-Trac

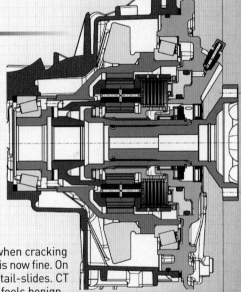

What it does
The electronic diff works by a system of clutches apportioning torque to each rear wheel as needed to keep the 458 pointing as intended, so rather than have a stability system annoyingly brake one wheel, the E-Diff accelerates the other. F1-Trac is the stability and traction system, its intervention reduced as you move up through Wet, Sport, Race, CT (traction) off and CST (traction and stability) off. E-Diff and F1-Trac are now controlled by the same software instead of just communicating by databus, so they can act more quickly and subtly.

How it feels
Invincible. In an F430 you'd likely use Race when cracking on because Sport intervened too much. Sport is now fine. On track, Race is also fine unless you crave big tail-slides. CT off, the E-Diff works harder and the car still feels benign.

Iniezione diretta di benzina
Translation: Direct fuel injection

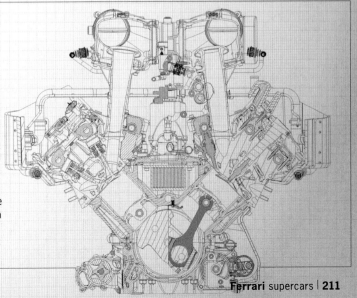

What it does
The key to the 458's extra power over the F430. It makes 562bhp at the 9000rpm peak when running at speed, 557bhp on the test bench without the ram-air effect of motion. Direct injection, including a second squirt at low speeds and loads, allows a high 12.5-to-one compression ratio and much greater efficiency. Graphite-coated pistons and a 'diamond-like carbon' tappet coating reduce friction, and the dry sump's oil scavenge pump also sucks air from under each descending piston to reduce crankcase windage and pumping losses.

How it feels
There's all the usual screaming drama at high revs, but the difference is the solid rush of torque right from ambling speed. The acceleration has a relentless, almost explosive feel, with a bombastically keen throttle response and an expletive of aural energy with every upshift. Deceleration is similarly abrupt, as if the flywheel weighs nothing.

The GTO returns

Everything you need to know about Ferrari's stunning 599GTO – and it's truly mouthwatering. **Richard Meaden** is your guide

Pictures: Ferrari

Of all the evocative

names in Ferrari's back catalogue, GTO is the one that brings you out in goose bumps. Reserved for Maranello's most special machines, only two cars have previously had those legendary initials bestowed upon them: the race-bred 250GTO of 1962 and the 288GTO of 1984. That surviving examples of the former regularly set new sale records at auction, and the latter is still regarded by many as the definitive mid-engined supercar, tells you all you need to know about the weight of expectation carried by the 599 Gran Turismo Omologata.

We've had a pretty good idea of what the 599GTO would be like from poring over the technical details and images that Ferrari has released of its experimental 599XX, but since that car is not legal for road use, quite how

extreme the GTO could or would be has remained a mystery – until now.

At the GTO's heart is a de-tuned version of the 599XX's 722bhp, 9000rpm, 5999cc V12, although with 670bhp and 457lb ft it's hard to accuse the GTO of going soft in an effort to comply with Euro 5 emissions standards. Boasting the same super-polished engine internals for minimal friction, the GTO's throttle response should be extraordinary, and complemented perfectly by the 60-millisecond gearchange times delivered by the six-speed paddle-shift transmission. With a 599XX-derived six-into-one exhaust manifold and careful acoustic balancing of the intake and exhaust sounds, it'll have an epic soundtrack too.

As you'd expect, the 599GTO's performance figures are something special. Assisted by

launch control, it'll hit 62mph from a standstill in a claimed 3.35sec, and although there are no official figures to confirm it, we'd estimate it'll go on to reach 100mph in 6.5sec and 124mph in less than 10sec. Top speed? 208mph.

Widespread use of carbon-fibre in the body structure, together with thinner-gauge aluminium and glass, a titanium exhaust and second-generation carbon-ceramic brakes all contribute to the impressive 1605kg kerbweight, which is 83kg lighter than a standard 599GTB. Aerodynamically the GTO incorporates many of the lessons learned in the 599XX, which in turn applied principles developed by the Ferrari F1 team. The aim – as always – is to generate more downforce without significantly increasing drag. This has been achieved thanks to careful sculpting of the front and rear, together with

'The GTO's performance should be on a par with, or even exceed, that of more traditional mid-engined hypercars'

Above: Body offers increased downforce levels. **Right:** new inside are longer shift paddles and a 'Virtual Race Engineer', which updates the driver on the car's status.

FERRARI 599GTO

SPECIFICATIONS

Engine
V12, front-mid, longitudinal, 5999cc

Power
670bhp @ 8250rpm

Torque
457lb ft @ 6500rpm

Transmission
Six-speed automated manual gearbox with paddle-shift, rear-wheel drive, limited-slip differential, VDC (Vehicle Dynamic Control)

Suspension
Front: Double wishbones, coil springs, adaptive dampers, anti-roll bar. Rear: Double wishbones, coil springs, adaptive dampers, anti-roll bar

Brakes
Ventilated carbon-ceramic discs, 398mm front, 360mm rear, ABS

Weight
1605kg

Performance
0-62mph: 3.35sec (claimed). Top speed: 208mph (claimed)

work to the car's flanks and flat underfloor. The result is 144kg of downforce at 120mph and bodywork that would look at home mixing it with GT1 racers at Le Mans. Now there's a nice thought...

While the extreme looks and magnificent V12 engine are undoubted highlights, it's the GTO's reliance on electronic dynamic-control systems that is likely to define the driving experience. Like current jet fighters, which wouldn't stay in the air without the quick wits and constant adjustments provided by powerful on-board computers, Ferrari's chassis dynamics philosophy is becoming increasingly dependent on its Vehicle Dynamic Control system (VDC) to extract the maximum performance from the car. Working in conjunction with the F1-Trac traction-control system and the latest-generation

magnetorheological dampers to harness the chassis' ultra-sharp responses, VDC will ensure that driving the GTO close to its limits will be a leap of faith as much as a test of skill.

The upshot is that the front-mid-engined GTO's performance should be on a par with, or even exceed, that of more traditional mid-engined hypercars. A lap time of 1min 24sec around Ferrari's Fiorano test track rather confirms this, as it means the GTO is 0.9sec faster than the Ferrari Enzo. Whether the GTO can successfully walk the line between extraordinary track car and engaging road car remains to be seen, but with more power, less weight and cutting-edge electronics to manage it all, the GTO promises to be a breathtaking experience, and a worthy addition to Ferrari's most hallowed breed of road car.

FERRARI FF

- NEW 6.2-LITRE V12
- 642BHP
- UNIQUE FOUR-WHEEL-DRIVE SYSTEM
- SPACE FOR FOUR WITH LUGGAGE
- 0-62MPH IN 3.7SEC
- 208MPH

Words: Henry Catchpole

Having howled up the Sella Pass only ten minutes before, it's something of a shock as we round a corner to discover our return descent now blocked. Although this is Ferrari's first four-wheel-drive car, an avalanche is too much even for an FF to drive over. A local assures us that a snowplough is already on the way, but faced with a choice of looking at a wall of lumpy snow for an hour or passing the time by heading back up the mountain for one more run through the switchbacks, there isn't really any contest...

The FF, as I'm sure you know, is the replacement for the 612 Scaglietti – Ferrari's four-seater. But because customers asked for a Ferrari that could realistically be driven every day, the chaps at Maranello decided to make the FF more practical and useable than any Ferrari before it. Such functional criteria have clearly dictated the FF's

breadvan/shooting-brake/M Coupé profile, and although it's a shape that will undoubtedly divide opinion, I happen to like it. It's a very well proportioned car.

As you walk up to it, you realise it is also a very large car; from the grinning grille to the double diffuser at the rear, it is just shy of five metres, or almost exactly the same length as an Audi A6 Avant. However, what the shape, combined with the split-folding rear seats, allows is for you to fit four people and their luggage inside for a weekend away, or three people and their bags for a week, or (perhaps most importantly) two people and their bicycles. It certainly comfortably accommodates Chris Rutter, Sam Riley and me, plus all their photographic and cinematic gubbins.

Of course, if the FF is to be considered a truly practical GT then it not only needs to be spacious

FERRARI FF
SPECIFICATIONS

Engine
V12, 6262cc
CO2 360g/km

Power
642bhp @ 8000rpm

Torque
504lb ft @ 6000rpm

Performance
0-62mph 3.7sec
(claimed)
Top speed 208mph
(claimed)

»

but it also needs to be able to whisk its contents across continents in comfort. This it will undoubtedly do. The roads in Italy's Südtirol seem to be twinned with those of Surrey – they are terrible. There is barely a yard that doesn't have a pockmark, crumple or crater. Yet for the first half an hour of driving, and whilst trying to navigate and generally survive the insane Italian traffic, I simply didn't notice.

The FF has third-generation magnetorheological (easy for you to say) dampers and they provide an incredible ride. Even with the suspension set to Sport rather than Comfort, not once did I wince or jolt – the broken tarmac simply slipped underneath us. It slipped quietly too; at a 100mph cruise on the autostrada there was a cocoon-like hush about the cabin and no need to raise even my mumbling voice to talk to the others.

There isn't really enough space here to do justice to the complexities of the FF's 4RM (*quattro ruote motrici* or four-wheel-drive) system, but I'll try. First you need to picture the layout of the drivetrain, the V12 set a long way back in the nose behind the front axle and a single propshaft running to the rear axle, where the seven-speed dual-clutch gearbox sits with the E-diff. It's a conventional transaxle arrangement, so how does power reach the front wheels? Well, ahead of the engine, over the front axle, is a very clever, very small Power Transfer Unit (PTU) containing two wet clutches – one for each front wheel.

This PTU draws power from the crank via an integrated gearbox and then apportions it to either or both of the front wheels when required. The front gearbox has just two gears, so the desired wheel speed is achieved by slipping the clutches. It's a system that means the FF is a

Top left: new 6.3-litre V12 has direct injection; power is up 109bhp over the outgoing 612's 5.8 V12, and is 31bhp up on the 599's 6.0. **Right:** brakes are CCM (carbon ceramic material) items; front discs are 398mm in diameter. **Below:** rear seats accommodate adults comfortably; central section can be lowered to allow long items such as skis to be pushed through.

'THROW THE FF INTO TURNS AND THE GRIP IS STUNNING – FAST CORNERS BECOME A TEST OF YOUR BRAVERY'

rear-drive car most of the time (and all the time above about 125mph) with the front wheels receiving power only when needed. How readily they start working depends on where you set the manettino: Ice, Wet, Comfort, Sport and ESC Off all make different assumptions about the level of grip available, and consequently how much work the rear wheels should do before they need help to keep the car stable. One of the main advantages of 4RM is that because it doesn't have a conventional centre clutch or a second propshaft, it weighs half what other four-wheel-drive systems weigh. Another advantage is that it allows torque to be distributed not only front to rear but also left or right, with the E-diff commanding the rear wheels and the PTU's two clutches dealing with the fronts.

What all this information can't tell us is how 4RM affects the driving experience. It sounds like an FF should still feel very rear-wheel drive, and fortunately Italian hairpins are a good testing ground to find out. The roads are bone-dry so it's ESC off, brake hard, first gear, sweep in wide and late, then get on the throttle aggressively... and the car simply fires itself out of the corner with supreme traction. I try it again, several times, and

power oversteer simply never materialises. What's just as flabbergasting is that the moment when the front wheels start helping is so seamless.

Usually in four-wheel-drive cars you can feel the rear slip before an obvious transition and change in attitude of the car as the power is shuffled forwards. But, with the FF, in the same instant that your brain is expecting traction to break and the rear to start moving, you find that instead of going sideways you're riding one continuous and enormous surge straight forwards. All 642bhp is simply deployed through the Pirellis, and the FF fires out of the corner with complete grip and maximum forward momentum. It's so extraordinary that I think it might out GT-R the GT-R.

The only time the car oversteers is in one right-left flick-flack with the chassis fully loaded in second gear, and even then there isn't any need to lift off as each time the car seems to stabilise the slide so early. Even on a piece of gravel road later, still with ESC off and deliberately flicking the car on the way into the corner, the traction is quite incredible. So, with all this traction, combined with all the practicality, is the FF still a proper Ferrari? Should we view it with the same suspicion

Above: optional second display ahead of the passenger can show speed, revs, chassis settings and other data.

that we view a Porsche Cayenne – a part of the brand in badge but not in ethos?

No. The FF is still definitely a Ferrari. Quiet though it may be inside when cruising, you only have to drop the window and plunge into a tunnel to be immersed in the properly spine-tingling bark of a Maranello soundtrack. The new V12, Ferrari's first with direct injection, might have been tuned to make 370lb ft (out of a total of 504lb ft) available at just 1000rpm, but it still makes its maximum 642bhp right up in the stratosphere at the 8000rpm limiter.

But it's not just the heart of the FF that is ⟫

'THE REAR TYRES SMEAR ACROSS THE ROAD, PUSHING YOU THROUGH CORNERS'

demonstrably Ferrari. The steering wheel looks like it has been lifted straight from a 458 and it feels like it too when you first turn into a corner. There is a fraction more weight, but it is still helium-light and incredibly responsive. This means that although the FF feels like a big car when you get in, it suddenly shrinks around you when you start really driving because the nose reacts like that of a much smaller, lighter model.

Throw the FF into turns and the grip is stunning – fast corners become a test of your bravery rather than limited as you think they should be by the capabilities of a 1880kg GT car. And don't think that because it won't do big lurid slides everywhere the FF is somehow boring. Right up to that point where the front driveshafts kick in and morph a showboating moment into forward momentum, the balance feels resolutely rear-drive. You feel the back tyres smearing across the tarmac and pushing you through corners, rather than the fronts in any way pulling the nose up the road.

By the time the avalanche has been cleared, we're seriously late for returning the FF to the hotel. Plummeting headlong down the mountain in a car as big as the FF, three up, could be terrifying, but it's brilliant. The third-generation CCM brakes are better than ever, giving reassuring feel (still that distinctive, slightly grainy sensation) right from the top of the pedal and never wilting despite the huge punishment of braking late and deep into mile after mile of downhill switchbacks. And because the brakes

Above: FF's steering wheel – like the 458's – has buttons for indicators, lights, wipers, dampers and stability control.

give you confidence, you feel happy to use all the power on the straights too, hanging onto gears and flicking the right-hand paddle just before the limiter for another whip-crack change, preferably with the window down next to a rock face (although now I think about it, I hope it wasn't that which triggered the avalanche in the first place...).

If you want a Ferrari that is absolutely the last word in driver involvement, one that will really test your car-handling skills over the limit of grip, then it's available in the form of both the 458 and the 599. But if you want a Ferrari that can carry more than two people and transport them almost anywhere indecently and intoxicatingly quickly, then an FF is the incredibly capable car for you. △

ABARTH 695 TRIBUTO FERRARI

■ FERRARI-INSPIRED 500
■ BEST NEW ABARTH YET

Engine In-line 4-cyl, 1368cc, turbo **CO2** 155g/km
Power 178bhp @ 5750rpm **Torque** 170lb ft @ 3300rpm
0-62mph 6.9sec (claimed) **Top speed** 140mph (claimed)
Price £29,600 **On sale** Now

IT'D BE EASY to smirk at the 695 Tributo Ferrari and even dismiss it as nothing more than a marketing gimmick aimed at extracting every penny from committed Ferrari fanatics. At £29,600 it's an irrelevance, right? Well, no actually. It's quite brilliant to drive and is easily the best of the Abarth 500 range. It's based on the Esseesse model, but here the tiny 1.4-litre turbo lump's wick has been wound up another 20bhp to produce a total of 178bhp, and with the addition of a variable-back-pressure exhaust it boasts a pretty manic soundtrack too, every upshift on the automated five-speed manual gearbox accompanied by a satisfying whump!

But it's in the corners you discover the biggest contrast. The Tributo is so much more responsive and precise thanks to uprated springs and well-judged dampers, so it's stiff but connected – you're never bounced across the road. The Michelin tyres are unique too, and offer much sharper and better-defined responses, while braking has also been improved with 284mm discs and Brembo calipers up front. Inside, a pair of Sabelt seats lock you in place beautifully.

So yes, it's expensive, but all that extra cash has been well spent – and thankfully this is more than mere badge engineering.
Roger Green

Above: Sabelt seats give superb support in all the right places; new 17in alloy wheels mimic those of the 360 Challenge Stradale.

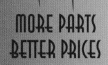

This page: Maurice
Trintignant's Ferrari 625
wins the 1955 Monaco GP.

222

Ferrari's F1 GLORY YEARS

By fair means or foul, Ferrari has had great periods – unrivalled in motor sport – of success in Formula 1. Here's how the marque did it

Words: Doug Nye Photography: The GP Library

Enzo FERRARI

He overcame a hard upbringing to create the greatest car marque the world
has ever known, ruling it in the uniquely tough, manipulative, emotional
and unpredictable manner for which he became famous

Enzo Ferrari was a hard-nosed wheeler-dealer. He was also a master manipulator of multi-talented people. His long-time chief engineer of the 1960s through to the 1980s, Mauro Forghieri, furrowed his brow when I once asked him what The Old Man's greatest strengths had been. He responded, with a thin and decidedly rueful smile: 'Mr Ferrari had a great understanding... of human weakness.'

'Oscar' Tavoni, Ferrari's team manager of the late 1950s/early '60s, told me that Enzo never lost his fascination with manipulating the great and the wealthy. 'He liked to see them dancing to his tune,' said Tavoni, 'yet once a wealthy customer offered enough money, he would sell them anything. He loved always to make the big score. The wealthy might have got what they wanted, and gone away smirking, but first they had left their money with him – Ferrari.'

It was in part this merchant, some say peasant, ability which founded Ferrari's greatness – and the world's most charismatic motoring brand. For decades *Il Drake* or *Il Grande Vecchio*, as he became known around Modena, had an almost unerring eye for an engineer who would contribute to building the legend. And before one engineer's potential had been squeezed dry, another would have been groomed and prepared to take his place. Once ultimately cast aside, that man's greatest potential would be behind him, trapped in Ferrari's pitiless filter.

Born on February 18, 1898, Enzo Ferrari was introduced to motor racing by his father, Alfredo, who ran a modest Modenese metal-fabricating business. The boy was ten when Papa took him to Bologna to watch the Coppa Florio motor race. Felice Nazzaro of Fiat won, and Enzo was hooked. Brief World War I service in the Italian Army ended when he fell victim to the flu epidemic of 1918; both his father and elder brother had died the previous year. Alone in the world, the recovered Enzo found a job in the Turin motor trade and developed friends who took him to CMN, for whom he drove in the 1920 Parma-Poggio di Berceto hillclimb. Now he was a racing driver...

His CMN friend Ugo Sivocci moved to Alfa Romeo and fixed Ferrari a job there. He became right-hand man to Giorgio Rimini, Nicola Romeo's closest aide, and drove Alfa Romeos in the Targa Florio, at Mugello and in other races. In 1924 he joined the works team for the French Grand Prix, but his nerve broke – the P2 GP car was beyond him, and he non-started. He recovered back in Modena, building his successful Alfa Romeo agency, and resumed racing in minor-league events in 1927. His agency attracted numerous wealthy clients, and at the end of 1929 he persuaded three of them – the Caniato brothers and Mario Tadini – to finance the establishment of the Scuderia Ferrari. This new team was to prepare, enter and run Alfa Romeo cars for such wealthy owners, so all they had to do was report to the right venue, on the right day, to find their cars present and race-ready, entries and accommodation arranged.

When Alfa's in-house works team was closed on cost grounds in 1932, Mr Ferrari manoeuvred his Scuderia into assuming quasi-works team duties. From mid-1933 until 1937 the Modena-based Scuderia was 'Alfa Sport'. From 1934 Alfa's GP cars could not match the emergent German factory teams in men, money and material, so in 1937 Mr Ferrari recommended building 1.5-litre Vetturetta class ('GP2') cars instead. He had them designed for him at Modena by a team under Gioachino Colombo and they emerged as the Alfa Romeo 158 'Alfetta'. Yet the Scuderia did not live to race

Below: Nuvolari in Modena, 1935, racing for Enzo's 'Alfa Sport' team. **Below right:** Enzo's son Dino, who would die aged just 24.

them. Instead, new Alfa President Gobbato took Alfa racing back in house for 1938. The Scuderia Ferrari was wound up and Ferrari returned to Milan to manage the new Alfa Corse factory team. He hated this loss of independence and walked out later the same year. One clause of his severance agreement was that he would neither build nor race cars under his own name for four years.

Instead he founded a precision machining business, Auto-Avio Costruzioni, in his old Scuderia HQ. Around Christmas 1939 he was visited by local aristo *Marchese* Lotario Rangoni and young Alberto Ascari – son of Alfa's long-lost great Champion driver, Antonio – who wanted Ferrari to build them Fiat-based sports cars for the 1940 Mille Miglia. AAC produced two otherwise anonymous '815' cars to suit, with Fiat-derived straight-eight 1500cc engines. At Brescia they ran quite well, but then Italy entered World War II, during which Ferrari moved his company to Maranello in the Apenine foothills to escape allied bombing. He manufactured copies of top-grade German machine tools, finessed his way around the fall of fascism and advance of Italian communism, and even before peace returned in 1945 he was laying the foundation for post-war car production... and the launch of his own Ferrari marque. △

Right: Alberto Ascari in 1940 in the AAC 815 built for him by Enzo for the Mille Miglia.

'He loved to make the big score. The wealthy might have got what they wanted, and gone away smirking, but they had left their money with him'

The Front-Engined Era 1947-1962

From tiny beginnings, Ferrari began a reign of giant-killing before turning into a giant itself – with all the attendant problems

Ex-Alfa Romeo, ex-Scuderia Ferrari engineer Gioachino Colombo was out of work in 1945, suspended and shunned by a highly politicised Alfa Romeo for too-enthusiast support of Mussolini. Such loyalty to a dictator was just fine by Mr Ferrari; Colombo was the man for him, and he was commissioned to produce a new breed of high-performance machine – in both sports and single-seater form – powered by a 1500cc supercharged V12 engine.

Through 1946 Mr Ferrari's tiny team developed its first V12s, then began racing them in primitive sports-bodied chassis in 1947. They entered the Grand Prix arena in 1948, fielding three new *Tipo* 125 *Monoposti* in the Turin GP – driven by Farina, Sommer and 'B. Bira'. They failed. Next time out at Lake Garda... Farina won.

Meanwhile Alfa Corse had taken a stranglehold on GP racing with its Ferrari-inspired cars in updated form. But post-war finance was always tight, and for 1949 Alfa took a sabbatical from competition – and the supercharged Colombo Ferrari V12s of Alberto Ascari – yes, him again – and Gigi Villoresi began winning GP races.

Having used up the butterfly-brained Colombo's original genius, and that of development engineer Busso to make these designs raceworthy, Ferrari massaged a perhaps greater engineer – Aurelio Lampredi – to take his company forward. A

Above, from left: Gonzales wins 1951 Pescara GP; Ferrari management at 1959 Dutch GP; winning the last Mille Miglia in 1957.

tough-minded and ambitious man, Lampredi did brilliantly by Ferrari. He shelved the highly strung supercharged 1500cc V12s in favour of new unsupercharged 4.5-litre units, and launched an unsupercharged 2-litre four-cylinder for Formula 2, in which 2-litre V12s had been campaigned, sans supercharging.

In the 1951 British GP at Silverstone, works cadet driver Jose Froilan Gonzalez drove Ferrari's 4.5-litre V12 *muletto* to defeat the returned Alfa Corse team, for the first time. 'I feel I have killed my own mother,' wrote The Old Man, self-consciously theatrical as ever.

Lampredi's unblown 2-litre four-cylinder Ferraris then carried Ascari to history's first back-to-back Drivers' World Championship titles in 1952 and '53. On their shirt tails rode sales of Ferrari sports and production cars, still built in what were really penny numbers, but generating revenue to feed Enzo's passion: racing. With headline-grabbing consecutive victories in the Mille Miglia from 1948 to 1953, at Le Mans in 1949 and in myriad high-grade sports car, Formula 1 and Formula 2 races worldwide, *La Ferrari* was on an amazing roll, the company's creator bestriding the motor-racing world like a colossus.

It took men of equal stature and hardness to cut him down. One such was Tony Vandervell, who made the Thinwall shell bearings that had cured the Ferrari V12's greatest frailty. Between

'Horsepower was God, chassis mere brackets that retained the wheels. Ferraris of the 1950s were seldom "easy" cars'

him and Mr Ferrari it was a pure case of diamond cut diamond. Lampredi was another hard nut. Yet when he failed to deliver the goods in 1955 against Mercedes-Benz and Maserati, he was overboard (to Fiat). By a stroke of good fortune Lancia went bust, and both its Formula 1 hardware and its great ex-Alfa engineer Vittorio Jano landed instead in Ferrari's lap.

Enzo had already separated production from racing, in conjunction with yet another hard man – Battista 'Pinin' Farina – to build and sell GT cars. The dominant Ferrari characteristic was 'unburstability' – engines and drive lines that were bullet proof, gearchanges that loved being used 'like the bolt on a rifle'. Horsepower was God, chassis mere brackets that retained the wheels. Ferraris of the 1950s were seldom 'easy' racing cars. Many drivers died in them, most doing something they adored. When works drivers like Luigi Musso and the Marquis de Portago were killed, Ferrari was pilloried. He grieved, but he went on racing. Since 1920 he had seen it all before.

The empire grew, and grew. His son Dino died from muscular dystrophy in 1956, aged just 24. The Old Man publicly agonised over his creation's destiny. Into the mid-1960s the public grievings fell away, and Piero Lardi, son of Enzo's mistress, Lina, was working at Maranello.

In 1956 the Pinin Farina-styled 3-litre V12-engined two-seat Ferrari *Berlinetta* took root, de Portago winning the Tour de

Clockwise from top left: Rosier in '53; Ferraris at Thillois (1956 French GP); Ascari in 1953 British GP; Fangio in 1956 Monaco GP.

France to give the new model its popular nickname. As a road/race 'supercar' the Ferrari 250GT would develop through the famously successful short-wheelbase variant in 1960-61 to the now immortal 250GTO of 1962-'64 – the most iconic road-useable Ferrari of them all.

The bad times for Ferrari were seldom far away. But the Lancia windfall plus Fiat financial backing – *por la Patria* ('for the Fatherland') – sustained Formula 1 fortunes in 1956 and '57, with Fangio winning another title for Ferrari in the former year, before Jano master-minded the four-cam Dino V6 engine that would bring Mike Hawthorn the drivers' title in 1958. Ferrari's own conservatism came home to roost in 1959-'60, when his faith in front-mounted engines, drum brakes and wire wheels proved near-fatal in the face of British racing developments – rear engines, disc brakes and lightweight cast wheels.

Still, as team driver Phil Hill recalled: 'Mr Ferrari was always busily stoking the fire under the boiling cauldron into which every racing driver worthy of the name would willingly leap...' The great Manipulator of Maranello would declare: 'My number one driver is he who won last Sunday' – like an automotive version of the Fat Controller he toyed with both staff and works drivers like chessmen on a board. Increasingly, in a developing age of big-money sport and major-league motor racing, Ferrari's in-house politics would do much more harm than good...

The classic
REAR-ENGINED
Era 1961-1974

When the front-engined cars began to be overwhelmed, a new era of 'Motore Posteriore' Ferraris took over – and began to dominate once more...

The demonstrable superiority of the new wave of rear-engined Grand Prix cars from Cooper, BRM and Lotus (1959-'60) simply overwhelmed the front-engined Ferraris that confronted them. Mr Ferrari had always had a unique power to influence the governing body, the FIA, in its decisions concerning the future of International racing. When 1.5-litre Formula 2 racing was launched in 1957, his Jano-conceived Dino V6 had begun to shine. It burned pump petrol instead of the exotic alcohol fuel brews standard in Formula 1, and when AVGas aviation spirit was specified by the FIA for Formula 1 (1958-'60), hey presto, Ferrari had just the ticket, ready developed to burn the stuff.

Dino development had devolved upon Ferrari's new chief engineer, Carlo Chiti, who came from an aeronautical background and who persuaded The Old Man to sanction major modernisation at Maranello. A wind tunnel was built, real progress was made and, early in 1960, the first rear-engined Ferrari emerged – the 2.4-litre Dino V6-powered 246MP – 'Motore Posteriore'. American test driver Richie Ginther drove it in the 1960 Monaco GP before it was fitted with a 1.5-litre V6 for Formula 2 racing. Team-mate 'Taffy' von Trips promptly won the F2 Solitude GP with it, defeating the Coventry Climax four-cylinder-engined Brits. For 1961, 1500cc Formula 2 was effectively upgraded to Formula 1 status, and again Ferrari was poised and ready, and Chiti's distinctive rear-engined 'Sharknose' 156s destroyed all opposition, Phil Hill emerging as World Champion after Trips' ghastly death – together with 14 hapless spectators – in the Italian GP.

Legal action against Ferrari for the de Portago 1957 Mille Miglia crash – which also claimed 12 other lives – had only just evaporated with the conclusion that road-centreline cat's eyes had slashed the sports Ferrari's tyres. Now legal action resumed against Ferrari – and others – for the 1961 Monza disaster. When pilloried by press and even the Vatican, Ferrari would pull up the drawbridge and adopt a stance of wounded persecution... while always planning, manipulating, researching and developing his next manoeuvre.

By 1962-'63 he was definitely feeling the chill once more. Formula 1 fortunes had dived, then recovered thanks to the shrewd signing of frontier-technology British engineer/drivers John Surtees and Michael Parkes. Sports and GT success had continued – against patchy opposition – and rear-engined Dino 246 sports-prototypes of 1961-'62 had spawned the 3-litre V12 rear-engined Ferrari 250P legends of 1963.

Enter Ford Detroit. To promote its wares before the new moneyed youth market of the 1960s, Ford lusted after Ferrari's ready-made glamour and capabilities. Ferrari proved a terrible old tease. He used America's advances to wind up Fiat, secured additional backing from Turin, and dismissed the Motown men. They swore revenge and – eventually – smashed Ferrari in the GT Championship of 1965, and at Le Mans in '66... and '67-8-9! The Old Man had always regarded Le Mans as the great promotional prize upon which he sold his road cars. After winning it in 1949, 1954 and 1960-'65 inclusive, he was stung. Worse, the ploy of roofing in the 250P V12 sports-prototype as a GT car to create the 250LM as replacement for the GTO line was rejected by the FIA homologation committee. Perplexed and enraged by such 'betrayal, The Old Man reacted to this sudden loss of manipulative success by handing in his entrant's licence... for a while.

Surtees and a new V8 Ferrari Formula 1 car had edged Maranello the 1964 World Championship titles, but into 1966 and a new 3-litre Formula 1 era The Old Man was struggling to make ends meet. His rearguard action against Ford in endurance racing was draining his coffers and the new Formula 1 V12 was a 380bhp cobble-up from sports car parts already on the storehouse shelf. Still John won the Belgian GP before being faced with an impossible situation engineered by *Direttore Sportivo* Eugenio Dragoni. John left the team in mid-'66 and Ferrari waved goodbye to another World title.

For 1967 The Old Man famously sank his dwindling funding into the 330P4 sports-prototype project, inflicting a 1-2-3 defeat upon Ford in the Daytona 24 Hours to avenge Le Mans '66, only to go down fighting back at the Sarthe that June. But not before the launch pad had been established for Ferrari's latest production *Gran Turismo* – the 365GTB/4 Daytona.

Yet by 1969 everything was going wrong. Ferrari built too few production cars to maintain adequate profitability. Formula 1 fortunes were slithering down the tubes. The flat-12 engine to replace the F1 V12s was teething badly. Ferrari swallowed his pride and approached Gianni Agnelli at Fiat. As an old friend, the younger magnate agreed to buy. The deal was done under the Italian legal form of *in vitalizio*. Fiat bought half Ferrari's stock for a fixed annual sum to be paid as long as *Il Drake* might live. Had he died in 1970 Fiat would have secured Ferrari very cheaply. As it was, the firm would pay for nearly 20 long years, which in general numbered some of Ferrari's finest, thanks largely to Fiat money and – where the production division was concerned – to Fiat management and investment in manufacturing machinery.

In F1 the flat-12 engine came good halfway through the 1970 season, and reigned dominant until halfway through that of 1971. Had those two half-seasons been just one, Jacky Ickx and Ferrari would have been World Champions. But Fiat funding was haemorrhaging into the sports car programme to confront the Porsche 917s. It failed. However, a 3-litre flat-12 'enveloping-bodied Formula 1 car' – the 312PB – emerged in 1971 and with a fine team it put all opposition to the sword through 1972 and won yet another title. In 1973 Matra fought back as Ferrari's F1 fortunes collapsed in disarray. Fiat winced at sports-prototype costs, and for 1974 the sports car programme was dropped – total concentration focused upon F1, and Niki Lauda and Clay Regazzoni came within a whisker of success. Just one more push was needed... △

For many years of Ferrari's history from 1969, financial backer Fiat fought shy of being seen to meddle – too publicly – with *La Ferrari*. Its input and control of the *Reparto Industriale* production operation was perceived as being both effective and benign. Its studious non-interference with the *Reparto Corsa* racing department was due as much to well-founded fear of the merciless Italian sporting paparazzi as respect for *Il Grande Vecchio* – 'The Great Old One' – Enzo Ferrari himself.

During 1974 Niki Lauda (right) had yet to become a fully fledged Formula 1 star, while his veteran team-mate Clay Regazzoni – in his second stint with Ferrari – provided invaluable support. Chief engineer Mauro Forghieri had been pushed aside in 1973, Sandro Colombo taking his place before Forghieri was hastily recalled! After thorough development of a new 312B3 model through 1974, Forghieri's group produced the 312T in which Lauda and Regga dominated the 1975 World Championship, securing Maranello both titles for the first time in 11 years. They repeated the Constructors' title in 1976 and

after Lauda's German GP fire Mr Ferrari doubted his ability to bounce back, engaging Carlos Reutemann as a potential replacement. Instead it was Regazzoni who took the bullet – partly because he dared market ladies' jeans with Ferrari's Prancing Horse badge on the hip pocket – 'He put our soul on a bird's bum!' is a fair presentation of The Old Man's detonation.

Lauda gelled with neither new DSs Daniele Audetto and Roberto Nosetto nor – most decidedly – with Reutemann, yet he and Ferrari repeated their World titles – Ferrari scoring the first hat-trick of Constructors' Championships, 1975-6-7. Lotus's revolutionary ground-effects cars re-wrote the form book in 1978, but Ferrari flat-12 horsepower told in startlingly ugly 312T4s driven by Scheckter and Villeneuve in 1979 – Champions again. A strategic decision was then taken to invest in new 1.5-litre turbocharged technology, so 1980's naturally-aspirated flat-12 312T5s proved a low-budget flop.

Turbo V6 technology with Gilles Villeneuve and Didier Pironi driving saw the French-Canadian triumphant at Monaco and Jarama. The 1982 turbo Ferraris were real challengers, and after

MODERN MARANELLO
1975-2011

And so Ferrari's Formula 1 effort really took off, admittedly in fits and starts — first with Lauda, then Villeneuve and Prost and, finally, Schumacher. So, what happens next?

'Would the old man have resorted to a judiciary had he found someone "spying"? I suspect not'

Villeneuve's death and Pironi's career-ending crash, Patrick Tambay and Mario Andretti shepherded Ferrari to another title.

Dr Harvey Postlethwaite brought composite construction technology to Ferrari at *Il Grande Vecchio*'s invitation, but in The Old Man's dotage – while he could still drink Harvey under the table – Ferrari became a house divided against itself. The old guard retired, leaving Fiat and family elements manoeuvring for Enzo's legacy. The increasingly eccentric Forghieri was ousted at the end of 1984, Postlethwaite prevailing as chief designer with Ildo Renzetti engine head. Into 1986 Jean-Jacques His – ex-Renault – took over engine development and The Old Man hired John Barnard from McLaren. Factional in-fighting tore the team apart before Gerhard Berger won the last two GPs of 1987. Harvey, latest DS Marco Piccinini and Piero Lardi Ferrari wanted to continue with 1.5-litre turbo engines. Barnard wanted 'atmo' V12s. Mr Ferrari backed him. Fiat's Pier-Giorgio Capelli was installed to run the racing team, Piccinini sidelined, Harvey left to join Tyrrell. And in August, 1988, Enzo Ferrari died, aged 90.

Fiat took full control. From 1989-'91 Cesare Fiorio became DS and Barnard's latest Ferrari 641 V12 emerged for drivers Mansell and Berger. Maranello required revolving doors as engineers and execs came and went. Pierguido Castelli, Enrique Scalabroni, Henri Durand, Steve Nichols and Paolo Massai each had their time in the sun. Alain Prost shone for the team in 1990 but was fired in 1991 by Fiat's latest *capo* Claudio Lombardi, for publicly criticising the car.

Fiat reappointed Luca di Montezemolo to head Ferrari overall, and Postlethwaite was re-hired, but in July 1993 – with Ferrari still unsuccessful – Jean Todt was recruited ex-Peugeot to run the *Reparto Corse*. Chassis were entrusted to Gustav Brunner and John Barnard, engines to Paolo Martinelli. Moderate improvement attracted Michael Schumacher from Benetton for 1996. Late that year, at his recommendation, Ross Brawn and Rory Byrne joined from Benetton, Barnard left, and from 1998 Formula 1 Ferraris were designed by South African-born Byrne, and run by Brawn. In 1999 Ferrari won its first Formula 1 Constructors' title since 1983.

The Schumacher Ferrari era had dawned – in 2000 he became Ferrari's first World Champion Driver since Scheckter in 1979. In the Byrne/Brawn cars Schuey and Rubens Barrichello brought Ferrari the Constructors' titles of 2000, 2001, 2002 plus 2003 (when Byrne eased off) and 2004. Michael won five consecutive Drivers' titles. Ferrari was well-beaten in 2005-'06 by Renault and, with Schumacher's retirement, Ross Brawn and Paolo Martinelli also opted for a quieter life. With Kimi Raikkonen and Felipe Massa confronting McLaren's finest, Ferrari took a heavily-tainted 2007 Constructors' Championship title (its 15th) and achieved the same position in 2008 – but to date that was its last World triumph. Coming fourth in the 2009 Constructors' standings and third in 2010, it has some ground to make up to return to those glory times of the new millennium. Will 2011 be its year...

Would The Old Man have resorted to a judiciary had he found someone 'spying'? I suspect not. He had his own ways of manipulating vengeance, and few dared test him. Perhaps the House of Ferrari he'd so painstakingly built was too conspicuously well-glazed for him to risk throwing stones. Part victory march, part tragi-comedy: what a record, what a legend, what a brand. △

It's a wonder that I've

ended up with such a long-term relationship with Ferrari. I succumbed easily to the charisma of the marque, although I was only seven at the time. I remember my first car being a Ferrari 625 GP racer in blue and yellow. It ran faultlessly, but then it was a die-cast Dinky so there was little to go wrong, apart from paint coming off the driver's helmet when it had the sort of massive accident only small children can engineer.

Later, in the late-'50s, I admired the cars in the paddock at Goodwood, but resisted any real plans for ownership due to the inevitable financial constraints placed on schoolboys. When fate decreed that I could finally indulge in spending on wine, women and singing, I foolishly frittered away much of it on cars. It was my own fault – I demanded a dealer and got Maranello Concessionaires instead of 'Terry the Pill'...

The best Ferraris go beyond the realm of being tools to ❯❯

NICK MASON
on the **250GTO**
(and the 275, the Daytona, the F40, the Enzo...)

What's it like to be a long-term Ferrari owner? Nick Mason reflects on some of the cars
he's been lucky enough to experience, and the passion they inspire
Photography courtesy Ten Tenths Ltd

become, if not art, at least high craft. Enzo Ferrari was a wonderfully flawed human being but he cared passionately. He wasn't an Ettore Bugatti, a Bruce McLaren or a Gordon Murray – that is, he wasn't a designer, driver or ground-breaking engineer – and yet he produced such wonderful cars, as well as a few really rather average ones. If he had been in politics in the same period I suspect Italy would have won WW2.

For me, the 275GTB/4 seemed the perfect starter choice. As often happens with real car nuts, it never occurred to me to actually try the damned thing before buying it, and I'm rather proud (in a weird way) to say this technique has generally worked well over the years. In fact, I tend to look rather suspiciously on potential buyers of my cars who insist on driving them, and I liked the fine print on one dealer's receipt that suggested the car was simply sold as a collectors' item and any driving activity couldn't possibly be considered as being covered.

In a world that had only just begun to discover the commercial aspects of psychedelic music, the 275 had many of the looks of a GTO without the impossible price tag. It looked a million dollars and cost a lot less. The four-cam was,

obviously, top of the range, and better than the two because it had a bigger number. I can't now remember where the model came from, but it felt by miles the most serious car I had ever owned.

They say that the two best moments of owning a yacht are the day you buy it and the day you sell. And, by God, the same was true of that 275. The view from the cockpit was magnificent, with acres of beautiful bodywork to worry about, leather seats and lots and lots of gauges. There was even a leather-bound instruction book, and the window catches hadn't yet fallen off.

The trouble was, the car was a disaster. Its two greatest faults were a tendency to wet its plugs, and brakes that at low speed with reduced servo aid were worse than a vintage Austin Chummy's. I became adept at parking on a hill to aid the bump start, and removing armloads of plugs that then had to be cleaned, or at least heated, over a gas stove. On one occasion when away from home the help of a rather smart Bristol hotel kitchen had to be enlisted to carry out this work. I was lucky they didn't come back with a pastry topping and a touch of garlic...

Those brakes tested nerve and leg muscles to the limit and ❯

Below and right:
275GTB/4 was Nick's first Ferrari, bought in the 1970s, but he never bonded with it as he did with its GTO replacement.

'The 275 looked a million dollars... Trouble was, the car was a disaster'

'No car is perfect, but the GTO comes close.
In terms of forgiveness for the driver,
it should be sainted'

'The 512TR formed part of a package that morphed into a competition Daytona – which easily qualified as being far less practical'

were an early form of Pilates equipment for strengthening the legs. One of the most memorable experiences was taking the car to Maranello Concessionaires for some advice. The well-spoken man who greeted me decided that the best solution would be to drive the beast. Apparently the brakes were excellent – well of course they were, for the salesman was Mike Salmon and we never travelled at less than full revs. Mike clearly had no time for doodling around in traffic, and couldn't imagine that I would either.

I later wrote to a titled bloke who I heard had had a mod done to sort out the problem. I got the most unhelpful letter back suggesting it might be a little complicated and pricey for the likes of me, but fortunately this turned out to be a unique experience. Like most enthusiasts' groups, Ferrari owners are usually only too eager to help. In fact, if I have a complaint, it's that any query frequently unlocks a raging torrent of advice.

Oddly, I don't remember my GTB/4 going, which probably shows that there wasn't that much love lost between us, but on the subject of 275s, I once had a friend in North London who used his as a builder's van. He manufactured a roof rack to carry plumbing fittings and kept the car in a side street. It looked terrible and he took great delight in giving short shrift to would-be purchasers who thought they had found a » bargain. He knew exactly what it was worth, and most impressive of all did a total engine rebuild in his bathroom, using the bath to expand the crankcase while assembling the engine. It was also noticeable that he had some trouble holding down a long-term relationship... It is possible there is a connection here.

In the years since the GTB/4, I've inevitably become a bit of a GTO bore, having lived with mine long enough now to see my status as an owner change from new rich kid to sad old sausage. No car is perfect, but the GTO comes close. As a drivers' car it has an almost perfect balance between engine power, brakes and suspension, while in terms of forgiveness to the driver it should be sainted. It also makes a great noise and has a sense of history permeating the cockpit, with a view over the bonnet that is just begging to include those Mulsanne marker boards whisking by.

The body is simply stunning. Jess Pourret, whose book *The Ferrari Legend: 250GT Competition* is to GTO owners what the Constitution is to Americans, records that, contrary to popular mythology, it was designed in-house at Ferrari rather than by Pininfarina. Whatever, it's purposeful but exotic enough to make a lot of chisel-jawed, steely-eyed guys unable to resist touching it – particularly when it's warm. (Bugatti tail sections are also susceptible to this and, post-VSCC Silverstone, will frequently need remedial work to the mild indentations in their top surface.) I have taken my

children to school in the GTO on a snowy day when nothing else would start, and we even used it for my daughter's wedding – fortunately the vicar was a proper motor enthusiast and felt that a side-exhaust Ferrari was by far the most suitable mode of transport for brides.

The car has generally been reliable. It dropped a valve on my first GTO rally in 1982, which was a bitter disappointment since they occur only every five years, but it's finished all the others – though on one occasion it needed support from Moët & Chandon's vineyard engineering facility to refit a propshaft. Otherwise most problems have been self-induced. Overheating in traffic was the result of using a lightweight radiator in an attempt to get a little more speed on the track and make some inroads against those damned E-type Jaguars!

There's nothing like such talk to bring out the rather thin-lipped, self-righteous tone in those who disapprove of the over-development of historic racers. I belong firmly to the group that believes it's entirely wrong to do all this development on anyone else's car; it would be OK only if I could do more to mine, but sadly the 3-litre GTO engine doesn't lend itself to the opportunity offered by some other competitors.

Having achieved the Holy Grail of GTO ownership, I ended up trying some other models in case I'd made a mistake. The closest competitor for me was the Daytona. It was terrific,

Below
Nick collected his F40 new from the factory – 'perhaps the most exciting car for a first drive'.

'Rear vision was marginal, but the design ethic was that no-one would be overtaking you' and in a way I still miss it. Mine was a left-hand-drive example – and, just in case it's still around, it should have two speedos that could be rapidly interchanged to allow for kph or mph. The fact that this also kept the mileage down was an added bonus...

Although a real Tarzan car to park (but a doddle on the brake pressure required), it was great on the open road. I did a lot of miles in mine during a six-month period working in France. In between recording in the Alps Maritimes and exhausting a number of sets of Michelin tyres on the steep route up to the recording studios, it set some fairly politically incorrect times for Cannes to Le Mans, and Nice to Spa.

One great feature was the cabin size. It actually had a boot with room for some luggage, as well as space within for all those bits and pieces that accumulate on long journeys. The air-conditioning struggled a bit, but it was only after that car had gone and I bought my very first new Ferrari from the factory that I realised just how civilised it was. In some ways the change was like moving from a manor house to an expensive but small flat.

After years of second-hand cars there was something very special about the factory visit. My dad had met Enzo, and even benefited from his friendship with the Commendatore when organising at short notice a drive and all the associated paperwork to co-pilot on the 1953 Mille Miglia. Although I came along too late to meet the great man, I did become friendly with probably the nearest person to him in the

organisation. Brenda Vernor is still the font of all Ferrari knowledge in Maranello. Not just the type numbers and history of the cars, but all the really good stuff about the drivers, the owners, their wives and girlfriends, and the machinations of Ferrari politics. There may be presidents and CEOs, but none would be as bold as Brenda in terms of the scurrilous gossip that helps transform the Ferrari experience from mechanical to human. If there are bodies buried, Brenda not only knows where they are, but what they are wearing.

It was unbelievably exciting to take my F40 – perhaps the most exciting car ever for a first drive – out of the factory gate and hammer up the autostrada. An over-long lunch had meant that Bob Houghton and myself hadn't quite bothered with the briefing about details like how to switch the dash lights on – or even the headlights, come to that. And a map wouldn't have been much use, as there wasn't a light to read it by.

The fitted luggage still delights me – a thin disc of leather suitable for an extra-large pizza or a low-rise sombrero, and a wedge-shaped briefcase that was clearly designed for a good chunk of Parmigiano-Reggiano. It's best either to pack light (that is, wear what you need) or to send the chauffeur ahead. Rear vision was marginal, too – the design ethic was clearly that no-one would be overtaking you anyway (I later had some better rear screens moulded). But despite these bugbears, in my opinion the F40 has made the transition from new supercar to genuine classic, which is not a journey

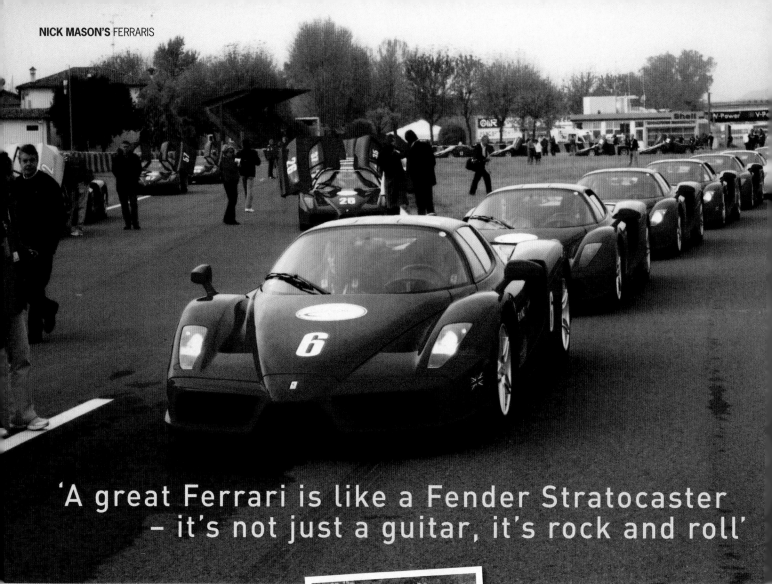

'A great Ferrari is like a Fender Stratocaster – it's not just a guitar, it's rock and roll'

that every design makes.

I also bought a 512TR new from the factory, but it never really endeared itself to me. Luggage space was inadequate and the cockpit was a bit too cramped, and I wasn't mad about the visibility. I think I felt I'd already had enough of that sort of car, and it formed part of a package that morphed into a competition Daytona – which had even less luggage space, no air-conditioning and easily qualified as being far less practical.

I had a couple of Dinos, and I still have a great affection for them. The silliest thing I did with one of mine was to hit an ice patch at the top of my street and slide its nose into the rear of another of my cars, pushing that one into the back end of the nanny's car. I hadn't the nerve to fill in the insurer's accident claim form. I could imagine the headlines: 'Rock drummer in three-car pile up'...

The second silliest act was to exchange a Dino for a Lancia Stratos. If you believe that if it looks right, it is right, this car might change your philosophy. For a lunatic rally ace it's ideal; for the rest of us it's a rather frightening fairground ride. I spent a lot of time looking at the road ahead through the side windows. The rather natty suede seats were the best bit of the interior – I still remember the almighty thump as the window fell down inside the door panel.

Oh, and then there was a brief flirtation with a 412. Auto everything and magnolia hide. Three-speed 'box and full four-seat

Above:
Nick now regrets swapping his Dino for a Stratos – 'a rather frightening fairground ride'.

capacity. This was some crazed notion about practical family motoring, I think, and it was soon packed off to a dealer.

Finally, there is the exquisitely impractical Enzo. I do have my differences with it. A really quick time around Fiorano is important, but Mr Schumacher should have taken it to the shops to discover that limited visibility at roundabouts creates just too much excitement, and too many insurance claims. And it is big – well, wide anyway. But it does go, and it has that sort of steering wheel you can enjoy even when you're not moving.

In fact, it's almost better when you're not moving. I was a little miffed to have it explained to me that, although the car had done only 740 miles, the new clutch that was already required was considered a consumable rather than a guarantee item.

Having said that, the car is now considered to have earned its keep after its appearance on *Top Gear* where, in return for the loan of the car, Jeremy's approach to the BBC's code of practice on advertising was ridden over rough-shod as he touted (or allowed me to tout) my then recently published book, *Inside Out*.

To my mind, a great Ferrari is a little like a Fender Stratocaster – it's not just a guitar, it's rock and roll, it's Hank Marvin, Eric Clapton or Jimi Hendrix. An instrument in the right hands to get the right results has to take on some element of romance. Gosh, the LSD's beginning to wear off, so hear endeth the sermon – if not on the mount, at least on the garage lift. △

EVERY FERRARI ROAD CAR

From the 64bhp 166 of 1947 to today's 642bhp FF, here's the lowdown on every road-going Ferrari from the very beginning

166 (1947)
The true Ferrari road cars started with the 166, which were developed from the 125 range of race-oriented models. All manner of bodies were built by various coachbuilders for the leaf-sprung V12-powered 166 chassis.
Total: 71. Power: 64bhp. Top speed: 125mph

195 (1950)
With model designation derived from the capacity of a single cylinder, the 195s were similar to the 166s but with a 2341cc V12 instead of the 166's 2-litre. Again, bodies were by various coachbuilders in several styles.
Total: 27. Power: 180bhp. Top speed: 130mph

212 Inter, 212 Export (1951)
Bigger engine and more power, but the same basic chassis for the 212 Export, while the 212 Inter had a longer wheelbase. Coachbuilt bodies were created by Vignale, Ghia, Touring and Pinin Farina.
Total: 106. Power: 170bhp. Top speed: 140mph

340/342/375 America (1950)
Based on an evolution of the 166 chassis, the America series of cars used a 4.1-litre long-block V12 designed by Aurelio Lampredi. The 342 was more of a tourer, while the 375 was a 4.5-litre. Various body styles.
Total: 41. Power: 300bhp. Top speed: 149mph

250 Europa (1953)
The first Ferrari built specifically for road use rather than adapted from a competition car. It was the only 250 to use the Lampredi V12 (a short-block version) and was based on the 166 chassis. Various bodies, most by Farina.
Total: 17. Power: 200bhp. Top speed: 120mph

250GT (1954)
The first volume Ferrari. It used the Colombo-designed V12, as used in the 166, and coil springs in place of the old transverse leaf springs. It was still a coachbuilt, with most versions made by Pininfarina.
Total: 130. Power: 220bhp. Top speed: 125mph

THE CHOSEN ONE

Ricambi America is the exclusive importer of Hill Engineering custom and re-engineered Ferrari

At Hill Engineering the primary goal is to produce a superior product. The philosophy has made them known around the
for precision engineering. From race-ready cam tensioner bearings to robust clutch release bearings, and everything in be
it is no surprise that Ferrari owners and shops demand Hill Engineering parts by name.

Ricambi America is proud to be the exclusive North America importer of Hill Engineering custom Ferrari parts.

RICAMBI
AMERICA

250GT Tour de France (1955)
A special 250GT to celebrate Ferrari's win in the Tour de France, with aluminium bodywork by Scaglietti and a tuned version of the Colombo V12. This is one of the all-time greats.
Total: 84. Power: 280bhp. Top speed: 137mph

410 Superamerica (1956)
To replace the 375 America, the Lampredi V12 was bored out to nearly 5 litres. The chassis was new and the brakes much improved. Coupé bodywork was by Farina, Ghia and Scaglietti.
Total: 38. Power: 400bhp. Top speed: 165mph

250GT Cabriolet/California (1957)
Scaglietti built the open-top versions of the Pininfarina 250GTs. The California had the Tour de France's tuned engine.
Total: 241/104. Power: 240bhp.
Top speed: 137mph

400 Superamerica (1959)
One of the last coachbuilt Ferraris, and powered by a Colombo V12 rather than a Lampredi. Most were built by Pininfarina in 'aerodynamic coupé' style. Disc brakes all round, too.
Total: 54. Power: 400bhp. Top speed: 160mph

250GT SWB (1960)
By cutting the 250GT chassis down to a wheelbase of 2400mm, weight was reduced, cornering ability improved and the looks of the car made more aggressive. A true great.
Total: 167. Power: 280bhp. Top speed: 167mph

250GT Coupé Pininfarina (1960)
Styled, as its name suggests, by Pininfarina, with a focus on comfort and convenience (there's no shortage of luggage space). Biggest seller yet.
Total: 350. Power: 240bhp.
Top speed: 126mph

250GTE (1960)
The first production four-seater from Ferrari, although the rear accommodation was all but useless. The engine, gearbox and front chairs were moved forward in the chassis to make space for the rear seats.
Total: 950. Power: 235bhp. Top speed: 120mph

250GT Berlinetta Lusso (1962)
The road-going version of the legendary racing 250GTO, the elegant Lusso is now one of the most sought-after Ferraris of all time. It used a three-carburettor version of the GTO's six-carb engine, making 250bhp.
Total: 350. Power: 250bhp. Top speed: 149mph

275GTB/GTS and GTB/4 (1964)
Essentially the 2400mm 250 chassis with a larger, 3285cc engine and a new body. The open GTS was less ornate than the closed GTB. Four-cam version followed.
Total: 456/14/350. Power: 280bhp. Speed: 162mph

500 Superfast (1964)
The replacement for the top-of-the-range 400 Superamerica, the 500 Superfast had a new 5-litre engine, the 330GT's chassis and an aggressive swooping body style. Lavish interior included air-con.
Total: 36. Power: 400bhp. Top speed: 174mph

330GT 2+2 (1964)
With much more sober styling than its stablemates, the 4-litre 2+2 330GT is often overlooked now, but it was actually a strong seller. Odd-looking twin headlights on early versions were soon dropped.
Total: 1075. Power: 300bhp. Top speed: 152mph

330GTC/GTS (1965)
Based on the 275GTB and GTS, the 330GTC and GTS (coupé and roadster) used the 300bhp 4-litre engine and, unusually for a Ferrari of the time, were available with alloy wheels rather than just the usual wire items.
Total: 600/100. Power: 300bhp. Top speed: 152mph

365GTB/4 and GTS/4 'Daytona' (1968)
This was the replacement for the great 275GTB/4. It surprised (and disappointed) many by eschewing the by-then-fashionable mid-engined layout, but turned heads by dropping the traditional front grille for a radical droop-snoot look. Rare GTS 'Daytona Spider' was one dramatic-looking roadster.
Total: 1284/122. Power: 352bhp. Top speed: 174mph

365 California (1966)
The 365 California was aimed squarely at Ferrari's most elite customers, hence the tiny production number. It was based on the 2650mm chassis, with a 4390cc version of the V12 engine putting out well over 300bhp.
Total: 14. Power: 320bhp. Top speed: 152mph

365GTC/GTS (1968)
These evolutions of the 330GTC and GTS received the 4.4-litre V12 powerplant, but were almost immediately made obsolete by the stunning (and technically much-improved) 365GTB/4 Daytona.
Total: 150/20. Power: 320bhp. Top speed: 152mph

365GT 2+2 (1968)
At more than 16ft long and weighing nearly two tons, this is one big machine! Along with its additional two seats, this 365 also had self-levelling rear suspension (a Ferrari first), air-conditioning and electric windows.
Total: 800. Power: 320bhp. Top speed: 125mph

Dino 206 GT/246 GT/246GTS (1970)
Never actually badged as a Ferrari, the Dino has slowly come of age, although the 2-litre, 180bhp 206 variant isn't nearly as sought-after as the 2.4-litre 246.
Total: 152/2487/1274.
Power: 195bhp. Speed: 152mph

365GTC/4 (1971)
Although rather less characterful in style than the Daytona, the 365GTC/4 was much more civilised to drive than previous 365 variants. At the time of the model's introduction, the integrated bumpers were highly innovative.
Total: 500. Power: 340bhp. Top speed: 162mph

365GT4 2+2 (1973)
The 365GT4 2+2 was totally different again from other 365s, and moved levels of Ferrari luxury up a notch or two. Thanks to the efficient use of the 2700mm chassis, four people could travel in comfort in this 2+2.
Total: 525. Power: 340bhp. Top speed: 152mph

365GT4/BB 'Boxer' (1973)
It took a long time for the Italian supercar manufacturer to produce a mid-engined grand tourer, but when the BB eventually appeared it universally impressed pundits with its clean, modern lines and the performance from its 4.4-litre V12 powerplant.
Total: 387. Power: 380bhp. Top speed: 188mph

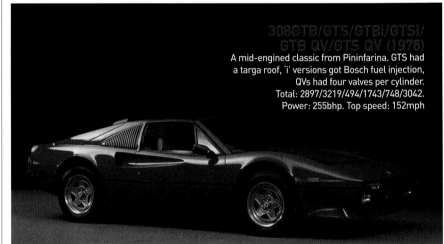

308GTB/GTS/GTBi/GTSi/GTB QV/GTS QV (1976)
A mid-engined classic from Pininfarina. GTS had a targa roof, 'i' versions got Bosch fuel injection, QVs had four valves per cylinder.
Total: 2897/3219/494/1743/748/3042.
Power: 255bhp. Top speed: 152mph

308GT4 2+2 (1974)
Styled, unusually, by Bertone, the GT4 was originally badged as a Dino, not a Ferrari. A 208 version, inspired by fuel-crisis tax laws in Italy, had a mere 2 litres. The GT4 was never as sought after as the following 308s.
Total: 2826. Power: 255bhp. Top speed: 147mph

400GT (1976) and 400i (1979)
A 4.8-litre V12 turned the 365GT/4 into the 400, with few aesthetic changes other than a front spoiler. Bosch fuel injection replaced carbs on 400i. First Ferrari available as an automatic.
Total: 501 (354 auto)/1294 (873 auto).
Power: 340bhp. Speed: 152mph

BB512 (1976) and 512i (1981)
By upgrading the 365GT/4BB with a 4.9-litre engine, and tweaking the styling slightly with a small front spoiler and NACA ducts in the sills, a true classic was created. Became the 512i when fuel injection was added in 1981.
Total: 929/1007. Power: 360bhp. Top speed: 188mph

Mondial 8 (1981) and Mondial QV/Cabriolet QV (1984)

Cleverly incorporated four seats into a sporty design, but looked unbalanced and needed more than 214bhp. Four-valve QV improved matters.
Total: 703/1145/629.
Power: 240bhp. Speed: 149mph

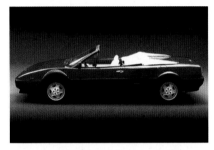

Mondial 3.2/Cabriolet (1985)

A 3.2-litre V8 (up from 3 litres) gave the Mondial some much-needed extra power to overcome its weight. Received Testarossa-style pop-up headlights at the same time.
Total: 987/810. Power: 270bhp. Top speed: 158mph

Testarossa (1984)

Evocative name came from the 1950s Testa Rossa (Italian for 'red head'); outrageous styling was testament to the excesses of the 1980s. Was a massive 1975mm wide. Five example of the roadster variant were built.
Total: 7177. Power: 390bhp. Top speed: 180mph

288GTO (1984)

Another true great, and definitely worthy of the GTO name. The 288GTO shape was based around the 308's body, but with a larger front spoiler, broader wings and a kicked-up tail. With light weight and 400bhp from the turbocharged 2.8-litre V8, it was seriously quick. Intended to go racing, it never saw competitive action due to changes to Group B regulations.
Total: 272. Power: 400bhp. Top speed: 190mph

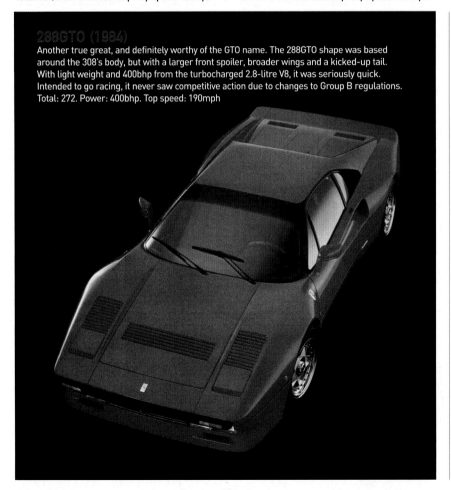

412GT/Auto (1985)

The 400GT grows up, getting a 4.9-litre engine, fuel injection and new ignition systems, and a still more luxurious engine with twin air-con plants – one for the front, one for the rear. Styling barely changed, though.
Total: 576 (306 auto). Power: 340bhp. Speed: 155mph

328GTB/GTS (1985)

A neat evolution of the 308, with subtly updated styling and the capacity of its mid-mounted V8 raised to 3185cc, giving an extra 30bhp. As with the 308 there was also a GTS version with a removable targa-type roof panel.
Total: 1344/6068. Power: 270bhp. Top speed: 163mph

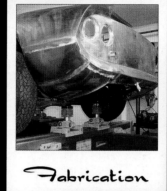

F40 (1987)
The 40th anniversary of Ferrari was celebrated with the launch of the wonderful F40, an extreme supercar with a 3-litre twin-turbo V8, composite chassis and bodywork, and a truly Spartan interior. While not as sophisticated as rival Porsche's fiendishly complex 959, the F40 seemed the more passionate machine and also trumped it for top speed, being the first road-going Ferrari to top 200mph.
Total: 1315. Power: 478bhp. Max speed: 201mph

512TR (1992)
The 512TR was a Testarossa that had been bestowed with extra power, thanks to fuel injection, and revised styling to the front grille and pop-up headlights.
Total: 2280. Power: 428bhp. Top speed: 195mph

F355B/GTS (1994)
As a successor to the V8 line of 308, 328 and 348, the 355 had plenty to live up to – and did so admirably. The F1 version had F1-style paddle-operated sequential gearchange.
Total: 4915/434. Power: 380bhp. Speed: 183mph

348 Spider (1993)
Aimed fair and square at the American market, the drop-top Spider was a pure roadster, which had a strengthened body to compensate for the lack of roof.
Total: 1090. Power: 300bhp. Top speed: 171mph

F512M (1995)
This third evolution of the Testarossa was the last Ferrari to have a flat-12. Power was upped, and there was a new look: headlights were no longer pop-up, fresh front grille and revised rear end.
Total: 500. Power: 440bhp. Top speed: 196mph

Mondial t/Cabriolet t (1989)
The Mondial range was updated in '89 with the 't' versions, which saw the transverse V8 engine turned 90 degrees to be mounted longitudinally, forming a T-shape with the gearbox.
Total: 840/1010. Power: 300bhp. Top speed: 158mph

348tb/ts/GTB/GTS (1989)
The 348tb and the removable-roof ts were replacements for the 328GTB and GTS. Testarossa-style side vents cooled the engine.
Totals: 2895/4230/252/137.
Power: 300bhp. Top speed: 174mph (GTB)

456GT (1994)
Undoubtedly one of the best-looking 2+2s ever manufactured, the 5.5-litre V12-engined 456 was available with manual gearbox (GT) and as an automatic as well (GTA).
Total: 1936. Power: 442bhp. Top speed: 186mph

F355 Spider (1995)
Converting the coupé 355 into a roadster was a big success. The hood featured a semi-automatic lowering and raising mechanism, synchronising movement of the hood, seats and windows.
Total: 3714. Power: 380bhp. Top speed: 183mph

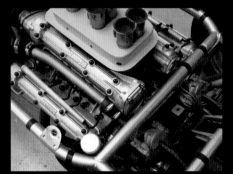

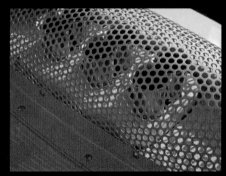

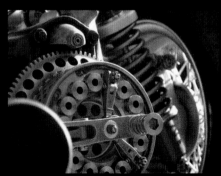

F50 (1996)

The idea of the V12 F50 was to produce the closest possible thing to a practical road-going Formula 1 car, so the F50 was built as a carbonfibre monocoque, with ground-effect aerodynamics and sequential gearbox.
Total: 349. Power: 520bhp. Top speed: 202mph

550 Maranello (1997)

A return to front-engined supercars with a front-mounted V12, long bonnet and coupé styling. Electronic dampers and traction control were firsts on a Ferrari road car.
Total: 3083. Power: 485bhp. Top speed: 199mph

456M GT/GTA (1998)

Despite appearances, the 456M was quite different from the 456. Although the V12 engine was unchanged, the suspension was heavily revised and electronically managed to work with the ABS.
Total: 3289. Power: 442bhp. Top speed: 186mph

360 Spider/F1 (2000)

Hood down, the 360 Spider harked back to classic 1950s barchettas, with twin roll hoops and fairings behind driver's and passenger's heads. But it was loaded with modern goodies, too, including a fully automatic roof raising and lowering system.
Totals: 2115 / 5450 F1s. Power: 400bhp. Top speed: 186mph

360 Modena/F1 (1999)

To counter the trend of ever-heavier new cars, Ferrari made great efforts to keep the V8-powered 360 as light as possible, with aluminium body and spaceframe chassis.
Total: 2630/6170 F1s.
Power 400bhp. Top speed: 186mph

550 Barchetta Pininfarina (2001)

After the strong reaction to the 360 Spider, Ferrari produced the 550 Barchetta with the same twin hoops and fairings as the 360. The difference, of course, is that the 550 had a front-engined V12 instead of mid-engined V8.
Total: 448. Power: 485bhp. Top speed: 186mph

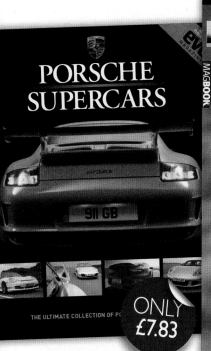
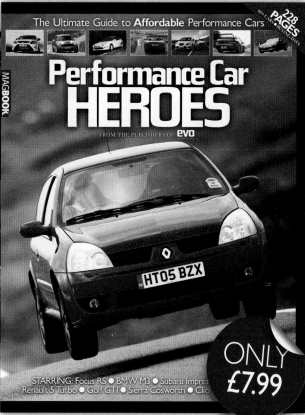
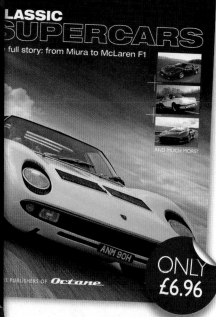

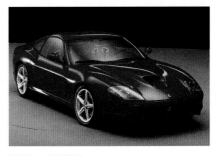

575M (2002)
Subtle styling changes, such as a smaller front grille, distinguished the 575 from the 550, but it was the bigger engine (5748cc), F1-type transmission and adaptive suspension that were the big changes. Total: 246/1810 F1s. 515bhp. Top speed: 202mph

Enzo (2002)
The ultimate! Like the F50 before it, the Enzo made great use of F1 technology, with composite construction, electronically controlled transmission (changes in 150 milliseconds) and the same output from its V12 as an F1 car. Total: 399. Power: 650bhp. Top speed: 217mph-plus

360 Challenge Stradale (2003)
The one-make racers in the 360 Challenge series inspired this fabulous road-racer, known as the Challenge Stradale (Italian for street). It had reduced weight and much of the character of the racers. A modern classic.
Total: 378. Power: 425bhp. Top speed: 186mph

612 Scaglietti (2004)
To commemorate the links between Ferrari and Scaglietti, the V12 612 Scaglietti was created. Ironically it wasn't one of Pininfarina's best shapes. Total: 3000-plus.
Power: 540bhp. Top speed: 199mph

F430 (2004)
The successor to the 360 was a technical tour de force, with (for the first time on a road car) an electronically controlled diff, plus F1 sequential gearbox and the usual traction control etc. Total: n/a. Power: 490bhp. Top speed: 196mph

F430 Spider (2005)
It came as no surprise that an open F430 would appear, and the car was as good-looking as you would have expected. Strengthening added about 70kg to the weight.
Total: n/a. Power: 490bhp. Top speed: 193mph

Superamerica (2005)
The name Superamerica has always been associated with the most prestigious Ferraris. This front-engined V12 was no exception, with a glass roof that could be electronically dimmed. Total: 559. Power: 540bhp. Top speed: 199mph

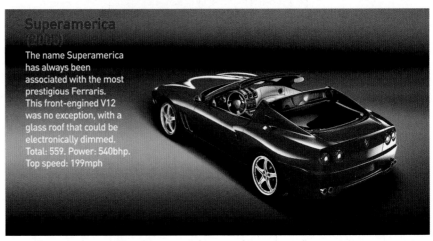

599GTB Fiorano (2006)
Combines high performance with top-end luxury. Its all-aluminium construction keeps weight down, and electronics aid stability, traction and gearchanging.
Total: n/a. Power: 611bhp.
Top speed: 205mph

F430 Scuderia (2008)
Hard-edged, race-oriented version of the 430, boasted lightweight panels, reduced sound-deadening and plenty of carbonfibre.
Total: n/a.
Power: 503bhp. Top speed: 193mph

California (2008)
'Baby' Ferrari, open-top, complete with mid-mounted V8 powerplant, seven-speed dual-clutch transmission and near-perfect 46/54 weight distribution.
Total: n/a.
Power: 454bhp. Top speed: 198mph

458 (2009)
Latest take on Dino theme, the mid-engined 458 – the marque's most powerful V8 road car ever – is as fast as the F40. Seven-speed dual-clutch gearbox – no manual. A real game-changer.
Total: n/a. Power: 562bhp. Top speed: 202mph

599GTO (2010)
A road-going version of the experimental, track-use-only 599XX: lighter than the standard 599 and with 50bhp more. This is the fastest road-going model in Ferrari's history, with a Fiorano lap time of 1min 24sec. Only 599 will be built.
Total: 599. Power: 661bhp. Top speed: 208mph

FF (2011)
Ferrari's first ever four-wheel-drive production car – and it's a four-seater. There's more room in this V12 GT's boot than in a family hatch's, too. Upwards of 200mph – and the kids go free!
Total: n/a. Power: 642bhp. Top speed: 208mph